'Andrea is the straight-shooting sister we all need. I can't think of a single woman who wouldn't benefit from *Make Some Noise*. This book is funny, relatable and a blueprint for empowerment.'
Laura Mckowen, bestselling author of *We Are the Luckiest*

'The ultimate guide to getting your shit together, written by the best shit stirrer I know. Andrea does it again with a book that is as equally thought provoking as it is transformative. Every woman needs a copy and should gift a copy to that friend that needs that little nudge to shine a little brighter and talk a little louder.'
Rachel DeAlto, author of *Relatable: How to Connect with Anyone Anywhere (Even if it Scares You)*

'Andrea Owen and her book, *Make Some Noise* are the slap on the ass you didn't know you needed. She'll take you from feeling as if you are somehow not "enough" to feeling perfectly equipped to stand up, speak up, and step all the way into your power. You'll want to buy this book for all the women in your life!'
Susan Hyatt, author of *Bare*

'Now more than ever, women need to come together, own our strength, rise up and empower ourselves and each other. This book is the essential road map to get us there. It's raw, relatable, activating, soul-stirring and a MUST read for e⸃
Shannon Kaiser, author of *Th*

D1434751

'I'm so excited for the reader that goes on this book journey. Andrea Owen does an incredible job of giving you a loving kick in the butt that encourages you to claim the life you truly desire and own the dreams you were born to fulfil!'
Christine Gutierrez, author of *I Am Diosa: A Journey to Healing Deep, Loving Yourself* **and** *Coming Back Home to Soul*

'Andrea Owen has done it again with bold wisdom from her heart. She points out the ways women stay small and at the same time offers compassion by reminding them it's not their fault – they're simply playing by the rules and narratives handed to them from the culture at large. Andrea is the sassy best friend that tells it like it is, but always with so much love.'
Christine Hassler, author of *Expectation Hangover*

'*Make Some Noise* is packed with tools that will help any woman who's ready to make some serious shifts in her life. Andrea's insight and energy come through from the very first page. You will not regret picking this book up!'
Lori Harder, author of *A Tribe Called Bliss*

'If you're looking for a powerful leader in the women's empowerment space, my girl Andrea Owen is it. *Make Some Noise* is full of insight, motivation, and tools and I can't wait for all women to read it. From taking up space, to asking for everything you want, you'll be equipped to grab your life by the hair and run with it!'
Jess King, Peloton instructor and life coach

MAKE
SOME
NOISE

MAKE
SOME
NOISE

Speak Your Mind and Own
YOUR STRENGTH

ANDREA OWEN

First published in the United States in 2021 by TarcherPerigee
An imprint of Penguin Publishing Group
A division of Penguin Random House LLC

First published in Great Britain in 2021 by Yellow Kite
An Imprint of Hodder & Stoughton
An Hachette UK company

1

Book design by Silverglass Studio

A CIP catalogue record for this title is available from the British Library

Trade Paperback ISBN 978 1 529 37081 2
eBook ISBN 978 1 529 37082 9

Printed and bound in Great Britain by Clays Ltd, Elcograf S.p.A.

Hodder & Stoughton policy is to use papers that are natural, renewable
and recyclable products and made from wood grown in sustainable
forests. The logging and manufacturing processes are expected to
conform to the environmental regulations of the country of origin.

Yellow Kite
Hodder & Stoughton Ltd
Carmelite House
50 Victoria Embankment
London EC4Y 0DZ

www.yellowkitebooks.co.uk

For Sydney
And for my mother,
and her mother,
and her mother,
and her mother . . .

CONTENTS

Author's Note

Throughout these pages some names of clients and women in my community have been changed to protect their privacy; otherwise I've been given permission to share their experiences using their real names.

Regarding the personal stories, I've changed some names. When possible, I consulted people who were there at the time and journal entries for validation. However, as we know, human memory isn't perfect, but I've written the stories to the best of my memory.

Letter to Readers

Dear Readers,

When the idea struck me to create this book, it was fueled by anger. Not only anger—there was a good portion of rage mixed in as well, like a volcano eruption.

Over the last handful of years I've taken a deep dive into my own trauma; walked straight into the storm that held past sexual assault, endless sexual harassment, and the choking feeling from being raised in a culture that told me to quiet down—that my voice, my spirit, my ambition, my most everything was too much.

This personal deep dive will likely continue for years; as it's taken four decades for me to face this rage, it will take some time to heal from it. The unraveling has been and will continue to be a rebirth.

When the time came to sit down to write, there was chatter that told me to wait. That I needed to get to a quieter place within myself to write this book for you—someplace more peaceful and subdued. That my anger wouldn't serve you, that it might scare you, and a prim-sounding schoolteacher voice in my head said, "Anger doesn't look good on you, nor does it sell books."

But a bigger voice, one that was louder and clearer, told me that you need my anger. Fury, rage, and rebellion *are* actually of service here. That by writing you this book, this is in service of *making some noise.*

My heart races as I type this to you, which makes me know this is true and right and I know you and I will connect on this truth. And if not, hey, no hard feelings, perhaps we're not ready to meet yet.

Your curiosity in this book tells me something. It tells me that you, like me, are tired, but still energized enough when it comes to bettering yourself. It tells me you're holding back in your life, at least a little (and might be afraid to admit it). It tells me that you have a fire that burns in you that may be a fierce quiet whisper, or it may be a full-on raging inferno, doused in gasoline. It tells me that maybe you're ready to burn the whole damn thing down and start over.

Most definitely, it tells me that you want something more for your life. You're ready for something to change and you're ready to let it start with you.

Maybe you read a substantial amount of self-help books, or maybe you picked this one up because it called out to you. Regardless, I'm going to take a wild guess and say you're hungry for something, and when you're hungry for something, you want to change the way you feel. There's an emptiness inside you that you want filled. Bottom line: You want something more for your life.

At the same time, changing your life has its challenges. Aside from it being work, we, as women, have been socialized to not make too much noise, to put everyone else before us, and to make everyone else comfortable. All of this at the expense of our own values, desires, and dreams. Many times, we don't even consciously realize this is happening. But unconsciously we know. It manifests as resentment, poor boundary-setting, lashing out, negative self-talk, unnecessary apologizing, people-pleasing, and approval-seeking. *And that feels like shit.*

In 2018, my second book, *How to Stop Feeling Like Shit,* came out, in which I chronicled the behaviors I just mentioned, which are very common behaviors for the thousands of women I've worked with over the last fourteen years, plus my own. We spend endless amounts of energy trying to contort ourselves into what we think people want and expect of us. Don't make others too uncomfortable, don't rock any boats, and never, ever make a scene.

We follow these "rules" because we don't want to be rejected. We want to fit in, be liked and approved of. We do these things because it's what we know and it's become, in a strange, twisted way, what's comfortable.

But, more important, we do these things because we live in a culture that tells women that no matter what, we are not good enough.

In working with many women who all want a better life—here's what I know to be true:

For women, moving away from behaviors that don't work for us anymore, letting go of core beliefs that convince us we're broken and not enough, laying a stake in the ground around our desires, is an act of MAKING NOISE.

I'm so fucking tired of women thinking there is something wrong with them for not having the confidence they need to go after what they want. I'm so fucking tired of women being afraid to use their voice to speak up in a meeting or when someone has harmed them.

And I'm so fucking tired of shouting "GIRL POWER!" and telling women they can be and do anything they want to, when the truth is if we want to find our true north and live our best life, we have to simultaneously work on bettering ourselves *and* push back on the culture that created the problem in the first place. These are not two completely separate conversations. We must do this in order to help create change for ourselves, as well as for generations to come.

For all the women who've been judged for their cleavage, clothing choices, or loud voices. For women who have been gossiped about for their choices of sexual partners (whether the gossip was true or not) and made to feel ashamed or even less than human. For the women who got passed up for promotions who never made it to the control center for the first moon landing.

For you, if you've ever felt like your life was an uphill battle. If you've been dismissed, harassed, abused, or dehumanized. There's nothing else to say about it except that it's unacceptable. It can feel all-consuming at times, like it's so much work and are we even making any progress?

The truth is, we are making progress. But we can't better ourselves and encourage women's empowerment unless we unlearn what we've learned from the beginning. Those old ways are not okay for us, nor are they okay for the women who will come after us.

This isn't a feminist theory book about how to smash the patriarchy. It's not about flipping tables, advising you to scream at and/or flip off your boss, or run away from your family and start a new life (even though at times you may want to do all those things . . . naturally). It's not about being a feminist activist. That's great if you are one or want to be one, but it's perfectly fine if you're not. *Make Some Noise* also isn't about the fast and easy way to living your best life. It's about looking at real-life stumbling blocks, drawing a line in the sand regarding what's not working, and helping you navigate in ways that make you feel like the absolute best version of yourself.

However, by doing things like taking up space, asking for everything you want, and not waiting for confidence before you take action, you are, in essence, disrupting the narrative of patriarchy and acting as a feminist. **Make no mistake, women's empowerment is an act of rebellion.**

It's our time to step forward. This starts at a grassroots level with you. It starts with you claiming your desires, claiming your voice, and CLAIMING YOUR LIFE.

This book is part rally cry and call to arms, part how to break out of what most of us have been taught as truth. I promise that you'll see yourself in these chapters—glimpses of your life that perhaps you thought no one knew about (I've been watching you).

Because may I remind you that this is it. There are no dress rehearsals or do-overs. Today and every day is the beginning of your life and it's up to you to live the shit out of it. All you have to do is tap into that hunger, believe even for a moment that you have the power to create what you want, and take some action. That's where I and this book come in, being your guiding strobe light to your most outstanding, kick-ass life.

Hugs, ass-kicking, and noisemaking,
Andrea

How to Get the Most Out of This Book

In order to change your life, you have to change your life. As obvious as that may sound, you might be surprised how many people don't realize the amount of action they have to take in order to get the things and the life they want. Therefore, you'll hear me talking a lot about taking specific action in the chapters ahead.

When I was first starting out on my own personal-development journey, I would read personal-growth books and write the names of my friends and ex-boyfriends in the margins. Pointing to certain traits and problems that *other* people had, thinking that if they would just change, their life and my life would be better. In other words, I liked the *idea* of change, and I especially liked it for other people. It took me about a decade to realize if I wanted my life to change, I had to change, and I had to do it myself.

I'm going to go ahead and assume you're here to change your life, and at the very least learn new habits that will bring you more happiness, confidence, and ease.

But when we're talking about the culture we've been raised in and the conditioning we've been exposed to, before we can learn and implement something new, we must first intentionally and consciously unlearn what we have been taught. To let go of what has become embedded in us, so we can move forward as better humans. Unlearning will be woven into each and every chapter of this book because no matter if you're a twenty-five- or seventy-five-year-old reading this book, you have beliefs, habits, and truths that are ingrained in you. If you want to change some things (which I think you do), unlearning needs to happen.

SPECIAL NOTE

There are many places in this book where I talk about the conditioning and socialization of women. I understand that not all who identify as women were conditioned and socialized exactly the same, and that therefore the factors at play are nuanced. Race, class, ability, sexual orientation, your generation, family values, and more can influence the lens through which we experience things, helping form our thoughts, beliefs, opinions, and behaviors.

This said, most of the time, I'm speaking generally, and for the sake of brevity have mentioned these nuances only a few times. But please keep in mind as you read that there are definite variations among women and there is no one specific way.

Last, as I did my best to get examples that represent an array of women, these examples are not a monolith as it may pertain to their specific race or identity group.

KNOW THYSELF

The origin of the phrase "know thyself" is debated, as is what it specifically means. Like most things, it's up for interpretation. To me, in connection to the world of self-help, to know thyself is to know your blind spots. To be self-aware enough to notice when you're engaging in behavior that doesn't serve you, not so that you can beat yourself up for it, not so you can change for good and never slip up again, but so that you can do your best to course-correct.

Sometimes when we read self-help books, we can walk away feeling worse about ourselves because the words turn into a mirror of what we don't like about ourselves, plus what we're terrified others will find out about us. We have so many other things to worry about, I don't want that for you. This book is not a place to blame and shame yourself or anyone else.

You may resonate with some chapters and not with others. Like everything in life, take what you want and leave the rest. All I ask is that this book be a way for you to know yourself. To look at the culture at large, how it's made an impact on you and how you show up in this world, how you want to show up better, and hopefully, this book shows you a better way.

THE
UNLEARNING

Since much of this work is about unlearning what feels instinctive at this point, I'm mapping out a framework that will help guide you through each topic. You'll see a text box in each chapter that will take you through four steps. In the next pages are the guidelines that you'll be following as you unlearn things like staying small, always being accommodating, and taking care of everyone else's feelings before your own. I've provided some examples as well.

And, hey, before we jump in together: This is the part where I turn to you, make eye contact, and grab you by the shoulders.

What we're about to walk into may be new to you, and it may not. You may already understand a lot of what I'm talking about or it may be a learning moment for you. Either way, the unlearning will likely be the part that is a lifelong journey. Any former cult member will tell you, the first step in leaving the cult is to have cognitive dissonance, when you realize *this isn't working anymore.* When the spoken or unspoken rules of "this is how things work around here" are questioned. We've probably all felt that in a relationship before, or a family or work situation (or maybe even in an actual cult), but the bottom line is that the unlearning begins when you're anywhere from uncomfortable with how things are going in your life all the way to a "fuck this shit, I'm out" type of feeling.

No matter where you are on that spectrum, let's get to work.

THE FOUR STEPS OF UNLEARNING
Step #1: Notice

As I always say, you have to name it to tame it. You can't clean up what you don't know is messy, so let's always start here. When we turn the light on in this metaphorical room that needs some cleaning up—in other words, when we start noticing—it can be jarring. We realize the air we breathe has been set up to keep women down and quiet and that many times, we've been actively but unknowingly participating in it.

As you read through this book and start paying attention to your own behaviors and tolerations, I encourage you to just notice. Some emotions might come up, and notice that, too. You can tell yourself things like "That's interesting" or "What a thought-provoking thing!" You don't need to make it *mean* anything. This first step is about awareness of what's happening.

During this noticing phase in each chapter, I highly encourage you to journal. You can grab your own blank notebook, or I've made it easy for you to work through each chapter by downloading your free *Make Some Noise* workbook at andreaowen.com/msn. From there, you can process your way through each of the four steps of unlearning from each chapter.

Step #2: Get Curious

Once you start paying attention and begin noticing your own behavior, I'm asking you to simply get curious about it. Think of it as going into your closet and looking in all your pockets. What will you find there? Who knows, but let's have zero expectations about it. Might find $100 or a chewed-up piece of gum. Either way, it will be something.

Getting curious is about asking questions, about digging deeper. Questions like:

I wonder why I think that?

That's interesting that I'm judging her for wearing that. I wonder what that's about?

Why am I so sarcastic when I argue with my partner? Is something else going on?

Is it odd that I assume my aspirations can't be a priority?

Why can't I talk to my parents about this?

Why am I so triggered by this? Is it at all about me or something else?

We, as humans, like to be right about things. It brings us certainty and control, and certainty and control bring us the feeling of safety. When we come to a conclusion or make an assumption, we close a loop, and that feels good.

But sometimes our incessant need for certainty and control can close us off from growing, learning about ourselves and others, and implementing behaviors that are better for us.

When we let in curiosity, we disrupt the pattern of judgments and assumptions about ourselves, other people, situations, the past, the future—literally everything. And guess what happens then? You can change your life.

My friend Elizabeth DiAlto asks this great two-part question: *What is my conditioning and what is my truth?* This is a question we'll revisit in many of the chapters you're about to read. This inquiry will ask you to examine the expectations, "rules," and ways of being you were brought up in, as well as how *you* actually want to be. Sometimes those two ways will be the same, but many times they will be different.

Once you start noticing your reactions and getting curious about them, you'll hopefully gain some clarity. For instance, if you assume something is wrong with you and that most other people have it figured out except you, ask yourself, "What if it weren't true?" or, "I wonder what would happen if I didn't believe that?" I'm not asking you to flip the switch and believe it's not true in one hot second, but to just do some thinking about what if it wasn't. Maybe you would be more apt to change, or not be so hard on yourself, or, I don't know . . . feel better and happier?

Curiosity brings clarity, but in addition, it has the capacity to change your life. It allows you to look at things from ten thousand feet away, which can help take the definitiveness and emotion out of it. From there, you can change your perspective and learn a new way of being.

Step #3: Self-compassion

One of the side effects of realizing how we've participated in a system that keeps us small or acknowledging how we've kept other women down (and thus ourselves) is feeling guilty, ashamed, angry, or any number of other challenging emotions. Which then can lead to beating yourself up about it. Thoughts like "How could I have had these unconscious feelings and judgments for so long? How could I have been so blind?" And, of course, you're going to feel however you feel, and I'll continually remind you, none of that is ever wrong.

So while you're all up in your feelings, I want to remind you that yes, this is part of the process, but if we're going to unlearn what we've learned for decades, if we're going to work on creating a new narrative about ourselves and our fellow women, beating ourselves up about it is not the way to get to a place of betterment or empowerment. It never, ever is.

Remember, the goal is to create an empowering narrative about ourselves as women, who we are, and what's possible. To make it okay to walk away from the box of conformity you've been conditioned to accept and to fit yourself into. This might upend your identity, make you understand or not understand your mother more, make you question other women's intentions—there could be myriad thoughts, emotions, and questions that come up during this time. Or maybe you've already gone through this process before, you've already done the heavy lifting here, but I believe the work is never done. You might still have unconscious biases around class, race, ability, or sexual orientation. Regardless, beating yourself up over it is a surefire way to keep yourself stuck and feeling hopeless about the situation.

If you think about it, it's a bit ironic. Here we are living in a culture that tells us we're not enough, that we need to do more, be more, and have more. And when we're beating ourselves up in the learning process of pushing against that same culture, it's as if we are taking a lesson from the oppressor and putting it back on ourselves. So let's not do that.

Cut yourself some slack. Realize you're human, a product of your environment.

Step #4: Keep the Momentum

Once you start noticing, getting curious, and even stepping into compassion, you'll understand new things, which is fantastic, and now the momentum will need to be established. It will ebb and flow, and many times the whole process will start over, again and again.

Part of keeping the momentum is talking about the unlearning and learning, because change doesn't happen in a vacuum. Talking about it can be with your therapist, your friends, your family, your children, your butcher, your baker, your candlestick maker, really anyone. I'm not recommending you become an evangelist and make it a full-time job to recruit everyone into your new way of thinking (although that can be a side effect of personal growth—rounding up people to join your club). In other words, it's not so much about convincing people of your new ways, it's about conversation.

For instance, if you start noticing how much you apologize for things you don't need to apologize for and you're consciously practicing stopping this, when you catch yourself about to apologize, say out loud, "I was about to apologize but realized I don't need to." Obviously, each situation is unique and sometimes it might be best to do this only with your partner or your friends, or perhaps at work with the appropriate people.

My client Tracie faced an example of keeping the momentum on the work she'd been doing with me. Tracie goes on the same couples' vacation every year with a group of her friends. She told me, "Every year, about six weeks before we go, a group text starts with me and all the women talking about how much weight we need to lose before we all get into our bathing suits for the beach. I'm so tired of this conversation. Not only am I tired of battling my weight, but I'm sick of seeing my beautiful friends upset about this. They're too smart and beautiful for this conversation." Tracie had gotten to a point where she knew body image was taking up way too much space in her mind. She got curious about it and did her own work on it. She'd worked on self-compassion, and now it was time to talk about it. Her assignment was to tell her friends, "Hey, this year, what would you all think about doing something new and not obsessing on our bodies? I care about you all too much to not say anything anymore." For some women this can feel like some kind of revolution. To speak up in service of one another instead of being of service to diet culture.

Keep in mind that as you journey through this process of questioning old patterns, some of the things you uncover may ask you to do some very emotional "heavy lifting," and I encourage you to seek out the help of a therapist, coach, or counselor—anyone properly trained and qualified to help guide you through messy topics. These old beliefs about who we are and our value can bring up trauma that you may not even know was there. This, again, will be a helpful place to journal your thoughts in service of your growth.

BURN IT DOWN

She had fire in her belly
and she used it to summon
her Truth.

She had fire in her soul
and she used it to remember
where she came from.

She had fire in her heart
and she used it to trust
the women who came before her.

She had fire in her spirit
and she used it to show
other women their own flames.

She had fire in her eyes
and she used it to burn
it all down.

She had fire in her every being
and she used it to blaze

a new path, a new way, a new life.

Andrea Owen

MAKE
SOME
NOISE

PART 1

SHIT TO START DOING

Start Taking Up Some Damn Space

In 2009, while very pregnant with my second child, I was finishing up my bachelor's degree at California State University San Marcos.

In one particular class, there was a formula that most of the students weren't understanding. We were let loose to figure out the assignment in groups, and I started asking my peers if they understood the formula and couldn't find anyone who did. The consensus was that we all needed more help, but no one wanted to ask for it. Our professor had explained it more than once, and apparently no one was willing to speak up on behalf of the class or even for themselves.

When our professor announced we'd have a test the following day on this topic, I raised my hand. "Professor," I said, "this formula is still unclear for us, and from what I can tell, none of us have a grasp on this material yet. Can we go over it again?"

"We've gone over it twice, Andrea," he replied.

Now, I don't know what made me feel like I needed to stand up in that moment. Maybe it was because I was speaking on behalf of the class, maybe it was because my ankles were swelling, but I hauled my big, pregnant belly up out of my chair, took a deep breath, and said, "Sir, for the last twenty minutes I've been trying to find someone in this class who understands the material so they can help me. No one does. To me, that says the material hasn't been taught to us adequately, and obviously I am not alone in not comprehending. I'm asking, on behalf of the class, if we can review it again."

I'll never forget the hushed silence that followed my request. I saw many heads look down at their desks as if they couldn't bear to make eye contact with me or with him. The discomfort was palpable. He stared at me for several seconds and I had no idea what was coming. I was starting to regret my choice of speaking up.

Right before I waddled myself out of the class to never come back to finish my degree, he said, "You're a tough lady. All right, we'll review next class and the test will be pushed back."

I highly doubt that if one of the young men had asked that same question he would have said, "You're a tough man." Who knows, maybe he would have, but what I felt in our exchange is that my professor was not expecting me to call out what I was feeling as a student, or make such a bold request.

I was not fearless in this endeavor. I knew it was a risk to take up this kind of space with my voice, and with my request.

Maybe you've been in that situation before, wanting to speak up and actually doing it like I did that day. Or maybe you've wanted to speak up, to make some noise, but didn't. Either way, I can almost guarantee there's been a moment in your life in which you've squashed your own form of bigness.

Maybe you get a promotion at work and contemplate posting about it on social media but stop yourself because you're worried people will think you're bragging. Perhaps someone at work tells a sexist joke and you can feel the response (and bile) in your throat but decide to say nothing. Maybe your father-in-law interrupts you on the regular and you let it slide every time.

There also may very well be things you're doing and you don't even know you are playing small and giving your power away. They've become so habitual and woven into your daily life that you do them as blindly as making your coffee in the morning. Whatever the manifestation of your playing small is, let's dig in and take a closer look.

WHAT DOES IT MEAN TO "TAKE UP SPACE"?

From an early age, many of us have been told we're "too much." Too loud, too opinionated, too sensitive or emotional, too talk-ative, too fat, wearing too much makeup, too something. In some way or another, whether it's explicitly said or we just catch the sub-tle message, we're essentially told we're wrong for daring to be our-selves. Everything from the big stress on the importance of "being a lady" or making sure we treat our virginity as the most revered possession we can ever have, to occupying as little space as possible, it's all part of the list of unspoken rules for women that we begin to learn at an early age.

Whether it's a raised eyebrow, a snarky comment online, or someone blatantly telling us to shut up, the vast majority of women have more than one example of being told to tone it down, or at the very least understand how we've learned to take up the smallest amount of space possible.

An obvious example is taking up space with our bodies. It's no secret that we live in a fat-phobic culture, naming thinness as the only body type that is valuable. That feminine achievement is won if we attain and keep a slender body.

Women are also more likely to get out of the way when walking down the street and a man approaches, as if it's a traffic law where one gender always has the right-of-way. There are countless memes about manspreading, and if there were an Olympic sport for apologizing for bumping into people, animals, and even inanimate objects, women would get the gold, hands down.

When it comes to our appearance, culturally we have a narrow view of what is widely acceptable and what is beautiful. For a woman to unabashedly express herself in terms of her image is an act of rebellion. Aging is another way women struggle to take up space. Once we hit forty, by society's standards we are deemed not as valuable as we used to be and begin to feel more invisible. To be an older woman and take up space with our voice, appearance, and opinions is in effect an act of defiance in a culture that tells us our time of relevance is over.

Race can add another obstacle around taking up space for women of color. Jessica Sharp, thirty-one, says, "As a millennial Black woman, I feel like I have to think about how I show up with a particular organization. I have to decide if I should show up as my full self. I know that there may be feedback that I am intimidating or 'a lot' and assume that if I were a white woman that feedback would be less likely to be received. I have to balance being myself with not being too much, because I am often fearful that I'll be perceived as an 'angry Black woman.' My age does not help—I sometimes feel like the room expects me to be more passive and quieter because I'm often the youngest in the room, although I'm equally as qualified as everyone else."

Expressing emotions is another way we, as women, allow society to tell us what's acceptable and unacceptable. I've talked to many women who've told me they don't know how to do something remarkably instinctive—feel their feelings. They've mastered numbing them out or dissociating. That, or they do feel their feelings, but they either can't or won't express them. They've successfully let the world tell them they're too emotional and/or sensitive. Therefore, they shove their feelings into a box, and generally shut out this innate expression that is crucial to their well-being, and also to their power.

Last, the best way we can take up space is to use our voices. Recent studies show that schoolgirls are more prone to do things like laugh off sexist jokes by their friends and not appear too smart (i.e., not raise their hand too much in class) in order to "not scare off boys, not appear bitchy or unsexy." This mentality and behavior continues into adulthood until we've created the proverbial box for ourselves. The box that contorts us into who we think we're supposed to be: compliant, malleable, and never taking up our share of space.

I worked with a client who told me she typically had ideas and opinions she wanted to share at weekly work meetings, but never elbowed her way into the conversation. When the meetings were over, she would spend hours rehashing them, imagining what she would have said and how she would have said it, as well as beating herself up for staying quiet. Week after week, she would have all the ideas and stories in her head swirling around, where they would stay.

All of this, my loves, is bullshit. If you could relate to any of this, it's not your fault, we've been trained to be this way. But it doesn't need to *stay* this way.

WHY WE DO IT

Whether it's obvious to us or just something we sense but keep buried—we know that to live one's purpose on this planet we must be the absolute full expression of ourselves, which includes taking up space in the world. So, if we know this, then why, oh why, do we not bust down the door to our lives?

Let's start with the fact that in the not-too-distant past, women had to stay quiet and insignificant in order to survive. My mother tells me one particular story of having a job in the 1960s where her boss would chase her around his desk "all in good fun," but she knew if she told him in seriousness to stop, she was at risk of losing her job, which, at that time, being a single mother to my older brother and sister, was not a great option for her.

To express ourselves fully, to go against cultural and societal norms and standards, is scary; I'm not here to tell you it's not. It's human nature to want to stay safe and be accepted by the group at large—whether that's your family, your friends, your community, or even your culture. Fear has crept in and created the behaviors of staying small.

In addition, it's likely the women who've come before you in your family have experienced trauma by accepting the challenge of taking up space, and you may have, too. The pushback can have consequences that range from minor to dire. I understand that the idea of taking up space may feel exciting at first, but when it comes to actually doing it, it may feel like the biggest risk you've ever taken, the most fearful thing you've embarked on by far. But you didn't pick up this book to learn how to crochet baby booties, so let's get cracking.

WHAT NOT TAKING UP SPACE IS COSTING YOU

Why does it even matter? Can't you simply go through your life playing it safe, not rocking the boat, not taking any risks? Yes, you can. You can do that and get to the end of your life, and when the time comes for you to take inventory of your one true existence, I hope to God you're okay with all of that.

Because regret matters. I can't stand the "no regrets" platitude, as it first and foremost tells us we should never have made mistakes or lament about our poor life choices. Personally, I regret not going to Australia to study abroad because a boy I was dating (he was thirty-two at the time, but make no mistake, he was a boy) didn't want me to go. That regret fueled me to *never again* make a decision about *my life* that was based on someone else's comfort.

Regret matters because, may I remind you, you just get this one exquisite life. And allow me to speak frankly here and say that regret fucking sucks. It sucks to walk out of a meeting wishing you would have spoken up or to have someone else say what you wanted to say first. It's the worst to turn forty and watch people in their twenties do the things you wanted to do when you were their age, before you had the responsibilities you do now. You know what regret feels like.

When we're talking about your existence, about your power, your sovereignty, there is not one that is more important to you than yours. So when you're thinking about taking up more space than you currently do but decide not to . . . think about what you'll regret. Think about the fact that when you say no to taking up more space in your life, you're saying no to you.

Another problem you create by not standing squarely in your own space and owning it is that you are modeling that behavior for other women and girls in your life. I have a daughter and know she is watching and learning. More than what I say to her, she pays attention to how I behave and the choices I make. Whether you have children or not, the next generation of girls matters, and how we behave will shape them.

One of the biggest losses that can come with not taking up space is one that may not be so obvious. It's not a smack-you-in-the-face matter, but more of a slow burn that has the ability to torch the house of your soul down to the ground. When we limit ourselves, our voices, and our lives, we are going against our values.

If you take even the slightest interest in personal development, even if you are just dipping a pinkie toe into these waters, then what's important about your life is that you take advantage of everything it has to offer you. This isn't a rule of self-help that gets you access to the party—this is a by-product of what happens when you decide you unequivocally understand that the fullness of your life is dependent on you living like you absolutely revere your time here on Earth. That means that what's important to you—perhaps it's authenticity, honesty, integrity, and courage—should be expressed in all areas of your life. You didn't come to this point in your life to be relying on personal characteristics like half-assing your existence and having it be "just sort of okay." You're not here to confine yourself to observe, wish, and hope you'll get the opportunity to shine like the light you are, and maybe if it all goes well you can live the good life.

I've broken down the solution to taking up space into two parts with three pieces of advice each. Starting with the "internal work"—things to do that require paying attention, self-awareness, and some reflection. Followed by what I'm calling "external work," which is all about taking action. I don't expect you to go out, kick ass, and take names without first undoing what you've become so accustomed to doing. Take your time, and accept that this might be uncomfortable, but is ultimately in service of your biggest, most badass self.

TOOLS PART ONE: DO THE INTERNAL WORK

1. Take Inventory

First, start paying attention to where you're making yourself small. We have to start here because much of our "smallness" has been conditioned in us from a very young age.

I had a personal epiphany recently within my own home. In my work, I preach about making yourself a priority, and I was proud to say I did that myself. I knew I was taking care of myself and even made time for a new hobby (to the tune of being the mother of forty-seven houseplants, in addition to two humans). Yet as my career grew, I found myself burning out. I was tired and irritable. What I realized is that, yes, I had made myself a priority, but I had equally made everyone else in my family a priority as well. I had allowed myself to be promoted to the manager of everyone's mental, emotional, and physical contentment.

What I had to do was take up space with both my voice and my own well-being. My lifelong conditioning told me it was my #1 job to first make sure everyone else in my family was comfortable, at the expense of my own welfare. That as a mother, burnout was just the price we pay for being categorized as a "good woman." That the more tired I was, the busier I was, the more I was rushing around for everyone else, the more it showed I was doing a fantastic job. But the cost was my life feeling like it was closing in on me, and I was pissed off about it. That anger boiled over into my family—which wasn't fair to them, because they never asked me to sacrifice myself for them.

Again, I had to start taking up space with my own needs.

By continuing the way things were going I was slowly killing myself, in addition to showing my daughter and son what it looks like to be a wife and a mother. I want them both to know that a woman can still be a "good mom" when she expects the other members of the family to learn to take care of themselves and all work as a team, rather than her scurrying around making it her life's mission to keep all the plates spinning.

For now, I'm not asking you to flip tables in anger, change your personality to be more gregarious, or run through the streets naked. All I'm asking is for you to notice all the ways you're allowing yourself and your life to be secondary to others'.

2. The Why

Second, now that you're clear on the behavior you're engaging in that's making you stay small, get curious about why you've stayed this way.

Who is benefiting from your being or staying small and playing it safe? Who or what is benefiting from you not speaking up? Have you not asked for a promotion, but you want to, and you're being passed over? Maybe it's something seemingly small, like the guy next to you taking over the armrest on a plane during the whole flight?

Or perhaps no one is directly benefiting from your playing small, but it's become your comfort level after so many years of acting this way. For instance, say you want to start your own side business, but it requires you reaching out to people to possibly be your customers and that's too far out of your comfort zone. So you procrastinate and find yourself scrolling for hours on Instagram. No one is actually benefiting from you doing this, but the obvious fact is that you're actively going against something you really want.

3. Question Your Objections

Third, question all your objections to taking up more space. You, because you are a normal human, have a fear of standing out. So let's get this out of the way: Yes, you'll get judged. Yes, people will have things to say about you expressing yourself more, about your going against the grain, about your being more brazen. Yes, there will be people who disagree with your opinions, who will call you out on your changes, who will be incredibly uncomfortable and displeased with your taking up space.

Your goal is not to avoid all of this. In fact, if you're ruffling feathers, you're doing it exactly right. The goal is to take up the amount of space that is your birthright. To treat your life as if you are the one in command of it. When people say, "Who does she think she is?" you respond with, "I AM THE BOSS OF ME, MOTHERFUCKERS," and if it's entirely inappropriate that you say that, in the very least you embody it.

Another objection that your smartypants brain will come up with is your fear of failing at this. What if you speak up in a work meeting about one of your ideas and it flops? What if you wear that amazing new outfit and it turns out you are way underdressed? What if you decide to fully express your emotions and your partner makes fun of you for it?

Again, all of this may happen. No one goes through life without putting themselves out there and once in a while getting their ass kicked. You were made for resilience (see chapter 8). No one dies from a little embarrassment, humiliation, or even a little shame. But your soul will slowly die if you continue to give your power away every single damn day.

TOOLS PART TWO: DO THE EXTERNAL WORK

Now that you've looked inside yourself in regard to this topic, let's look at what you can do out there in your everyday life.

1. Taking Up Space with Your Body and Appearance

Since you've become more aware when you do things such as trying to shrink yourself in an airplane seat instead of taking up the space your body actually needs, or trying to squeeze past people who didn't hear you say "excuse me," etc., in lieu of repeating yourself more loudly so they can hear you, spend a week making your physical space a priority. Embody the attitude that you belong in the driver's seat of whatever area you're in—whether it's your seat on the train, a crowded elevator, or the sidewalk.

How you physically hold your body matters. You may have heard about Amy Cuddy's research that shows using body postures associated with dominance and power ("power posing") for as little as two minutes can increase testosterone, decrease cortisol, increase appetite for risk, and cause better performance in job interviews. In other words, adopting postures like the Wonder Woman pose, "tits up," or leaning back in your chair with your feet on the table (which I don't necessarily recommend for a work meeting) can make you feel like a boss.

Another tool that can be used when you're working on taking up space with your body, appearance, and also your emotions and your voice, is to have a Board of Directors (BOD), which is a tool my colleague Susan Hyatt gave me. Imagine you can appoint anyone who will manage and direct you, who will hold only your best interests at heart, and who you can turn to at any moment when you're afraid of taking up space and/or are unsure of what to do next. These can be real or fictional characters and can be *anyone* you admire for what they stand for, the action they take, and the kind of space they take up in the world.

To name a few on my Board: Jennifer Lopez, Billie Jean King, and Wonder Woman. When I find myself afraid to send a proposal for a big project, I ask myself, "What would JLo do in this situation?" And I know damn well that JLo might feel the nervousness, but she'd send the proposal and have a dance party afterward. So that's what I do. The best version of yourself *demands* that you take up space. Jennifer Lopez didn't achieve a successful dancing, acting, and singing career by shrinking and letting her fear take up the most space. It's important to have people you admire near you, and this is a great way to remind yourself that your best self is only a series of brave choices you make every day.

Maybe you have Michelle Obama, Joan of Arc, or Ruth Bader Ginsburg on yours. Your Board of Directors is not up for judgment from anyone; it's whomever you would *love* to have as your mentors and guides. Make a vision board with cutouts of your BOD, make a picture collage on your phone and save it as your screen saver, and tell your friends about this so you can remind one another about your BOD when you find yourself not knowing what to do.

2. Taking Up Space with Your Emotions

Throughout history, women have been told their emotions make them hysterical and unrestrained. Naturally, there are instances when emotions can overwhelm the best of us, but for the most part, women are stereotyped for not being able to control bigger feelings like anger and frustration.

Emotional intelligence matters. It teaches us to use our emotions to our benefit, to get curious about them and cultivate self-awareness and self-management of them, as well as foster healthy relationships with empathy and strong communication. I'm not at all saying to go hog-wild with your emotions and allow them to take over your thoughts, words, and behavior. If you did that, you might not have any friends and possibly get fired from your job.

However, think about how often you hold back emotionally. How often you limit your emotions in order to make others more comfortable, and that then becomes a hindrance to yourself, your relationships, and even your personal expression. In a society that normalizes holding in something as innocuous and natural as a sneeze, somehow we've translated that into accepting that "bigger" emotions like anger and frustration are wrong, when they're not. They are natural; anthropologists tell us that feelings and emotions help us to survive, are part of evolution, and are connected with self-awareness, self-consciousness, and the ability to empathize with others.

From the start, after you've examined where you hush up your feelings, use that as a stepping-stone to be more expressive in those areas. For instance, if you feel strongly about a particular issue at work but hold back in meetings or in conversations out of fear that you'll be perceived as too dramatic or intense, let loose instead. Show your passion and enthusiasm. Allow your body to lead the way. Have your words create your message and your energy show your eagerness for whatever it is you're fired up about (see chapter 10 on confidence for more on this).

In your relationships, take a step forward by giving yourself permission to express your feelings. If you typically push down tears of sadness or overwhelm, let them flow. If it's joy, shout it from the rooftops. If you convey that you're indifferent about things that you do in fact care about, you're not only cutting yourself off and making yourself small, but you're rendering yourself unimportant. Your feelings and emotions matter and are worthy of expressing (see chapter 14 for more on how to express your emotions).

3. Taking Up Space with Your Voice

Ah, the coup de grâce, taking up space with our voices. This isn't about being loud and boisterous, unless that's your inherent way of being. It's about understanding that your words and expression matter.

Let's start by talking about interrupting. It doesn't matter who's interrupting you, or where you're being interrupted, the interruption should be addressed. There are a handful of ways to approach this. You can keep talking when someone interrupts you and simply ignore the intrusion. Or say, "Let me finish, please." You're still polite, while at the same time acknowledging their interruption and making it clear that you're not finished yet. Kamala Harris showed us a perfect example of this in the 2020 U.S. vice-presidential debate, where when she was interrupted, she smiled and said, "Mr. Vice President . . . I'm speaking." She wasn't rude or insulting, but on the contrary was direct and unwavering. *This* is claiming your voice.

It can also be empowering to help other women when they are interrupted. I was once in a brainstorming meeting with two colleagues and one of the women interrupted the other two or three times in our meeting. When it was over, I asked the woman who had been cut off if she had noticed and she said no. Apparently, she had gotten used to this other woman breaking into the conversations. I vowed then to never again allow this to happen, but rather gracefully say, "I don't think she was finished," or, "Wait . . . you were saying?" to the woman being interrupted. This is taking up space with your voice, and helping other women do the same.

Your opinions matter. Let me say that again: *Your opinions matter.* I recognize that the current climate we're in can feel intense and risky. Sharing your opinions on social media or with strangers may not be the best first place to start expressing your opinions more vocally. Start with your family, start with work, start with your friends.

Many times, we tell ourselves we need to wait until we have all the research for rebuttals, in case someone disagrees with our opinion. This is not the case. No one ever died from not getting the last word or feeling like your argument is weak. If you have an opinion, it's yours, it's important and it's your obligation as a team member, employee, partner, and/or living, breathing human being to speak up. The absolute worst that can happen is that you'll learn new information and change your mind or be presented with new information for you to dig into and research. The challenging feelings that come up with a counterargument to your opinions are just that: feelings. To not express your opinion at all and to stay silent is far worse on your spirit in the long run than facing challenging feelings.

Years ago, I was on a date with a man I'd met online. In emails and on the phone, he was hilariously funny, and I couldn't wait to meet him in person. While sitting across from me at a restaurant he was telling me a gut-busting story, and at one point in surprised response to something funny about his story, I said while laughing out loud, "Shut the fuck up!" and continued to laugh. He immediately got a solemn face and said, "You're too nice and pretty to use language like that."

My immediate response was surprise, anger, and shame. My silent thought was, "Well, then you need to get into your time machine and go back to 1950 to find yourself a wife." However, I gave no snarky response, nor did I even respond with a kind disagreement to his opinion. On the contrary, I slept with him that night when I didn't particularly want to. This was long before I realized how often I was giving away my power. On that date I handed it all over to him practically wrapped up in a bow.

If you're on a date, or speaking with a new coworker, or anyone, for that matter, and they tell you their opinion about you and it's flat-out wrong, please, for the love of all that is holy, do not make the same mistake I did. A simple reply is, "I don't share that opinion," with a smile on your face (or your middle finger in their face, either way). Or even, "Thanks for sharing that, and here are my thoughts on the matter . . ." The reason I didn't respond on that date was because a) I was a little shocked by his response to my lively outburst, b) I still wanted him to like me and didn't know what to say to save face (even though after that I didn't like him anymore), and c) I was worried about disagreeing with him for fear that it would make him uncomfortable.

God forbid we make someone else uncomfortable by defending our own opinions.

Another example of where our opinions matter is at the doctor's office. First and foremost, women more often than men are dismissed when telling doctors their symptoms (and even more so for Black women), and many times will resist even going to the doctor in the first place for this reason. Second, you know your body best, but sometimes second-guess your own symptoms or worries. *You must listen to your body.* Our bodies are the wisest parts of ourselves, giving us messages if we listen. Give your doctor your opinion about what's happening to your body, and if you feel dismissed, express this. If still you are getting nowhere, find a new doctor. Again, your opinion matters, especially when it comes to your own health. This is what it means to take up space.

Look for other women who do these things and befriend them, follow them on social media, read their blogs, listen to their podcasts, be in and around their energy. We've all heard, "You can't be what you can't see," and this is a perfect illustration of something we need to notice more in our lives—women unapologetically taking up space in their lives.

THE
UNLEARNING

NOTICE: Both shining bright and taking up space can feel like changing your whole identity. Notice where you have any resistance to the advice I've given above; that may be a clue on where to start. For instance, if you balk at being more outspoken with your opinions, notice that, and get curious. It's not about completely changing your life right away; progress starts with awareness first.

Think about any regrets you have in your life. Were they about playing small and not taking up space?

Look at where you hold back in taking up space with your body, your appearance, your voice, and your emotions. It's not about becoming someone different than you are in order to take up more space, it's about getting to know your authentic self, who might be afraid of the consequences of taking up space.

GET CURIOUS: Now that you've identified some places in your life where you try to take up as little space as possible, ask yourself, Why do you feel the need to do this? Where and from whom did you hear messaging about this? What was modeled for you growing up? Do you have judgments about women who take up lots of space, and if so, what are they?

What is it costing you to not take up more space? What are your fears if you do take up space?

SELF-COMPASSION: As you start to notice and get curious about your possible lack of taking up space, you may find your inner critic chiming in about wasted time, what you "should" be doing, and other soul beatings. This is about your growth, and awareness can sometimes be the hardest part. If you're feeling down on yourself about this, here's your reminder: The great news is that now you know. Now you know, so you can use the tools you have (and many more to come) to take up some damn space in this world because we need more of you!

KEEP THE MOMENTUM: As I mentioned, first comes knowing where you might be "small" in your life. Take this inventory and look back to connect the dots as to why you're doing it—why you've felt safer not taking up space rather than being more of your real self and going after all the things that you aspire to be, do, and have. Then it's about slowly chipping away at old belief systems. You won't bring them all down at once; it's one belief, one action at a time that will create more energy in the direction you want to go.

"Taking up space" might not look the same to you as it does to the next woman and the woman after her. *You* get to define that. As long as it feels expansive and badass to you, you're on the right track.

2

Start Shining Too Bright

"She thinks she's *sooooo* hot!"

As I sat on the curb, my friend Amber slowly rode her bike in a circle as she talked about another girl in our fourth-grade class. I don't remember exactly who she was talking about, but I distinctly remember feeling shame, even though she wasn't talking about me. In that moment I very much understood that thinking you were hot was a thing we did not want to do. I hoped no one thought of *me* that way, and I certainly hoped none of my friends were talking about me like Amber was talking about this other "hot girl."

This conversation is burned into my memory with fear. That seemingly innocuous exchange took place with my friend when we were nine or ten years old, but a story was made up in my mind. The story was that to take up space, to act confident, and to garner attention were all bad things and deemed you unlikable. Further, that we, as girls, were supposed to dislike these ways of being in one another, and it was up to us to talk about one another, especially when it came to matters of someone "acting all hot." That it was up to us to make sure we all knew what lane to stay in and to never move into territory that would get us excluded.

This example is one of many small experiences I had that taught me from a very early age that we were not to act like we wanted attention, or what I like to call "shine too bright." Since we learn this when we're young, these narratives can stay with us forever. These small stories live in us, and can seem harmless all by themselves, but when you add them onto the mountain of messaging that we get throughout our lifetime, the conditioning that tells us we need to act and behave a certain way, the outcome of "smallness" manifests at work and in our friendships, and it can show itself in even just naming our goals. It pops up in how we speak about ourselves silently in our heads and out loud to other people, and plays out in our romantic relationships. In other words, this conditioning and socialization, if not intercepted, engulfs us and is expressed in every aspect of our lives. So the more you know it, the more intimate you get with these stories and experiences, the better you are at unraveling them and creating new ones.

In our need to belong as human beings, I learned that to "act hot" would make me different, would make me not belong, and therefore was one of the scariest things to be, even if it was perceived only by others—even if *I* didn't believe this to be true about myself. This is one example that the vast majority of girls and women are bombarded with on a regular basis in terms of how to be.

Acting hot, shining too bright, making a scene, upstaging others, showing off, causing a stir . . . these are all things for which I have done the work to unravel what they mean to me, and I wish now, as a grown woman, I could list them in my bio as "hobbies include." But rare is the woman who grew up in a world where those types of things were okay, let alone discussed. And even more rare is the woman who grew up in a world where these things were encouraged and celebrated.

FEAR OF OUTSHINING OTHERS

The nervousness, fear, or sheer terror of standing out too much or shining at all is the feeling most of us can relate to and nod in agreement about fairly easily. You may even be able to think of a story from your childhood of hearing gossip about someone who "brags too much" or "thinks she's so pretty." But this fear isn't where it ends, just the fear of shining too bright. Another layer deep is the fear of *outshining* others.

In the book *The Big Leap,* author Gay Hendricks talks about what he calls the Upper Limit Problem, or ULP. In short, we reach Upper Limit Problems when we feel so incredibly uncomfortable stepping out of our comfort zone. This can be going after a bigger job, putting our art out into the world, speaking up, raising rates or asking for a raise at work—really anything that requires more attention from others, a risk, and, you guessed it, acting all hot. Upper Limit Problems come up all over the damn place for women—our ULPs look like litter in a public park that nobody has paid attention to for a long time.

I had a client once, Michelle, who was struggling to take action on sending out an email for her new consulting business, inviting people to work with her. As I strategized with her, I had a hunch and asked her what she was afraid might happen if she sent the email. Or what might happen if she had success and her business continued to grow. While I coached her around these two questions, what we both realized was that it wasn't about the thing that she was failing to take action on—getting the words right to send out the email—it was her fear of shining, or even, in her case, outshining her sister. She admitted she was worried about her sister, who'd recently lost her job. Michelle feared that if she had success with her business, her sister would feel worse about herself. She said she would feel embarrassed and even ashamed about having success while her sister was struggling.

We are taught to not outshine other people, because, if we do that, we are making them uncomfortable, we are showing off, and we are not doing what we're "supposed" to be doing. What we are "supposed" to be doing is taking care of everyone, making sure they're happy, and certainly making sure that everybody likes us.

These are not "lessons" we make up out of thin air. Research shows that both men and women view certain traits differently based on gender. In 2018, the Pew Research Center published a study that revealed how Americans describe what society values (and doesn't) in each gender. Traits that were viewed as more positive for women were: beautiful, kind, and compassionate. Words that were viewed as negative for women were: aggressive and powerful. I'm sure no one is surprised that when it came to men, the word *powerful* was seen as positive.

To shine is to garner attention. To garner attention is to be powerful. To be powerful is still an enormous risk for women.

That risk can be exacerbated depending on things like race, because of stereotypes. For instance, my friend Rachel Luna, a naturally energetic and gregarious forty-year-old Latina author and coach, told me a story about an experience she had in high school as she was dating a young white man. Rachel says, "I was so excited to meet my boyfriend's family at a party they had thrown. After being there only a few minutes and being my natural enthusiastic self, I felt discomfort in the room, and felt I should tone it down. Later, when I asked my boyfriend what his family had thought of me, he told me that they thought I was sweet, but that I'm not the kind of girl he should marry, but instead, the kind of girl to have fun with." When Rachel pressed him as to why she wasn't the marrying type, he told her, "Well, because you're Latina and a city girl, and my family thinks I should marry someone like us." Rachel confessed that this devastating experience impacted how she showed up in her future relationships.

What's also important to understand here is that it's not just that we fear outshining people because we might make them uncomfortable. In many cases, it's also because we're afraid of people feeling threatened by us. It's like an unspoken crime for women that we dare not commit.

How many times have we hidden our accomplishments, our celebrations, our bigness?

Maybe you are gregarious and spirited like Rachel, maybe you have a loud voice and a thundering laugh, maybe you have an outgoing personality. Perhaps you love to wear colorful or tight clothing or you're the first to have the answers or ideas or you give your opinions freely. And if any of those ring true, I'm assuming you've been told to turn it down, that you come off as intimidating, or that you have resting bitch face. (Now that we're talking about it, why is RBF even a thing just for women? Why is there no equivalent for men?)

As a woman, I learned to read a room. If I felt like I was getting especially excited about something, and felt very much "in my Andrea-ness," I would glance around the room to gauge people's reactions, to watch their body language, and to see how they were looking at me, looking at one another in split-second glances, and then I would behave according to that, whether I was surrounded by strangers or people I knew. I think about the amount of energy that I spent worrying how I was coming across, worrying that people were thinking I was too loud, that I was too boisterous, that I was taking up too much space. I could probably fuel a rocket with all that energy I spent taking inventory and worrying.

Maybe your superpower is that you're extremely intelligent, or ambitious, or that you feel beautiful when you show your cleavage. Even if you don't have a loud, gregarious personality, I know there are other ways you have probably felt that you might be making other people uncomfortable. Women tend to do this with their intelligence—they are brilliant, and they excel academically and/or in their careers, and that might be an area where they are afraid to outshine people. Maybe they were told to not make their siblings look bad, or perhaps it was your friends you didn't want to make uncomfortable, and maybe it was no one—merely the fear of transcending others and what that might mean for them and for you.

THE DAMPENING OF YOUR SOUL

I'm certain that many of you reading can pinpoint somewhere in your life where you have felt uncomfortable, felt like it's best not to outshine anyone else, and that you need to tone it down in some way or another.

And like you'll hear me say in this book more than once, you can live your life just fine and ignore everything I'm pointing out. You can go about your job, your romantic relationships, raising your kids, and everything else, and it'll be okay.

But I know you didn't pick up this book to just be okay. To live a little life and be just fine. You picked up this book because something whispered inside you, "I need this. I want to live bigger. I want to shine."

I want to make it clear that this can be scary. I would never berate you for what you've been doing—downplaying your accomplishments or playing it safe in order to not be seen as "too much" and to not make others uncomfortable. I do it, too.

And at the same time, I need to remind you that this is your one, true life. This is it—not a dress rehearsal, not the choreographed dance "full-out" before the performance. This *is* the performance.

Tamping down your brightness and bigness slowly but surely dampens your soul and, if it goes on for too long, can crush it. I know that sounds dramatic, but for the love of all that is holy, this is your life—we're not talking about the brightness and bigness of your new kitchen lighting; we're talking about the bigness and brightness of your *life*.

For too long, women everywhere have been giving in to societal "rules" that tell us to dim down. And the time is now for all of us to not only declare that we're done with that, but to do the necessary work involved to make changes and shine on.

TOOLS

At the end of our lives we want to know we did our best. Not necessarily that we crushed it and kicked ass every single moment of every single day, or that we shone as much as our favorite celebrity or any other woman we admire. But real-life success in terms of your self-growth looks like this: We become aware of the ways we sabotage ourselves—we know that it's not our direct fault, but we realize the ways we self-sabotage and understand that we do it because that's what we were taught would keep us safe.

(That's something I want you to remember—for women, many of the behaviors and mindsets I'll talk about in the upcoming chapters are not things we do because we are broken, or not smart enough, or not having a "high enough vibration." We do things like try to not shine too bright, not ask for what we want, and numb out of our lives—all things you'll read about—because we've been conditioned to do them. We believe they work to keep us safe, keep us from failure, ridicule, criticism, and judgment. And sometimes they work for a little while until we feel the pull in our hearts and souls that we don't want that for ourselves anymore. The voice inside us is either whispering or screaming, telling us enough is enough.)

If you do get to the end of your life and you've crushed it, bravo! But most of us step into shining our brightest by taking small steps to do so. Little, incremental actions that lead up to the brightest star you can imagine.

SHINE ON

The first thing I'd love for you to think about is that hiding yourself out of fear of being perceived a certain way or outshining others does not in fact make it better for others. It's not a zero-sum game, where your gain automatically means less for other women. In fact, when women who know you and care about you see you shine, it's inspiring for them. It shows them it can be done and gives them hope and motivation.

Second in helping you shine bright is to identify where you are tamping down your own brightness now in your life. Maybe you do it at work. Let's say you're in a work meeting, you have an idea, and you're afraid to raise your hand because you're always the first person to raise your hand and give an idea and brainstorm. You think to yourself, "Maybe I should give someone else a chance . . . but no one else is raising their hand . . . I'll see if someone else raises their hand, even though I have this fantastic idea . . . Maybe I should give this idea to my coworker and see if they want to be the one to volunteer it . . ."

Thought processes like that are ones to pinpoint and notice. Your discomfort in raising your hand is definitely something for you to take note of.

Or maybe you're not taking credit for things that you actually did at work, or someone gives you a compliment on a work project and you make sure you tell that person about three other people who helped you with it, even though all they did was sit in on the meeting and scroll through their phones. What is it at work that you're doing where you are afraid of outshining others? Where are you not fully showing up, for fear that you will make people feel threatened by you, uncomfortable, or that you will make them dislike you? This isn't about throwing your coworkers under the bus or taking credit for something that isn't yours—it's about noticing where you undermine yourself, where you don't take credit for things that are rightfully your doing, or don't step fully into your best self for fear of shining too bright.

Perhaps you tone it down with your appearance. If you're familiar with the TV show *Schitt's Creek,* you'll know the character Moira Rose, played by the brilliant Catherine O'Hara. Moira was a wealthy woman who lost everything but managed to keep some of the clothes that she had from her former life, including many wigs. In one scene, she attends a party where she's incredibly overdressed in an unabashed gold lamé dress with a giant bow on the front of it. People stare at her and make comments about it, and someone gives her an obviously fake compliment and she accepts it as genuine.

I love characters like this on TV and in movies, and the truth is, if I saw a woman like this at a party, I would probably at first stare and perhaps (even though I hate to admit it) make a comment about her eccentric attire. Because we're socialized to look especially at women like this as different, attention-seeking, weird, and an easy target to make fun of. So how about we catch ourselves in those moments, understand it's our conditioning that's making us think that, and alternately choose to focus on their confidence? Moira Rose doesn't care if she makes people uncomfortable; she doesn't care if people feel threatened by her appearance or by her presence in general. She loves her own style and embraces it wholeheartedly.

In terms of your appearance, do you sabotage yourself so that you don't outshine? Do you try to tone down your expression so as not to make other women feel uncomfortable? Or tone it down to try not to garner attention from men? It's no secret that women who show lots of skin are judged for it, both by men and by women. My mother has lived her entire adult life with double-D breasts and told me she never liked showing her cleavage because "no good ever came from it." I'm pointing out the obvious here to say it's undeniable that we have always lived in this no-win situation of understanding it's part of our "duty" to be attractive but not to overstep into "too much." Think about where you fall into that. More specifically, think about and name where you try to toe the line in an effort to try not to draw too much attention to yourself in terms of how you look, and/or where you try to not eclipse others.

Or perhaps you try to not shine too bright in your friendships. A few years ago, I had to take a good look at how I was doing this. I had a close friend with whom I was feeling like I had to stay at the same pace in terms of our careers. I had made up in my head that I needed to be her "pacer"—as if we were running a marathon and she had asked me to stay with her as we ran together. This is a thing in running; you can ask or even hire someone to pace with you and make sure that you don't fall too far behind or go too fast, so as not to run out of energy. But we weren't running a marathon, we were both running our own businesses.

The real fear was that if I succeeded more than my friend did, then I would leave her behind, she wouldn't like me anymore, she'd think I was being a show-off, she'd think I was being too ambitious, she'd think I was being too smart. Additionally, I would make her sad and feel bad about herself. All of these stories, although for a long time unconscious, seeped into my decisions and were sabotaging my own success. I was basically putting a fire hose on my own fire, and my friend had never asked me to do that. She had never said, nor would she ever say, "I want you to keep pace with me. Stop writing books, stop it with all your success, wait for me to catch up!"

This friend has always celebrated my success and my ambition. My success only made her feel more inspired and motivated. But I was completely making up a false narrative about this. The story was: If I am too successful, I will leave people behind and I will be alone.

I confessed all of these feelings with this particular friend. I owned and took responsibility for my thoughts and feelings, and was able to let go of this notion that I needed to take care of her by not "leaving her behind."

Next, look at your romantic relationships. Maybe your partner has a high-profile job and you've made up an unconscious story that there's only one person who can be the "star" in the relationship. In a heterosexual family, typically it's the wife who is the supporter. While the meaning of the expression "Behind every great man is a great woman" is clear, its origin is less so. The first documentation comes from a quarterback in 1945 talking about his comeback as an athlete and giving credit to his wife; however, it's rumored that this idiom was being expressed long before that decade. Even if you didn't grow up with traditional gender roles being the norm in your family, we all learn to some extent that that's our "job" as women—to be the nurturer, the helper. I'm not at all saying nurturing and helping is bad; it's a great thing as long as we have the capacity for it. My point is that many times we think we shouldn't shine as bright as our male partners do because it would take something away from their success and we dare not emasculate them. This can also happen at work if you work with men.

THE BIG WHY

Now that you've identified *where* you do this, the second part is to identify *why* you are doing this. Get out a pen and paper and start writing.

Maybe it started when you were young. Perhaps you had a sibling who wasn't as smart as you, so you learned not to be celebrated as much, or to feel uncomfortable when you received compliments. Or maybe you grew up seeing traditional gender roles, where women were meant to be the primary caregiver in the family and never ask for help. Where moms just stayed in the background and that was their job. Or maybe you've tried to shine bright and been judged for it, ridiculed or teased, or been told, "Don't get too big for your britches."

When you get all these stories and memories down on paper, you might look at them and think they're ridiculous. The client I mentioned before, the one who was afraid of outshining her sister, said, "I make up a story that there's only so much shiny-ness to go around and it's like a box of a dozen donuts. Everybody gets one, and I don't want to take anybody else's donut. I'll wait and see if there are any left over for me; I might have some, but there probably won't be any left over. I would rather it go to all those people that I love and care about, so I'm just going to stay back here and hide and not shine."

In other words, "This will keep me safe, this will keep everyone else comfortable in this comfort zone that I am so used to, even though, in the end, it feels like shit. Even though at the end of my life, I'm going to look back and say, 'Damn it, I should have shone like a huge glazed donut and then ate it!'"

It's the *why* that's what I want you to look closely at, poke, question, and once you gather more information about your unique experience, you can look at these stories that you've made up, connect the dots, and do more inner work. Maybe you need to do inner-child work, family systems, or even trauma therapy. Bring this journal or notes that you took to your therapist, and/or you can bring this to a conversation with your friends, the ones who appreciate these kinds of conversations.

Because the world needs more shiny women, whether you love to wear gold lamé dresses with bows on them or not. It needs you to not hide, it needs you to come out from worrying about making people uncomfortable or worrying if they're going to feel threatened by the space that you're taking up and the shine you are putting out there.

You could be twenty-five years old, sixty-five, or somewhere in between, but no matter how old you are, you have had years of conditioning. The good news is you can still 100 percent unravel these stories and create new ones in your life. It will not be linear, and it will not happen overnight. I know a lot of you get excited and think, "Oh, I figured it out. I'm creating a new story and I'm on this trajectory to know that I'm the damn hot girl, and it's all going to be great!" Although I *love* your enthusiasm, this will be a journey. But now that you've done the work of identifying it, you're well on your way.

Your life, your being, is a light. And that light is a gift that was bestowed onto you when you were born. A gift for you to relish in and a gift for you to share with the world.

Other people who judge are struggling with their own gift, or they have also been conditioned to dampen and hide the light of others. It rarely, if ever, has anything at all to do with you, but more so the other person thinking they are following the "rules" of social conditioning. Or perhaps they are trying to take out their own pain on you, typically unknowingly. Maybe they see something in you they envy, they see light in you that they feel they cannot emit. They long to shine their own light, but cannot; therefore, something inside them makes it okay to judge yours and try to make you hide. Again, it's not about you.

We, as women, have a special kind of light that was meant to radiate. Just as the sun was meant to warm the earth, you were meant to shine, to step fully into yourself and illuminate others.

THE
UNLEARNING

NOTICE: Notice where you find yourself holding back, whether it's with your opinions, your success, your appearance, your anything. Pay attention and acknowledge the stories or narratives that you've made up to be true over the course of your life.

Does this happen at work? If so, be specific. Does this happen in your romantic relationships either past or present? What about with your appearance? More specifically, do you find yourself holding back or hiding when it comes to your accomplishments, your opinions, or anything else? Get it all out on paper.

Remember, this step is about observing only, not necessarily coming to any grand conclusions.

GET CURIOUS: Where do you think these habits came from? What was the message or even the unsaid "rules" from your family of origin? If you find something there, where do you think your parents came up with these rules?

What about your past relationships? Did you ever date someone who tried to make you wrong for shining bright? Did this happen in your friendships, whether it was your own doing or someone else's?

Think about your conditioning in general. Now that you've poked around in your past, think about other things, like the media you consumed. What did you think of female TV or movie characters who did in fact shine? Did you admire them? Fear them? Judge them? Nothing is wrong with any of your answers to any of these questions; this is all helpful for you in getting to the bottom of why you think and behave the way you do.

SELF-COMPASSION: As you start to realize where you've held yourself back, have compassion for yourself. You might uncover a whole mountain of stories that don't feel good. You're not alone here—many, if not most, women have been conditioned to create stories that holding back will keep them safe. As I mentioned, you're not wrong for believing these things, and as a reminder, you've been conditioned to believe shining too bright is not okay, and neither is outshining others. This is about unlearning those beliefs to adopt new ones.

KEEP THE MOMENTUM: Like all the chapters you'll read in this book, this is a lifelong quest. While the first thing I encourage you to do is start having this conversation with yourself, also start having these conversations with other people that you know will get it and that you trust. Start noticing when you're with friends and you or someone else says, "I wanted to speak up, but I didn't." Or if you or someone else pooh-poohs their accomplishments or tries to bypass their own big dreams. Women shine more brightly together, so I encourage you to bring this up with your friends in order for you to learn to be vulnerable with one another about this topic, as well as help one another to create your own support system of light and radiance.

Keep noticing when, where, and with whom you tamp yourself down. Keeping the momentum is all about using these steps repeatedly, as the unlearning process will continue throughout your lifetime.

It's easy to get bogged down thinking about all the obstacles we have to overcome, and my hope is that you see that, and keep the focus on how you can take small steps to make some noise in your life. Your changes inspire others!

3

Start Asking for Everything You Want

If women asked for the things we truly wanted as often as we apologized, we'd have a lot of happier women in the world. But it's not our fault.

We've been raised to not ask for seconds at dinner, promotions at work, or oral sex from our partners. We start our requests with "Sorry to bother you . . ." or give people an out when we make an ask, such as "I'd love if you can get that done for me by Friday, but if you can't, no worries, I can just do it." When truly, if they can't get to it by Friday, we surely will worry, and we'd rather get a Pap smear every day for a month than do their job on top of ours.

We tend to not ask for help around the house from our partners, and instead take it on ourselves and then feel resentful. We hesitate to ask for help at work with projects when the work is simply too much. We'd rather work longer hours and stress about it than ask for a hand or more time, and often we don't even realize we're doing this.

At the root of it, we are regularly worried about putting people out, about inconveniencing them, or about asking for more than what we think we deserve. We don't want to be categorized as difficult, pushy, or bitchy. That, or we don't even recognize we can ask for help in the first place, or that things are up for negotiation.

Women's empowerment begins with women asking for what they want, period. It's foundational. You can't be empowered while unnecessarily apologizing all over yourself or wishing and hoping things will fall into your lap. Think about how shitty it feels when the ask bubbles up in your throat, the moment passes, and it feels too late to ask. And as you'll hear me repeat over and over in this book, you don't not ask for what you want because you're weak or too stupid to know better. You don't ask because it's the norm in our culture. It's in the air we've all breathed since we were born. "Good girls don't ask for too much, good girls are selfless not selfish, and good girls just make do with what they get."

Well, I'm here to tell you that the vast majority of us are done settling for crumbs, and if you're not done settling, we'll fight for you, too.

I understand that it can feel uncertain asking for things when you've spent a lifetime not asking beyond what you've deemed "acceptable." I get that you can feel motivated and excited to read about how to ask for everything you want and at the same time feel afraid that it won't work for you or that you're too timid to start asking, or worried how people will react or what they'll do. But if nothing else, while you read the rest of this chapter and even the rest of this book, I want you to imagine the "what-if." What if you could take what you read here and decide to apply it? If this truly feels foreign, understand that you don't have to take action in this moment, you need to decide. Then, after a while, you take small action. Those small actions can turn into big actions, and that can and will change your life.

Asking for everything you want feels bold because *it is* bold. It's taking a stand against what it means to "be a "good girl." It might make people question you or even be afraid of you. If you're hesitant or even terrified to start asking for what you want, let's explore that.

WHY WOMEN DON'T ASK

Let's talk about why you don't ask for what you want, so you can more easily unpack it to move into asking. The short answer as to why we don't ask is because we're afraid. The longer answer will be uniquely yours. I've narrowed the fears down into five different scenarios. Here's the list of all the things we're afraid of when it comes to asking for what we want, as well as some tools on how to turn things around:

Fear #1: Afraid of How We'll Look to Others/of Being Judged

As I mentioned before, you might have a belief that women who ask for too much are everything you don't want to be. Perhaps the words you might use are *greedy, bratty, spoiled, entitled,* or *selfish.*

Melinda, forty-one, says, "I have a very hard time asking for anything. I don't want to offend anyone or look selfish or greedy. I've been told before that the way I ask seems fishy because I'm so nervous. For example, I recently emailed a coworker, 'We were thinking of going away from June 4 to June 12. Are you okay with that? I can change it if you wanted that week off.' I drive myself crazy trying to accommodate everyone else!"

Melinda is an example of being more concerned with how she is perceived by others and what they think of her, as opposed to getting her own needs met. It would be amazing if Melinda could plainly declare, "I'm *done* putting everyone first, and I give zero fucks what anyone thinks of me! From here on out, I am my first priority!" That's great for a cute Instagram meme, but it's fleeting and never really helps in the long run. Melinda, like most of us, has learned from a young age that her first priority is other people, before her own. While certainly it's important to be flexible and considerate, women tend to bend so far over backward, we get used to that position and stay there, and some of us bend so far we end up snapping.

If you're worried about being seen in a negative way, first check what *your* assumptions are of women who ask for what they want. If you think women who ask are "bad," ask yourself, Is that your conditioning or is it the truth? It's important to get clear on that and check your judgments. If you assume women who ask for what they want are greedy and thinking only about themselves, simply ask yourself, "What if I could choose another perspective?" Maybe that perspective is: Women who ask for what they want are confident. They are smart in that they know what they want in order to not waste the time or energy of others. You don't have to completely flip the script on what your beliefs are right now, but rather recognize your disempowering beliefs and look at another perspective. When you find a perspective you could get on board with, it's about sitting with it and reminding yourself of it until it becomes your new belief.

Fear #2: Afraid of Being and Looking Vulnerable

Asking for what you want is vulnerable, and humans tend to not like that. But the other option is not getting what you want, so you decide.

Let's unpack this—the obvious is that being vulnerable is uncomfortable, but most things that are worth getting are worth feeling uncomfortable with for a little bit. Typically, uncomfortable conversations aren't as difficult as we think they'll be, nor do they take as long as we think they will. They usually last between five and fifteen minutes. Personally, I've made myself physically sick with anxiety before hard conversations or requests, only to realize later that they were only about 20 percent as bad as I had made up.

There is absolutely no getting out of feeling vulnerable on this one. You have to get to the point where the pain of not asking is worse than the pain of feeling vulnerable for a little while.

Fear #3: Afraid of a "No," Which Could Lead to Conflict

If I had a dollar for every time a woman told me she's "conflict avoidant" or uses the excuse "I hate conflict" as to why she didn't ask for what she wanted, I'd have more Birkin bags than Cardi B. No one actually likes conflict, and if they do, they're kind of an asshole. While it's natural to try to stay away from conflict, some people are extremely conflict-avoidant, to the point of making up in their heads that even the risk of a "no" isn't worth the possible conflict. Or, if you grew up in a house with lots of conflict, you might be the type of person who equates getting your needs meet with combativeness.

If you're afraid of conflict, ask yourself where it's coming from. If your family-of-origin story revolves around conflict, maybe it's time for some trauma therapy. It's not just about telling yourself you're safe before you walk into your boss's office. While that can help for many people, if you don't work on your childhood wounds of feeling unsafe, the weight of those feelings will keep circling around like vultures over a dying animal and will continue to be a somatic, full-body experience. You deserve to feel safe, and trauma therapy can help.

Or maybe you don't have a family background of conflict but you're still afraid of hearing "no" and the shitstorm that will create in your head if and when it happens. Ask yourself this: Like the fear of feeling vulnerable, do you want what you want more than the discomfort of hearing no? If the answer is no, see the preceding paragraph about how the fear of conflict is ruling you—you may want to consider digging deeper. If you're willing to give up what you want in order to avoid a "no," conflict may have a bigger hold on you than you think. If your answer is yes, that you want what you want and you're willing to take the risk of a "no," then maybe all you need to learn is how to ask, which is what I'll dive into in a minute.

Fear #4: Afraid of a "Yes," and Then We'll Have to Level Ourselves Up and Really Show Up

This coincides with the fear of success. If your boss says "yes" to giving you more money or a promotion, or if your partner says "yes" to couples counseling, then you also have to show up more, which may test and shake your confidence.

Let's first talk about your success, your yes, your up-level. What if you ask and get what you want? Hooray! This is great, *and* you might be shaking in your boots about having to show up to a new, bigger situation. Know that while you may have some embarrassment about the fear of success (I mean, who doesn't want to be successful?), it's not that you're afraid of having more money, better relationships, or more opportunities—what you're afraid of is the results of that.

More money or a promotion at work might mean more pressure. If your partner gives you what you want, you might feel like this is the healthiest relationship you've ever had, and that might lead to being more vulnerable, or that you're not used to a great relationship and you feel it's destined to fail. Perhaps you fear the uncertain next level after that, if this new thing is sustainable, or the fear of judgment from others.

While the fear of failure seems more obvious, the fear of success is more common than you might think. If this is you, first know that you're normal, and that in the decade-plus I've been doing this work, most of the women I work with fear success in some way. Part of the reason is that we tend to not be encouraged to be "successful" in our culture's definition of success. It's typically reserved for boys and men.

Second, one thing you must do is take small action toward what you want in terms of your success. You're attempting to retrain your brain about how it thinks of success, and therefore changing the way you think of asking for what you want. For instance, start asking for projects at work that are a small step above what you normally do, rather than asking for a huge new project. In other words, you're taking baby steps outside of your comfort zone in place of huge ones. The point is to prove to yourself that you can and will ask for what you want, and that success is not scary and won't lead to your ultimate demise, which is what your subconscious might be attached to.

Fear #5: Afraid of Not Asking Correctly and/or Being Misunderstood

Many times, we don't ask because we don't know what to say. Do we write on a piece of paper to our boss, "Can I have 10k more a year? Check yes or no"? It can feel awkward at best and terrifying at worst if we're not prepared.

Plus, there's an assumption that what you want can be asked for in only one of two ways:

1. Apologetically and timidly
2. Demanding and confrontational, with a side of ultimatum

Women tend to get categorized as "demanding" when they freely ask for what they want. They are called difficult, bossy, intimidating, and hard to work with. There are stereotypes that we're all familiar with. Hence when we do ask for things, we do it as softly as possible.

III

Coinciding with several of the above fears is an example from Andrea Lee, a fifty-year-old Canadian-born entrepreneur of Taiwanese descent. Andrea's story shows how both culture and race can have an impact on some women's ability to ask for what they want. She explains, "In 2003 my first mentor, Thomas, died suddenly. He was a leader in our industry, beloved by hundreds of thousands, and had only a back-of-the-napkin will. The business went to a white man who had not been actively involved in the company. As general manager and one of very few Asian women in my field at the time, I had thrown myself full-throttle into running the business, but . . . I was only a contractor.

"A white woman who had been a content creator with Thomas raised her hand to say, 'Hey, I should see a share of his estate,' and she was given a meaningful payout, just like that. No red tape, no lawyers, no apparent contention. I was shocked. First, how bold of her in that moment of mourning to do that. But then, very quickly, an internalized 'be a good Asian woman' voice kicked in.

"But at the same time, this wasn't fair. Why was I being overlooked? Was I supposed to also ask? No way, that's impolite and disrespectful, now is not the time. Besides, if that person got a meaningful payout, it should be very obvious that I am due one, too, right? I was working way harder, running the whole company, and had been with Thomas longer and, although that was its own reward, I would be financially rewarded in the end, right?

"I was severed a few months later, even though I had worked to ensure the business delivered its promises as best it could in the months after Thomas died.

"What made me not raise my hand to ask for a share of the estate? Why did I agonize over how used I felt by myself, never telling this story to anyone for fear I would be seen as demanding and entitled? I had internalized the cultural forces that told me to stay in my place. I was a woman, and an Asian woman at that. It was expected that I be quiet and polite. Add to that the patriarchal forces of North American culture which I'd been brought up in—don't rock the boat, nice girls don't cause conflict, someone will take care of me, be seen not heard, and, well . . . the result is probably not a surprise.

"As someone who did not recognize those forces were in play, I thought it was just me and my flaws. Insecurity, shyness, inadequacy, or was it a lack of talent? Those were certainly present. But these elements were actually secondary to the bigger conditioning that I've since unlearned."

WHERE TO START IN RELATIONSHIPS

But there is a middle ground in asking for what you want that can be direct and kind. I had a client named Melissa whom I coached on my podcast. She had written to me about wanting to have more time to do more self-care for herself. She wrote, "I am struggling with sticking to routines that involve taking care of myself physically and mentally and figuring out what is actually of priority." Once we started the session, it turns out the topic really was that she was doing the lion's share of the work and needed to ask her husband for more help. The truth was, she *had* expressed to him that she needed more help from him, and he responded with telling her he was too tired after work.

The thing that struck me wasn't so much the obvious situation, which is not an uncommon one. But rather that she translated this problem into something she needed to fix on her own. That she felt the struggle she needed to remedy was being able to stick to a routine to take care of herself. That's the part that made my head explode. She was working full-time, raising two daughters, and essentially taking care of a third person, her husband, who was fully capable of not simply taking care of himself, but doing his share of the work with all the chores and child-rearing.

Melissa's homework was not to find and stick to a better plan to take care of herself (that would come later), but her homework was to have a loving, serious, and clear conversation with her husband that him pulling his weight was not up for debate. That his "being too tired after work" was not a valid excuse, but was hurting their partnership and her.

Melissa is one example of the fact that, generally speaking, we as women would prefer to do twice the amount of work, and neglect our well-being and basic self-care than have uncomfortable conversations with our partners about helping.

Now, I understand this is complex and nuanced for most. For those of you reading this who are single, I implore you to have this conversation *before* you get married or decide to be in a committed relationship. Statistics show that by the time a couple enters marriage counseling, the problem has gone on for many years, and in too many instances, the woman already has one foot out the door. Dr. John Gottman, emeritus professor of psychology at the University of

Washington and executive director of the Relationship Research Institute in Seattle, says, "Couples wait an average of six years of being unhappy with their relationship before getting help." Please don't wait until it's an emergency in your relationship.

In this example, what might be helpful is for you and your partner to have an honest conversation about gender roles. What do you both believe a wife or husband "should" do? No one gets to be wrong when you're talking about what you learned growing up and what you brought into the relationship in terms of your beliefs. You both need to start there if you're going to really hear each other and see where you're both coming from, and then hear each other about what you want. If your beliefs and then expectations are completely far off from each other's, that is then the problem you need to solve, and also to decide if some of those problems are deal breakers.

Another example is Robyn. She says, "I am afraid to ask for what I want in my current relationship. I want a level of transparency and complete open communication—this matters to me, and it's how I build trust with someone. In the past, I've heard 'Why does that matter?' and 'Why should that be important to you?' The statement that hurts the most is 'It's in the past, so it doesn't matter.' So I never ask the questions anymore. I never say it, because it is an uncomfortable conversation.

"I have always felt wrong for asking this or wanting to know it. I think that maybe there is just something wrong with me or that maybe I am crazy for wanting to know.

"As a result, I quit asking. In my current relationship, I can feel it becoming a problem. I have questions that I don't ask. I feel a wall that is between us and the trust and communication isn't there. Then I shut down, I make up stories in my head, lash out, get pissed off, and I feel like leaving the relationship. I feel all sorts of negative things because I am afraid to ask. I am afraid to hear that my wants are irrelevant. I am afraid to feel bad for wanting to know a certain thing in order to build a strong relationship."

Robyn's story is a common one. She's clear on what she wants—her desire is to have a stronger connection with her partner and to have conversations that show each other deeper parts of themselves. She understands it's not an easy discussion. When she's tried, she gets pushback from her partner and essentially a "no."

It's not that Robyn needs to get her way by having her partner tell her everything—there might be things that are too painful for him, and he may need to do his own work before he can share with her. But she's being completely shut down, which is making her question her own instincts, her own sanity, and she feels like something is wrong with her. She makes it about her, and it's actually about her partner. He is the one who's refusing to go deeper, and that's the real issue. Not Robyn.

The thing that also strikes me about her story is that she says she's afraid to ask again, afraid to feel bad for wanting to strengthen her relationship, and the kicker: *afraid to hear that her wants are irrelevant.* This, my friends, is the crux. Because when we're afraid to hear it, we're afraid it might be true.

For those of you in this situation or even if you could relate to Robyn, consider in this moment me taking you by the shoulders and staring into your eyes. I need to tell you: Your wants matter. It's normal and healthy to want a deeper connection with your partner. If your partner won't let you in, and puts up emotional boundaries that seem normal in a coworking-relationship kind of way, but not in an intimate-partner, spend-my-life-with-you way, that's on them and it's their responsibility to seek help in learning to be vulnerable with you, not on you to stop asking and settle for the scraps they give you.

I understand this puts Robyn in a bit of a no-win situation. If she keeps asking her partner for what she wants, she'll get pushback, or if he never opens up to her like she wants, she continues to feel lonely and not have the intimacy she wants. If she makes this issue a deal breaker and he never changes, she'll be forced to consider leaving.

My advice for Robyn is to really consider how she wrote out her problem. Many times, in these situations we think about the problems we have with our partners, when we're not getting what we want, and then make excuses. "But they are really supportive of me going back to school" or "My parents and my friends really like them." Trust me, I'm the queen of learning things the hard way, and maybe Robyn is, too, but I will tell you if you're asking for your emotional needs to be met and your partner hands-down refuses *and* refuses to work on it by reading books about it or going to a relationship counselor or therapist, and basically digs their heels in and makes *you* wrong, they are choosing their fear of intimacy over what's actually healthy and beautiful in a romantic relationship. The partner probably has their own stuff to work out, and that's their responsibility and a gift to *both* of you when they do so.

In the examples of Melissa and Robyn, they're asking something big of their partners. I, too, have been in this situation in my current and my first marriage. In my first marriage I would ask, plead, yell, threaten, and rage, never got what I wanted, and that marriage ended up in divorce.

Not wanting to make the same mistake in my second marriage, I knew I needed to fix my communication. To make a long story short and tidy, a couple of years into this marriage I brought a particular ask to my husband and, at the end, added this: "This is a big deal, what I'm requesting. I'm not asking you to move mountains with your progress, but I am asking for you to try and for me to see you are trying with progress."

"That sounds like an ultimatum," my husband responded.

"It's an ask and a boundary. It would be shitty if I came to you ten years from now and said I was leaving, and you never knew previously how important this was to me and how much of a deal breaker it is. I love us and you too much to not give you a fair opportunity to grow."

I had to make clear the seriousness of my ask. I wasn't asking for fun to see if he would jump if I asked. My ask was based on my values and what I knew was important to me in an intimate relationship, as well as seeing the mistakes I had made in my previous marriage and wanting to learn from them as opposed to repeating them.

And since then he began to work on it, *we* began to work on it. It wasn't the fast progress that I'd wanted, but I made a commitment to acknowledge his effort and love for me and for us, as well as give him the dignity of his own process. That conversation was about seven years ago, was one of the most important conversations of our marriage, and we are worlds further than we were then.

These types of asks come from a place of love, compassion, understanding, and knowing that what I want is important and it matters. That what I want comes from a place of my values in a relationship, which are love, growth, trust, intimacy, and support. We both slip back on this sometimes, but now we both know what that looks like and can have an uncomfortable but fundamentally important conversation in order to help our marriage.

FRIENDSHIPS AND WORK

I'll talk a bit more about asking for what you want and the art of negotiation at work in chapter (I highly encourage you to read more about that; check the Recommended Reading section of this book). Next is knowing how to ask for what you want in the other areas of your life: your relationships, friendships, kids, neighbors, Peter, Paul, and Mary.

Even though I want you to ask for everything you want, I never want you to walk in thinking you have to be demanding, intrusive, combative, or rude. Even your body language matters when you're making an ask. Briefly putting your hands over your heart and tilting your head slightly while you're asking looks very different than if you lean backward and cross your arms over your chest. One is kind and open, the other defensive and puts up a barrier.

Say your friend asked you a couple of times if you could watch her kids when she started her new job since you work from home and your schedule is flexible. You were happy to help, but she's not paying you, and it's becoming difficult to manage your own job (not to mention you *really* loathe changing diapers). You want to tell her you can't anymore, but you're nervous, you're not sure if she has any other childcare options, and you don't want things to get awkward in your friendship. So you procrastinate and silently curse as she drives away yet again while you chase down her toddlers. For free.

When it comes to having these conversations, there's a process, and it always starts with kindness and gratitude.

If you're pissed and resentful going into the conversation, even if it's righteous, coming from that place will be harmful to the dialogue and automatically put you at odds with the person you're asking something of. Leave those emotions at the door *and* ask yourself if your anger and resentment is partly (or wholly) based on the fact that you've let things go for too long and should have had the conversation weeks (years?) ago. If that's the case, remember that's not on the other person, but on you.

Start with kindness, perhaps gratitude even, and then go into what you're asking for. After that, offer a solution, if you have one and if it's applicable. For instance, in the situation with your friend, it might sound like this:

"Friend, I love watching your kids, they're so fun to hang out with, and I'm so happy about your new job! I know it was so stressful when you lost your job during the pandemic. I love helping you, and to be honest I won't be able to watch your kids after next week. I wish I could, but it's become a strain on my schedule. I'd love to help you research childcare places in the area—can I do that?"

Notice you say, "I love helping you AND . . ." Not "I love helping, BUT . . ." The *and* carries a different meaning and tone. The *but* tends to negate what you just said. This is a small thing that carries a big impact.

Important possible addition to note: "I should have told you this weeks ago, and I'm sorry I didn't. I was worried you wouldn't find anyone else and I felt bad. That part is on me." This is optional and only really necessary if you've been putting off an important conversation and ask for a long time. For example, perhaps you and your partner have always had "traditional gender roles" where they have a full-time job and you work part-time or stay home with kids. Then maybe you start working more or get a part-time job as your kids get older. But you still do the majority of the work around the house. You want to ask for more help, and maybe you drop hints, but nothing changes.

Years pass. You get more resentful. You complain to your friends. You get passive-aggressive with your partner. "Oh, look, shoes left out again. I'll pick them up and put them away, no need for any of you to help me. You all relax." Everyone stares at their phones while you sigh audibly. And maybe you've snapped a couple of times over the years and have blown up at your partner. Acted like someone you're definitely not proud of.

In this case, I would for sure advise adding the part taking responsibility for not asking sooner in a healthier way. The entire ask might sound like this: "I know when we got married/decided to live together we both knew this was a team effort. That we both would help each other out so each of us feels the amount of work we do feels fair. And for a long time, it's been weighing on me that the distribution of weight does not feel fair. I should have brought this to you sooner, and for that I'm sorry. It's not fair for you to try to read my mind. And I need you to know the gravity of how much this has been harming me. I know if this keeps going it has the ability to break me, but I love us too much to let that happen. That's why I'm bringing this to you now."

As you can tell in that script, you're owning the fact that you didn't tell your partner when you first started feeling resentful, you're reminding them about your partnership, and you're emphasizing that you're communicating this because you're committed to the relationship, not merely trying to get what you want. Both are true.

From the place where you've asked for what you want, you let it land. You might feel discomfort in the silence—the space where you've put your vulnerability out there for a response. But it's up to them how they respond. Your goal is to show up with honesty, confidence, and love. That's the only thing you can control. The rest is up to them, and in the end, if you show up as your best self, no matter the outcome, it's a success.

WHAT WOULD *SHE* DO?

Think of someone—real or fictional—that you know would ask for what she wants. Maybe a mentor of yours, or maybe it's a fictional character. Claire Underwood in *House of Cards* or Daenerys Targaryen from *Game of Thrones* might be good choices, or Annalise Keating in *How to Get Away with Murder.* We'll dive more into this tool in chapter 10 when I talk more about confidence, but for now I'd love for you to grab one or two people or characters in your mind.

When it's fictional, I invite you to think of characters who aren't necessarily nice but who are known for asking for everything they want. Think of this as an "associate," someone who perhaps you don't want to emulate or embody *all* the characteristics of (especially if she's a lying, murderous backstabber), but only the way she focuses on what she wants and asks for it. The goal is for you to get into the habit of thinking like she does in terms of opportunities for yourself. To ask yourself, "What would _____ do in this situation?"

Because at the end of the day, if you don't ask, the answer will always be no, and no one is going to ask for you. And if you don't ask, you are giving away what might be yours.

THE
UNLEARNING

NOTICE: Part of the unlearning around asking for everything you want is moving away from believing that asking for what you want is wrong. Pay attention if you find yourself not wanting to send your food back at a restaurant even though they put a rare steak in front of you and you're vegan. Notice when you procrastinate on asking for a raise even though you know a guy in your department with less experience makes more money than you do.

If you're not ready to take action on any of these things, start making a list on paper or on your phone of all the things you want but you're currently unwilling to ask for, and what it's actually costing you. Maybe it's not always costing money, but rather costing you your self-confidence, self-esteem, and self-trust, and it's going against your values. Once you see all the ways you aren't asking for what you want, you can't unsee it, and that's the point.

GET CURIOUS: Before reading this chapter, what were your assumptions about women who ask for everything they want? What did you think of them? Are you judgmental or do you envy them? If you have judgments, what are they, specifically? If you admire women who do ask for what they want, what is it that they do that you think you can't emulate? Is there anything about them you think you could also do?

Do you think asking for what you want is something you could, would, or should never do? If not, why not?

If you are afraid to ask for what you want, what exactly are you afraid of? Did someone tell you that girls were supposed to behave a certain way when it came to asking or even wanting things? What do you remember about that?

These questions might take time to sit with and answer. Curiosity is best not rushed, but is the key to clarity so you can start to unravel and unlearn old patterns and stories and relearn new ones that get you on a path to putting yourself first.

SELF-COMPASSION: If you're suddenly coming to the realization that there've been a million things you've never asked for and you're beating yourself up for it, you can cut that out right now. Most likely, you've been trained to never ask for more than what you need and/or only ask for what you think you deserve, and sometimes not even that. You're having to unravel decades of conditioning, and it won't happen overnight.

If you find you're being hard on yourself about this, try this mantra: "I am now aware, so now I can work on changing my thoughts. I deserve to be able to ask for what I want."

Compassion, like most things, is a tool that must be utilized regularly and consistently for it to work. It's key to "staying on task" in place of letting your negative self-talk get in the driver's seat of your processing and learning.

KEEP THE MOMENTUM: The number-one way to keep up the momentum on this topic is to start asking for what you want. Again, don't demand, ask with kindness and, where applicable, professionalism. Once you get clear on the areas of your life where you could ask more for what you want, notice and get curious about your conditioning around this; I invite you to talk to the women you grew up with—your friends, your sisters, even your adult friends who grew up similarly to you. Ask questions like "Do you think you hold back in asking for what you want?" Or "Do you think there are things in your life you want that you wonder 'Why bother?' and then don't ask for?" Start the conversation. Not to complain about it, but to investigate it. Change starts with conversations like these.

In addition, notice and celebrate your progress and wins! Even if you don't get what you want, your asking is part of your going after what you deserve and is a means to build confidence.

4

Start Accepting Challenges as Life Invitations

You know when you hack into your boyfriend's email when he's away at rehab and you're pregnant with his child, because you have a feeling something isn't right (I mean, the fact that he's away at rehab might be the first clue), and then see email after email in his inbox from a woman he's in rehab with, a woman you met during the heart-wrenching "family week," when you spilled your guts in front of her and everyone there? And you know that feeling when you know what you're going to find when you open the emails in his inbox from her to your boyfriend, and you don't want to read them, but you can't not? And you also see all the emails that you've been sending him, although those are unread?

So you open the emails from her to your boyfriend and read about the torrid relationship they're having at the inpatient rehab center, including their plans one night to slip away down to the ping-pong tables where no one could see them, and that that, according to the romantic emails back and forth, was where they had their first kiss.

And then as your mouth hangs open, you read the emails he wrote back to her, the same tender lines he used on you about being "twin souls," as well as their discussion of her financially supporting him after they leave rehab. And you know that feeling of dread seeping into your body as you realize that along with cheating on you in rehab when he promised he'd work on his recovery so you can both start over, have this baby, and move away together, leaving the city you've lived in your whole life—but now you realize that he was using you financially and now that you're out of money and onto his lies, he's moved on to another woman to manipulate and use?

And then you know when the feeling of dread turns to terror, as you've been here before, twelve months prior almost to the day, discovering your husband (a totally different guy, in case you're confused) has been cheating and he plans to leave, too?

So then you suddenly find yourself on the floor in a heap, phone to your ear as you babble to your sister on the other end, *"It's happening again, it's happening again, it's happening again,"* and realize she's on the other end crying, too?

No? Yes?

You might not have the same circumstance or even your own proverbial "rock bottom" like I did. But I'm guessing you know what it's like to feel as if your life has kicked the shit out of you.

I don't remember much in the days that followed reading those emails. I do remember calling the rehab center, screaming at them for allowing this to happen, desperate for someone to blame. I recall laughing hysterically at one point, the whole situation seemed ludicrous, like it was happening to someone else, that it was all a dream in which I was the star of a very sad Lifetime movie.

I was still legally married to my ex-husband, the one who had gotten our neighbor pregnant *on purpose* and ran off to start a new life with her, complete with a new house, their new baby, and a new puppy. So I dated this new guy, a David Duchovny look-alike who made me laugh and made me feel like I mattered. Only to find out months later that he'd lied about having cancer throughout our entire relationship, had an opioid addiction, and had been using me the whole time.

I won't lie—it was terrible. The absolute worst. That day, as I picked myself up off my bedroom floor, I knew my life would never be the same, and it wasn't only because I knew me and my baby's father wouldn't be together and that I wasn't getting this romantic story that I had hoped for. It was because I knew my life was about to change, and that my life was also asking something of me. To show up like I had never done before, to lean on myself instead of a man, and to not just step, but ascend into my power.

This was an invitation. I wish it had come through as a text message from the Universe filled with high-five emojis, but apparently I needed a body slam combined with a punch in the face to get the message.

You might be thinking about your own difficult time, or maybe even thinking of the spring of 2020 when we all faced the COVID-19 global pandemic, the catalyst of racial injustices that year, and the rest of the hardships that followed. I would never argue with you and tell you to not feel that those things are hard. They are, and you must honor the process. And once you've gone through that and feel you're ready, working on changing your perspective from feeling like your circumstance will break you to how it will make you can change everything.

I promise you: This work and perspective shift have the capacity to change your life.

POINTING FINGERS WON'T HELP

When I went through my personal crisis, it was easy to put blame outside myself. My ex-husband for cheating and leaving me, my boyfriend for lying, cheating, and leaving. The rehab center. I even looked for ways to blame my parents for how they raised me, and my friends for not warning me enough. Why wasn't someone or something coming to my rescue?

It was also easy to blame myself. How could I have been so stupid? If I were smarter, sexier, and more successful, this wouldn't have happened. I obviously didn't know how to pick partners. Why was I so bad at relationships? The reasons were endless as to how I got there.

For some, blame is a way to evade the hurt. Sprinkle in a little numbing out and disconnecting and, voilà, you've found the perfect recipe for running farther and farther away from the problem rather than facing it head-on. And you know what? Sometimes that works. Sometimes that eases the pain, allows us to wallow and garner sympathy from others, and we need that. Lord knows I bathed happily in the sympathy I got and loved recruiting people to Team Andrea. I reveled in making my exes wrong and me right, and for a short time it made me feel powerful and happy.

Until it didn't.

In the back of my mind I knew that this was an invitation. Life was tapping me on the shoulder and asking me to show up. For a while I wasn't ready; it was easier to keep slinking back, to blame, to numb, to disconnect. The truth is, it's scary to move out of that place. We feel we have more control if we play the blame/numb/disconnect game. People understand that and sometimes even expect it. Until, finally, we have to get to that point when the tapping on the shoulder becomes something we can no longer ignore.

We must start to ask ourselves three important questions:

What is life asking of me?

Who do I need to become?

What do I need to walk through in order to not only rise to the occasion, but to come out a better woman on the other side?

Because you must move from a place of blame to personal responsibility and understand the difference. Yes, you might have made the biggest mistakes of your life, and those decisions might have been tinged with self-sabotage. Maybe those mistakes had dire consequences. Maybe you knew better and didn't do better. But they still haven't invented time machines to go back and make different choices, so beating yourself up for it and blaming yourself for your current situation and pain is of no use to you or to anyone else. It's time to take radical responsibility for where you're at in your life.

THE MEANING OF LIFE

I'm a firm believer that the meaning of life is all about our connections with other people, as well as the entire journey itself. People get all hot and bothered about finding their purpose, when I'm over here preaching that your life, your path, is your purpose. Not to keep going in circles, but to keep moving forward.

When we stay stuck in our struggle and never reflect on what we learn, that's where we stay stuck. Spinning our wheels in a place of blame or martyrdom will keep you caught in the same place, and I know you didn't pick up this book to do that. No, you came here to change your life. You came here to use what you have. What you have is a lifetime of things that have happened to you—joyful things, boring things, and everything in between. And then there are the difficult things. Difficult things are the things that will make you. Difficult things are the places you'll have to go in your heart, mind, and soul to face, process, and heal. And that, my friend, is a meaningful, incredible, and fulfilling purpose.

TOOLS

When you find yourself anywhere between rock bottom and wanting a slight kick in the pants, it's always helpful to ask yourself some powerful questions—in other words, learn how to coach yourself. Circling back to those three questions—I'd love for you to ask yourself and truly ponder. If the answers come quickly, that's great; if you need to sit back and reflect, that's good, too. The point is to lean in to the questions and investigate what's true for you. You can download a no-cost workbook of these questions at andreaowen .com/msn.

What is life asking of me? "I need to go find myself" is a common phrase uttered when people break up (maybe when they don't want to tell the truth of "I don't love you anymore"), after they graduate high school and aren't sure about college, or really anytime in life when they don't know what's next.

This is why people go on pilgrimages, take "breaks" from their partners, go on personal-development retreats. Because we feel lost and we're looking.

What we're actually looking for are our personal values. We either have never found them or know them and have moved so far away from them that we don't know who we are and what we stand for. When I had left my relationship in my twenties multiple times, life was asking me to walk away from my boyfriend. To be alone long enough to discover what was important to me, to connect with who I was meant to be. But at the time I was too afraid to do any of that.

So now, for you, what is your life asking of you? What do you want to be important to you? Not what your parents, or your job, or your family thinks should be important to you, but what do *you* want to be the driving forces in your life? If you're feeling stuck in your challenging circumstance, you are likely valuing status quo (because it feels too scary to change) and familiarity (because the uncomfortable has become comfortable), and feeling lost (because you're used to it). You're not wrong for valuing these things, and it definitely isn't intentional. But no matter what and no matter where we are in life, we have a set of values that we are acting on. Your behavior relies on it, whether you know it or not.

Is your life asking you to be more courageous? To live with more integrity and honesty? To lean on your spirituality instead of trying to control? Is life asking you to be more curious instead of black or white? Or maybe it's asking you to look at things like self-trust and self-respect instead of letting your thoughts and behaviors be on autopilot.

So, again, what is your life asking of you? Not the "just think positive" kind, but more so the question: In order for you to show up and be proud of who you are, what do you need to do?

Who do I need to become? Every once in a while, I get an email from a woman who wants to hire me to coach her daughter. The mother feels her daughter needs guidance and direction and she wants me to personally lead the way. Having children myself, I understand the hopes, the fears, and the worry, but I will always say no to these requests.

People who come on board to work with me have to be ready to change their life. Maybe these daughters are ready, but there's something about going at it of your own accord, as changing your life never truly sticks when it was prescribed by someone else.

I can't answer the question *Who do you need to become?* for you. In order to do so, you must be willing to look back and declare what you'll need to let go of. What parts of yourself are you willing to see as unhealthy coping mechanisms, or trigger responses to hurt, shame, and fear? Or, perhaps it might be helpful to let go of relationships that are harmful to you or to set boundaries around them. It's not that you'll never again fall back on these behaviors, but once you can see what they are, you're more likely to have power over them as an alternative to them having power over you.

Who do I want to become? This may be similar to the question above, but it can shift your thinking from what you need to do to get to where you want to go to dreaming bigger. Do you want to become the woman who feels the discomfort of shining bright and does it anyway? Do you want to become the woman who asks for everything she wants? Do you want to become the woman who blows past her financial goals?

Once you're clear on who you need to become, start envisioning what's possible for you. Notice if your inner critic jumps in with negative commentary, and politely ask it to piss off.

What do I need to walk through in order to not only rise to the occasion but also to come out a better woman on the other side? Fear and uncertainty go together like Nutella and a spoon, but are not nearly as delicious. When you're in your life crisis/challenge/crappy situation, you'll be facing fear and uncertainty. Things didn't go as planned, you've perhaps never dealt with anything like this before, and maybe your heart is broken, and you don't know what's next. And when you're in the depths and muck of it, it's not the time to ask yourself what the lesson is. When I was going through my own difficult time, I would have thrown a drink in anyone's face who asked me, "What do you think being dramatically dumped twice in a row is here to teach you?"

However, once you've gone through the shock, anger, sadness, and whatever raw feelings that come up, then it's time to really look at what you need to walk through.

But I don't want to jump over the emotions, because one of the things that you'll certainly need to walk through are all of your feelings. Typically, we like to bypass them. Numb them out with food, alcohol, busyness, exercise, our phones, really anything that will allow us to run away without actually packing our bags and faking our deaths. Contrary to popular inner belief, your feelings will not kill you. The truth is that your body is actually the smartest part of you, always trying to get to a place of homeostasis. A component of that process is to express and emote. When I was first separated from my ex-husband, I was so scared and heartbroken, I spent the first few months drowning in booze, benzos, and bad love. I would cry in the bathroom at work and scream in my car. My feelings came out in bursts, but I was making it especially difficult on myself.

What we all need to do in challenging times is to trust that our body knows how to process what's happening. It's normal and healthy to sit in the feelings and emotions. To ride the wave of them and to ride it all the way to the shore.

Whoever or whatever hurt you may end up being your biggest teacher. Not that what they did or what happened was good or okay, but that the outcome served you in some way. There are some instances when this is complicated, like the loss of a child.

And perhaps if that's your life challenge, the invitation is to live life fully in honor of your child. As you think of your life challenges, you don't have to think about what the lessons are, but rather what are the invitations.

Bonus question. You may or may not want to ask yourself the question: **How did I get here?** This is only helpful if you're willing to connect the dots to prevent you from ending up there again, such as getting into a heap of credit card debt with nothing to show for it, or saying yes to a relationship with a known addict when you are in recovery.

But if you think this will bring you down a path of beating yourself up, then you might want to skip it.

ON CONFIDENCE

If there's one thing I hear that women want more of when it comes to personal growth, it's confidence. They want to do more new things, say what's on their mind, take action toward their goals, and build resilience to keep getting back up. I'll go much more into that topic in chapter 10, but something I'll keep repeating to you is that confidence isn't curated by purely searching for it and being confident.

Confidence is conceived through courage. Being brave enough for two hot seconds in order to do the thing builds your confidence muscle. This doesn't happen when your life is all unicorns farting rainbows; this happens when, you guessed it, life punches you in the face.

Think again to one of the hardest times in your life. What happened? Someone dumped you, you lost your job, got passed up for a promotion, or didn't get the job you had three interviews for.

Maybe you had a miscarriage, your child got a special-needs diagnosis, you got a chronic illness . . . the list is endless of what that could be for you.

As I mentioned above, because you're human, you were sad, angry, disappointed; felt sorry for yourself; grieved—whatever you needed to do. And then what?

Listen, those feelings ebb and flow. It's not that you get ten days to be sad and then you need to pack all that up like your winter sweaters and shove it into the back of your closet. The challenging feelings may come and go, but once you get through that initial fall-on-your-face-in-the-dirt moment, you—and only you—decide what you're going to do next. In the world of personal growth, there are various quotes about pain. A popular one is something along the lines of: There are two types of pain in this world. The pain that hurts and the pain that changes you.

Essentially, one type of pain is the pain that is simply suffering. When Kelly Clarkson sings, "What doesn't kill you makes you stronger," I can't help but think that sometimes the things that make us feel like they're killing us continue to make us feel like they're killing us. It can feel like endless suffering. Our challenges feel burdensome and we fall apart like cheap one-ply toilet paper that's trying its best, but it's just not cutting it.

Then there's the pain that changes us. Whether we've been underestimated, dumped, or treated poorly, or someone we love dies—we all have the option to transform the pain we've endured into something that can propel us forward. This can be the entry point to confidence. By accepting the invitation. By walking through the fire of your pain, hurt, and suffering, and asking it to serve you in lieu of it kicking your ass and leaving you facedown.

THAT DAMN DOWNWARD SPIRAL

The last tool I'll leave you with is for you to pay attention the next time you go off the deep end about anything. For instance, if you get feedback that is less than stellar at work and you dive deep into beating yourself up. Or you start seeing someone you met on a dating app and they ghost you. You keep thinking, Is it me? Why does this keep happening?

In that moment, you're cordially invited to ask yourself how you want to show up. With fear and dread? Or with grace and grit? You are more than welcome to spend some time in fear and dread. (Tell them I said hi, as I've spent plenty of time there, too.) Assuming you'll then be ready for grace and grit, investigate your thoughts and emotions around what happened. What is in your control and what isn't? Ask yourself the questions from this chapter—what is life asking of you, who do you need and want to become, and what do you need to walk through? Maybe life is asking you to practice resilience (more on that in chapter 8), or patience. And last, look to your imaginary Board of Directors from chapter 1 to fire you up and push you through.

THE
UNLEARNING

NOTICE: First, pay attention to where you are blaming others for your challenges, problems, and struggles, and if you're blaming yourself. If you stay in blame, you stay stuck. You may have made bad choices and people may have done shitty things to you, but it's over and you can't go back and change things. Understand that the only place of control you have in your challenging situation is the perspective you take in it. Do you want it to solely be a hard thing that happened, or do you want it to be an invitation for a better life?

GET CURIOUS: How did your parents or caregivers shape you when it came to facing challenges? Did they crumble or react drastically? Or never talk about them? Did you have a single parent who against all odds was successful? Connecting the dots may be helpful for you to both have compassion for yourself and to understand that you are doing what you learned and seeing the new story you want to create in terms of life struggles. If you're resistant to answering the questions I posed in this chapter, ask yourself where that resistance is coming from. If you're used to staying in the struggle, maybe you get lots of attention there, or it's become a habit, so no wonder you've stayed. Your curiosity might then lead to asking yourself what's at stake if you continue to stay stuck in your struggle.

SELF-COMPASSION: You may have it down to a science when it comes to beating yourself up for past mistakes. It's what you're used to, and you may even be convinced that's the way to not make the same mistakes again. That your inner critic is your motivator—the one who keeps you in check.

I'm here to tell you that's not true. Your inner critic—the voice that beats you up and is especially hard on you—is a part of you that's afraid. Afraid of failing, afraid of being perceived in a negative way by others, afraid of making the same mistakes again, and on and on. No one beats themselves up into betterment or into not being afraid; that's not the way to go. Having compassion for yourself and understanding and accepting your humanity is how you heal and move forward.

KEEP THE MOMENTUM: Understand that literally everyone has challenges and faces struggles in life. It can feel lonely when you're in it, as if you're the only one who carries burdens like you do. But if there is one thing that we all face, it's life's trials, albeit to varying degrees. Process the feelings as an alternative to avoiding them, and then ask yourself how this struggle can make you stronger and better. When you're deep in the thick of it, it's probably not the time to have a spiritual experience about the whole thing, but time will bring you the capacity for the learning lesson and the gift of newfound wisdom. With each difficult experience that you've walked through brings strength, resilience, and your personal and profound power.

5

Start Getting Your Money Shit Together

The topic of money can be as loaded as your burrito when you say yes to everything at Chipotle. Delicious, but if not handled right, it has the potential to be a giant mess.

Let me say this from the start: This chapter is not about how to invest or save, or the best advice for getting out of debt. There are plenty of other books and experts on that. This is about the fact that money equals power, and I want you to have more of both of those things. Our relationship with money tends to be an emotional topic. I'll address both of those issues because we, as women, need to talk more about power and what it means to us, as well as untangle any emotional baggage we have around money.

|||

Let's start by *feeling* into the topic of money. There is some debate about whether the way we handle and manage money has any deeper meaning to it. Some argue that managing money is something we learn, plain and simple, in terms of spending, saving, debt, and investing. While that may be the case for some, for many, many women, it's not that simple. For most of us, money is not completely about money. It's not purely about getting to buy what you want, when you want it. Money is layered, weighty, and can feel intense. And the less we unpack that, the less money we have and/or the less we manage our money well.

When I wrote the outline of this book and knew the foundation of it was how women can best step into their own power and move against the restrictions our culture has taught us, it became obvious I needed to talk about money. I have seen many women, myself included, improve in so many areas of their lives, creating better relationships, speaking up, and asking for help, but they ignore their relationship with their finances or, even worse, sabotage themselves financially. Generally speaking, women are so good at taking care of everything and everyone, except their money. Often, we like the *idea* of making more and managing our finances, but when it comes to facing it and taking action around it, we don't.

It wasn't until I did my own internal work with the emotional side of money that I realized the impact this work has. And when I looked around me, I realized so many other women need to do this work as well.

At this point you might be clear that you need to work on your money issues, but in case you aren't sure, let's break it down. Check off if you struggle with any of these things regarding money:

- [ ] You can't or won't talk about it (or if you do talk about it, you get very uncomfortable).
- [ ] You know you could probably make more of it or you undercharge for your services.
- [ ] You let your partner handle all the finances and have no idea what's going on there.
- [ ] You live beyond your means.

☐ You ignore your money (i.e., you don't face your debt or even your bank account).

☐ You hoard your money in constant fear of losing it all.

☐ You feel shame or embarrassment for financial mistakes you've made in the past (that you may or may not still be paying for).

☐ You feel shame or embarrassment for not educating yourself more about managing money.

☐ You've never had a conversation with another woman about saving or investing for retirement.

If any (or all) of that is you, you don't have a problem with money itself, you have a problem in your relationship with money. Make no mistake, all of us have a relationship with money, just like we have relationships with people. And just like some of us have dysfunctional relationships with people, we also have massively dysfunctional (and sometimes completely shitty) relationships with money.

So buckle up, and let's bring to light something uncomfortable.

YOUR INDOCTRINATION ABOUT MONEY

Several years ago, my husband and I needed to find a babysitter so we could have date nights. I got a few referrals and noticed the same thing with the majority of the girls I spoke to or texted with when I asked how much they charge per hour. Instead of telling me how much, they'd say, "Ummm, however much you want to pay me is fine." This caught my attention only because it was the response I got from most of the young women.

It got me thinking . . . when my daughter is old enough to babysit, do I want her to reply this way? Do I want her to be okay with whatever, even if they offered to pay her with magic beans, handing it all over to someone else to decide? Would I deem her as too young to be able to name her price? Or do I think it would be disrespectful of her to tell an adult what she charged?

On the other hand, I could ask her to think about it ahead of time, set a price, and be able to back up what she charged by telling them the value of what she brings as a babysitter. Then teach her to negotiate, such as get paid more if she did extra chores around their house or brought learning games with her. Would I want to teach her that it was in fact respectful for her to politely tell them her hourly rate in a way that allowed her to build confidence in herself and in her negotiating powers?

I posted my thoughts around this on Facebook, it was shared hundreds of times, and it even caught media attention. My main message was this: Babysitting is commonly a first job for girls, and we need to help set them up for success in future jobs and to not be afraid to ask for what they deserve. In response to my Facebook post, the majority of comments were from adult women saying, "I've never thought to teach my daughter this," and, "No one ever talked to me about this when I was young."

In contrast, when I posted and especially when it was shared, I also got pushback, people saying that thirteen- or fourteen-year-old girls are too young to be telling an adult how much they charge, that they should leave that to the grown-ups. I don't know what century those people are living in, but having raised toddlers, I know that if you've ever tried to potty-train a small child, or get them to eat their veggies, or go to bed, small children understand negotiation.

This is about money, and it's about more than that. Especially with girls, we need to send the message that they are smart enough, and that they matter enough to be able to think for themselves.

Tweens and teens are not too young to know their own personal values and what that looks like. If we can teach them this when they are adolescents or young teenagers, this will only pave the way in a positive trajectory for them to ask for what they want from a place of respect and being well thought out.

Whether you have daughters or not, you're here now and probably thinking about things you didn't and currently don't ask for, as well as your relationship with money. As I mentioned in a previous chapter, your empowerment begins with what you request, and that very much includes money.

NOT YOUR GRANDMA'S MONEY

If I had to guess, I'd say that your mother and grandmother didn't have power over their money. I'm making a generalization here, but in most of the women I come into contact with, this is the case. In the generations before us, it was unusual and many times rare to find a woman who was self-made or who even had control over her finances.

Since beliefs tend to be passed down like Grandma's banana bread recipe, and it's no exception with money, consider yourself endowed with the pleasure (and possibly pain) of being the generation that elicits change around this topic. This doesn't mean you have to be rich or become an expert at finance in order to change what's been passed down. All it means is that you can do the mental and mostly emotional work it takes to change your relationship with money and pass it down to any young women who are your daughters, nieces, other family, or friends.

Like excavating any problem or blind spot you have in your life, a great place to start is when you were young. Get out a piece of paper, or better yet, a notebook, because this might be several pages. Ask yourself the following questions:

1. What is your earliest memory of your parents, parent, or other caregiver talking about money? What was being said? Were there feelings or emotions happening? In other words, did you get a sense there was more happening than simply the words? (It doesn't matter if you interpreted correctly or incorrectly, just write down what you remember.)

2. What did your parents explicitly teach you about money and personal finance? Did they tell you to save all of your allowance for a rainy day, college, or something else? Did you even get an allowance? Did they let you spend it however you wanted and make no suggestions?

3. Did your parents fight or disagree about money? Or spend it in large amounts without teaching you about it? Did they talk about credit cards in a positive or negative way? Did you grow up with a single parent who was always worried about money or made comments about money in regard to your other parent?

4. Did you have a job when you were in high school? Why or why not? What kind of work ethic was taught to you and how was it connected to money?

5. Did you grow up seeing women in your life handle money? If so, did they handle it well or not well? Did you ever see or know a woman who worked in banking or finance?

6. Did you know anyone wealthy or rich, and how did you know they were wealthy? What did your parents or other adults say about those people, or even wealthy people in general? Did you know any wealthy women? If so, what was their

positioning? Put differently, were they self-made or did they come into money another way? What did you think of this?

7. Did you often hear, "Money doesn't grow on trees," "We can't afford it," or "Money is tight"? Or anything else in regard to money?

After you've compiled all of these answers and maybe gone down a tear-filled memory lane (sorry, not sorry), I want you to go back and write out what stories you've made up in connection to what you wrote down. Based on your answers, what stories do you make up about:

- Money in general
- Women and money
- Wealth, saving, and investing

We're going to dive deeper into the concept of making up stories in a future chapter, but for now, this shouldn't be a stretch for you to connect the dots in terms of what you learned as a child and how that's translated into your thoughts, beliefs, and actions today.

We'll circle back to that in a moment, but first, a quick story. If you're my age, you might remember those Disney storybooks that came with a small record. When you played the record, you could hear the story read to you and a little charm would ring out when it was time to turn the page in the accompanying book (I feel like this could make a comeback for audiobooks). My favorite one of these was *101 Dalmatians*. I was probably five or six years old, poring over this book, both reading and listening. Cruella De Vil was a millionaire—the first fictional rich woman I would encounter. She was a millionaire with a name that was a pun, combining "cruel" and "devil," and did the evilest thing my child brain could wrap my head around—she skinned puppies. Even as an adult, my opinion is she is the cruelest of all the Disney characters (and a quick Internet search agrees with me). My, and probably hundreds of thousands of other little girls', first introduction to a wealthy woman was horrible. A terrible, heinous woman who hurt little animals . . . but she was rich, *and* this is how she accumulated wealth.

You may think, "Does that really make such an impact? It's only a Disney movie!"

Maybe it does, and maybe it doesn't, but I cannot name one woman I learned about growing up, fictional or not, who was wealthy and did good things. And especially not a woman who was self-made. If I did learn of a wealthy woman, she got that way from being the wife, daughter, or widow of a wealthy man. Bottom line: We had none or very few role models of wealthy women. And *that matters*.

So when you're answering the questions above, and then writing out the stories you've made up about money, women and money, wealth, saving, and investing, I want you to think about everything that could have and did indoctrinate you to believe about money, and, thus, your power. This might vary depending on your age, race, religion, class, ability, etc., but your story is uniquely yours, and it's important for you to unlearn old beliefs and relearn new ones about your money.

IT'S MORE THAN JUST MONEY

While it's important to get clear on your relationship with money, it can also be extraordinarily helpful to dig into your relationship with debt, as well as saving and investing. You may have a not-so-great relationship with money but have a long love affair with debt. Maybe it's an on-again, off-again thing going on, where you decide you're done, work hard to get out of debt, then immediately get yourself back in. Trust me, after paying off $60,000 in debt myself, knowing how good it feels to have it all paid off, then deciding, "Well, $10,000 in debt isn't so bad," and going back in—I know what a complicated relationship with debt looks like. It's truly like a bad boyfriend or partner. You know they're not good for you, but you can't help yourself in getting back together. Getting clear on your relationship with debt can help you get clear on the big picture with you and money.

And maybe saving and investing feels bewildering or "something other people do" or, more specifically, "something men do." In Amanda Steinberg's book *Worth It: Your Life, Your Money, Your Terms,* she cites a 2016 Fidelity study and says, "Most of the women surveyed (82 percent) were confident managing household finances and budgeting. But their self-assurance plummeted when asked if they could handle planning for their long-term financial needs (37 percent) or selecting the right financial investments (28 percent)." She goes on to state that about three-quarters of the women in the study wanted to learn more about money and investing, but that most refrained from discussing their finances with most everyone. One of the biggest reasons, the women in the study said, was that it was uncomfortable for them or they were raised to not talk about finances.

In my twenties I thought financial advisers were for rich people, and I certainly was not one. The only real reason I had a financial adviser is because my former in-laws set us up with one (let's be honest, it was for their son, and because we shared money, I was there by default). I sat in on meetings I didn't understand, never asked any questions, always felt intimidated by words like *portfolio,* and didn't know how the stock market worked. I felt like I didn't belong.

The financial adviser stayed with me when I got divorced and then remarried (I did get a new one, fresh start with a fresh marriage), and it wasn't until I was forty that I finally stopped turning away from my money. I stopped ignoring his calls, I stopped ignoring my own questions and confusion, I stopped ignoring my money. I had always felt like "If I only make X amount of dollars, how do I even qualify for this?" And what "this" was was taking care of my money. "This" meant looking at the truth of it and the power of it. Looking at the power I was throwing away by ignoring it all.

The bottom line that I want you to get crystal clear on is: What narrative do you have about you and *your* money? What do you make up about earning and spending money? All of those beliefs, whether you're conscious of them or not, are dictating your livelihood, your future, and your power. Once you become conscious of them, you can begin to change your narrative.

WE NEED TO TALK

As you start to work on your money stories, the next thing you need to do is learn to be comfortable *talking* about money. As the Fidelity study mentioned, women tend to be uncomfortable talking about money, so the less we talk about it, the less we manage it well, and the less we manage it well, the less we have. I don't know who it was who decided it was taboo or "in bad taste" to talk about money, especially for women, but let's all agree that's a bunch of bullshit that's as outdated as when people thought smoking was good for them. This antiquated belief that it's impolite to talk about money has made it okay to talk about getting our pubic hair waxed off by a stranger to our besties, yet we don't talk about finances. It makes no sense.

Since money is the currency we use for virtually everything, when you think about it, it's mind-blowing that we don't talk about it pretty much all the time, except to complain about how broke we are.

If you hesitate to talk about money, I'd like for you to spend some time thinking about what it's costing you to avoid the conversation. How much money are you leaving on the table by not asking for raises and promotions at work, by not raising prices after years of being a service provider, or by letting your partner handle all the finances? If your answer is "I don't know," there is definitely money being left behind that should be yours. You would never take a pile of cash that you earned and set it on fire. So let's make a pact to work on being able to talk about money.

In the late nineties, I had my first "real job." I squealed to my friends that I had my own desk with my own phone extension. It was a salaried position for $27,000 a year. It never even occurred to me that I could negotiate for more pay when I was offered the position. Never. I assumed that "you get what you get" and that I should just be happy that I beat out the other young women who'd interviewed for the job. No one had ever talked to me about this before.

As the months went on, more and more was asked of me that was not in my initial job description. I was working long hours, far more than forty a week, and one day as I was working on a Saturday (and no one else was there in the office but me), I took out a calculator and calculated that I was making less than minimum wage when I factored in the extra time I was putting in. Still, it never occurred to me that I could negotiate my job role and then ask for more money. Rather, I thought, "That's not fair!" and sat back and pouted.

In their book *Women Don't Ask,* authors Linda Babcock and Sara Laschever claim that men are eight times more likely than women to negotiate their starting salaries when entering their first jobs out of college. Over the course of her working life, this seemingly small oversight by a woman could equate to hundreds of thousands of dollars left behind by the time she's ready to retire. What would you like to spend hundreds of thousands of dollars on during your retirement? A second home? College money for your kids or grand-kids? Open a big-cat sanctuary? What you spend it on doesn't matter; what matters is you need to start learning to negotiate salaries and raises so you can have it.

In the Recommended Reading section of this book, you'll find resources that go in depth on how to do this, whether you're at a corporate job, you work in sales, or you own a business and set prices for goods and services.

My main point here is that because we were primarily raised to not talk about money, we don't grow up learning how to negotiate pay, let alone even know we can in the first place. In essence, we feel it's a topic that doesn't "belong" to us as women. And that, my friends, needs to change.

MONEY IN RELATIONSHIPS

A close friend of mine and her husband keep all of their money separate and have done a fantastic job of working out systems in regard to their finances that feel good and fair to both of them. They've both had ups and downs financially, when one person couldn't work for a period of time, or when one of them made more than the other, and they help each other out when that happens. The key to this type of success? My friend has said many times that it's communication and the willingness to grow as individuals and as a couple.

You may be married or partnered, but even if you're single, this is something you need to think about if and when you're in a relationship. *Especially* if you're single, please, I beg you to start the conversation early about earning, debt, investing, spending, everything that has to do with money. Don't wait until you're married to find out how much debt your spouse has. Don't wait until you're ten years into your relationship to find out their views on saving for retirement. And if one of you plans to stay home with children and not work, don't wait to find out how the money will be handled in terms of distribution and spending. If you've seen this person naked, you should find it reasonable to talk about money. Relationships are intimate, and so is money.

When it comes to partnerships, if you're in the beginning stages of a relationship, start the conversation now. Make it known to your partner that healthy finances are important to you—even if it's something you aspire to and your goal is to get your finances in order.

TALKING TO THE EXPERTS

If you don't have a financial adviser yet, ask your trusted friends, family members, coworkers, or managers for a referral. Put it on your to-do list now. Google is rife with things to look for and ask them, and notice if you feel uncomfortable or anxious, or have any other "small" feelings about this. This might be a new thing for you, and it's a topic that you've been conditioned to stay away from. Walk toward it anyway, knowing there are many, many women with hands on your back, smiling broadly as we welcome you into the world of taking charge of your money and your future. This is the same for 401(k)s and other investments at work. Ask your employer about it. It's common for people to blindly enroll without totally understanding what's happening. It might feel awkward asking questions, but this is literally their job: to help you understand and to answer your questions. Once the awkwardness passes and the clarity steps in, so does your power.

The bottom-line belief that I want you to lean in to here is that talking about money isn't bad. The shame or discomfort you may feel is the conditioning that's been handed to you by your parents, your family, and our culture. It doesn't have to belong to you anymore. If you want to speak things into existence, before you speak money raining down on you, you need to speak your money stories, beliefs, and all the emotions that surround it.

POWER

In her book *Women & Money*, Suze Orman says, "You are never powerful in life until you are powerful with money."

Let's all let that sink in for a minute.

The thing that stands out the most in this quote is the phrase "powerful in life." I mean, it sounds good and motivating, right? But what does that really mean for us? Especially now, as a global pandemic and civil unrest have ripped through the United States and been felt in other countries, too, what does it mean for a woman to be powerful in her life?

I've thrown out the word *power* several times in this chapter and will continue to do so throughout this book. This is as good a time as any for us to have a little chat about it. If you're going to fix your relationship with money, you must work to fix any dysfunctional relationship you might have with power.

Pause and think about how you react to the word *power*. What does it make you think of and how does it make you feel? Do you feel drawn to talking about it, reading about it, and learning about it? Or does it make you recoil or feel nervous or not want to think about it? Does it make you think of men who've hurt you or society at large? Does it make you think of women you judge or don't want to be like?

When you think specifically of women and power, what narratives are at play for you? Do you believe with power, we are inherently backstabbing and conniving? Competitive with other women, cold and calculated?

Although these are widely known stereotypes about women, studies show this is not statistically true. In fact, many people believe that it's only men who are interested in power, and not women. On the topic of stereotypes, some people assume there are vast differences in the ways men and women establish, maintain, and express power. But the truth is, studies have shown that increasing women's participation in leadership positions decreases corruption, as women are less involved in things like bribery.

Just as you have core stories and beliefs about money, you likely have core stories and beliefs about power. I'd love for you to spend some time thinking about what that is, and answering some important questions:

If you could define power and make it feel good to you, what would it look like?

If you had more power, what would you do with it? If you had more influence, where would you direct people?

When you think about your values, how could you honor and lean in to them more if you had more power and influence? For instance, if you had disposable income, could you donate to organizations you love that do work in the world that you believe in? Could you donate to politicians who back policy change that matters to you?

This is power and influence.

If you struggle with the words *power* and *influence* (and I mean beyond a social fashion blogger's influence), I invite you to not skip over the first question I posed here. Redefine or define for the first time what those words mean to you. If *power* feels negative to you, you get to make it positive.

Women historically don't hold as much power as men do. As I mentioned in a previous chapter, studies show that when both women and men are asked, the word *powerful* was seen as a positive virtue for men but a negative for women. It is woven into the DNA of our conditioning and our socialization. That's why, on our way to change this culturally, you must start with yourself. Journal on it, create a manifesto, paint about it, whatever you need to do to define or redefine what power means to you, because you do in fact have it, deserve it, and have the ability to gain more and to do great things with it.

Ruth Bader Ginsburg said, "Women belong in all places where decisions are being made. It shouldn't be that women are the exception." To be in the places where women are making decisions requires us to be comfortable with power.

When you're thinking about your own definition of power, and especially if you're struggling here, I encourage you to do a quick Google search for "Brené Brown's power within PDF." Brown's research on leadership is extensive. Here's a snapshot:

What makes power dangerous is how it's used. Power *over* is driven by fear.

Daring and transformative leaders share power *with*, empower people *to*, and inspire people to develop power *within*.

Of course, I feel that all the chapters of this book are important to your rising up and changing our future. They are important for women specifically, for change to happen both for you on a personal level and culturally, but money has the ability to move mountains. No one can deny that whoever has money has power, and whoever has power has the capacity to help get who they want elected to office (or be in office themselves), can contribute to charities they want to lift up, and generally has more options.

Whoever you are reading this, you either run your household, run your job, run a business, or even regularly run your mouth, so you can run your relationship with money.

THE
UNLEARNING

NOTICE: Where do you get triggered by money? Are the stories and beliefs you have about money holding you back from asking for a raise, causing you to spend beyond your means, preventing you from saving or investing, or anything else that sabotages your financial health? Pay attention to when you say "I can't afford it" (even if you really can't) or "Must be nice to go on that vacation." Or anything else that makes you feel left out, like you're missing out, or that you can't "get there" to where you want to be financially. Paying attention to these thoughts will help you notice where you're taking action (or not taking action) that directly affects your finances.

GET CURIOUS: Use the questions in this chapter to journal—I asked a lot of them. It's imperative in your unlearning old conditioning to examine what you believe so you can learn new beliefs.

Additional questions are: Why do I feel this way about investing? Why do I think I don't save? What might happen if I asked for more money?

Come from a neutral place and know this is your jumping-off point. It's not about getting the answers to your introspective questions right; it's about digging around in the couch cushions for answers (and maybe loose change) to see what might come up, in an effort to get to a new and better place with your relationship with money and, thus, your finances. It's never too late to create a healthier relationship with money.

SELF-COMPASSION: After you do the work of answering the above questions, you might come to some huge revelations. Maybe you realized you've been leaving money on the table by not increasing your rates or ever asking for a raise when you know you deserve one. Maybe you're fifty and haven't started saving for retirement because it's been less painful to ignore it than to face it. Or perhaps you've realized you've always viewed wealthy women as money-hungry bitches and have wanted no part of that.

First, know that you're not alone. Plenty of women have their hang-ups about money, and although you might not be able to fist-pump about it yet, my hope is that soon you'll realize that the first step is always awareness, so now you know! Second, show yourself some grace. Money is loaded and there is still likely work to do. Beating yourself up won't get you through your money issues, and it surely won't make you wealthier.

KEEP THE MOMENTUM: The most important thing here is at the same time you're working on your relationship with money, if you haven't already, start talking to a financial adviser that you trust, and/or a trusted friend who knows more about this than you do. Start small, learn step-by-step, and sooner than you think, you'll be an expert in terms of *your* money.

In addition, talk to your friends about the topics you read about in this chapter—specifically, your friends who are women. This is a conversation that is not done enough in female circles. It's not about bragging regarding how much money you have in order to "one-up" one another. It's about making money a topic of regular conversation, like we talk about our hair or the memes we see on Instagram. Plus, it's about unlearning generations of assumptions and stereotypes that women don't talk about money.

Making noise in your life is directly connected to your own personal power, which in turn is directly connected to money. Make your money work for you and talk about how you're doing it.

6

Start Remembering Your Built-in Wisdom

In 2006, I started dating a con man. Obviously, I didn't know he was a swindler at the time, but I did know something was wrong right from the very beginning.

On our first date I sat across from him at the restaurant, and I had the feeling something wasn't right. He seemed too good to be true, and I couldn't explain it beyond that, so I ignored it.

On our second date, the stories he was telling me sounded odd, and there were other red flags popping up as well (such as him telling me he could see himself marrying me and me having his children on our second date), but I ignored those, too.

Several months later, and with probably hundreds of flaming crimson flags ignored at that point, I found myself in Tijuana, Mexico, in the middle of the night, standing outside a taxi on my way to get illegal drugs with this man. You see, he had told me for months that he was sick with cancer, and since he had no health insurance (because he was too sick to work, and his family had disowned him because, according to him, they were mean and terrible), we had to go south of the border to get his controversial, not-approved-by-the-FDA, available-in-Mexico, and also unpronounceable-so-I-couldn't-google-it "cancer medication." We had been going down there regularly all summer, always during the day, and one day he was especially sick. Since it was nearing the middle of the night, all the legitimate pharmacies were closed.

As we walked down a dark back alley, my boyfriend saw two men, walked over to them, and from twenty feet away I heard him say the words I knew in my heart were true, but had somehow ignored in all of my denial, blind trust, and just plain never wanting my gut feeling to be right: "Hey, do you know where I can get any OxyContin?"

The men and my boyfriend exchanged more words, they pointed down the street, and my boyfriend and I continued to walk.

Which brings me back to the taxi.

There I was, as he held the door open for me to get in the cab. Everything was screaming inside me to turn around and walk back over the border and go home. Everything shouted, "THIS ISN'T SAFE, GIRL, GET OUT OF HERE!" in my body, and I knew it wasn't only the fact that I was getting illegal drugs in the middle of the night in a foreign and many times dangerous city with a man I should not be trusting. My body was telling me *everything* over the last several months I had been with him was unsafe. I remember at that moment thinking, "If this goes bad and I get raped and murdered, no one will know where I am." None of my friends or family knew where I was, as I hadn't told anyone about our weekly trips down to T.J., because, oh, I don't know, I knew it would sound fishy.

"I don't want to get in the car," I said softly, looking down.

My boyfriend stepped toward me, softly pulled my face up in his hands to look up at him, and said lovingly, "I would never do anything to put you in danger."

And even though I didn't believe him, I got in the car.

I sat in the backseat as we drove in silence, filled with rage at him, but mostly at myself. What had happened to me? What had happened to the young woman who inherently knew she would not take shit from anyone? How did I end up in the back of a cab on the way to a drug deal in Tijuana, Mexico? My wake-up call was interrupted as we arrived at apparently the drug dealer's house; by some miracle, we didn't have to get out the taxi—perhaps the driver took pity on me and would do the deal for us. My boyfriend turned to me in anticipation because it was *me* who would be paying for his "cancer medication." As I forked over a handful of twenties, I also handed him any ounce of inner wisdom and strength I had felt bubbling up before. It was easier for me to shove it down and hope those feelings would die.

It was more than that particular night. That whole relationship and so many moments in other romantic relationships I was in, I constantly put my partners' feelings and comfort before my own. Somehow along the way I had mastered pleasing, proving, performing, and perfecting, all in an effort to be accepted, validated, and loved.

It hurts to tell this story. It hurts to remember how lost, insecure, and desperate I was. That I was willing to override my screaming intuition, to trade in my personal sovereignty for a mess of a relationship that I knew had no future. And for what? Why?

The answer to that question, plus how to learn to hone your intuition, is what we'll get into. My hope is that by remembering your experiences where you've ignored your intuition, you can gain insight from that, understand your conditioning, and learn a new and better way.

WHY WE IGNORE OUR INTUITION

No one in my life explicitly told me, "It's your duty to put other people's feelings and comfort before your own; you must please and accommodate everyone even to your own detriment," but it was something I learned. Many times as children, we are told to sit on various laps that we don't want to (including but not limited to Santa Claus), or to hug Uncle Frank when we *really* don't want to because we always feel creepy when we do, or maybe the fact that he's a stranger feels awkward. Or when we watch our mother ask our dad if she can go out for mom's night or spend $100 on a dress for a wedding they're invited to. When we grow up and don't listen to our bodies when we're hungry or full, and again don't listen when we know that a relationship is terrible for us and they won't change no matter how hard we try to change them.

On the contrary, maybe your uncle Frank wasn't that creepy, and perhaps your mom mostly did what she wanted to do, but it's not about each individual situation and if you can relate to each or not. It's about the collective experiences we've all had, that our mothers had, that our mothers' mothers had. Without a doubt, we have come a long way from generations before us, and there is still *so much* work to do.

Part of that digging in is working on what we believe to be true—beliefs that have been passed down from our families, and from all the women who've come before us. Many of us have the belief that one of our most important duties as a "good woman" is to put others before us and to not make anyone else feel ill at ease. So when we *do* hear our intuition talking to us and acting on it requires us to likely make someone else unhappy or uncomfortable, we bypass it.

In my story above, in order for me to listen to my inner wisdom, I would have had to tell my boyfriend "no," which would have upset him. I didn't have the self-confidence, self-love, self-trust, or any tools whatsoever for me to deal with the consequence. It was easier for me to live with ignoring my intuition and putting my safety at risk rather than do what the smartest part of myself—which was my body—was telling me to do.

And I know, dear reader, that you, too, have stories like mine.

Yes, there are exercises you can do to hone your intuition, which I'll get to, but we need to back up before we start slapping Band-Aids on the bigger problem. When it comes to honing our intuition, it's not always about learning how to hear it. That's part of the problem for some of you, but the primary issue is we don't act on it because, as I've mentioned, we've been taught both to always put others before us (and to act on our intuition often means making others unhappy and uncomfortable) and to not trust ourselves.

Sometimes we don't act on our intuition because to do so would also mean we have to take painful and difficult action. I didn't break up with the con artist because I was ashamed of where I was in my life: a woman in my thirties with a previously failed marriage, no husband, and no kids (which is another thing our culture brands us as being wrong for). It felt less painful to stay in a relationship I knew was unhealthy and doomed as opposed to walk away and start my life over.

I believe you *do* hear your inner wisdom, and because the risk is high for acting on it, many times women put a muzzle on that voice. I also believe our natural state as women is to be certain about what we want, what and who are good for us, and to be able to make decisions in confidence. I believe we are born this way and it's conditioned out of us. In order for us to remember this built-in wisdom, we must tease out the problem and create a new belief system, as well as practice listening to our intuition.

INTUITION AND TRAUMA

If there's one thing I know about changing your life, it's never about seeing and understanding that we're doing something we want to change, deciding to change, and then it magically happens. Especially when you're having to unlearn what you've inexplicably been taught your whole life, these changes come in layers.

Before I even get into this, I want to talk about how trauma plays a role. My friend and colleague Terri Cole, psychotherapist, teaches about how chaotic childhoods can play a role in how we grow up to listen or not listen to our intuition. She says:

> For some adult women who experienced sexual abuse as children, they can have the experience of being confused by their intuition or feeling like they don't hear it at all. Perhaps the mother tells the kids they should be grateful their stepfather has stepped in to take care of them, even though he's abusing the children while their mother is sleeping. What ends up happening is the child's reality is consistently being denied.
>
> It can be the same in families with addiction. For instance, there's a big blowup that happens—circumstances and patterns depend on the type of family—but almost all have this collective denial, a "we're going to have a silent agreement that we're not talking about what happened last night, okay?" The broken dishes, the yelling and fighting, etc. The child gets up in the morning and sees that

everyone's being normal and having breakfast. So they understand that's how the family handles these things . . . we don't talk about them.

Many times, in families where there is abuse and/or addiction, without even saying so, there is a sense that all must be kept quiet. Children sense and feel shame, understand something is wrong, and wonder if they did or are doing something wrong. This can happen as children or even adults, because we are constantly trying to make sense of our experiences.

In some families when things are traumatic for a child—be it addiction, abuse, neglect, etc.—when the child tries to get help from their parents, and it's their instinct to get help from their primary caregivers, sometimes they are told things like "You have a vivid imagination" or "That's not what happened." Those responses make them feel like their instincts are not only nonexistent, but wrong.

Families can deny the child's reality, whether it's with words, their own denial, or their behavior. The child grows up creating patterns and internal stories and beliefs about what's safe and what's not. Even when they're taken out of the environment and put in a safe one (and being in a "safe environment" is subjective—people in oppressed groups many times don't feel safe even if it looks safe from the outside), they can tend to not trust their instincts or even care about them.

This isn't necessarily only in adults who grew up with childhoods that were obviously traumatic. Maybe your family was highly focused on outward appearances, so you grew up to be a perfectionist, type A, and a people pleaser. Or a very religious family with high expectations, and being virtuous was an important value for women. And sometimes there is minimal or no trauma, but in your childhood, you may have learned that adults are always right, and you have grown up learning not to trust yourself. This kind of upbringing can make it complicated to trust your intuition. When your focus is always on the outside, it can be difficult to focus on your inside.

Susan, forty-seven, says, "I have ignored my intuition continually throughout my life. Relationships, work, you name it. Sometimes to evade the truth to myself. I've been scared to ask for things, as I worry it will upset the apple cart (even though I know full-heartedly the worst-case scenario rarely happens). Me continually ignoring my intuition has been one of my biggest faults in terms of self-care, and is possibly holding me back from being my best to clients, my husband, and friends.

"Growing up, my dad had diagnosed borderline personality disorder—plus my brother was the golden child. My dad was both verbally and physically abusive to me. My mom has been diagnosed with bipolar depression, and she left my dad, thus leaving me and my brother with him. I was also sexually abused repeatedly.

"With a dad who has borderline personality disorder, you are continually sensitive to mood changes, and you do everything possible to not set him off. You become numb to the pain, and go into survival mode. I know for me I have PTSD and anxiety, and those filters make it hard to decipher gut feelings."

Susan's story is a clear example of someone who feels challenged by listening to her instincts, because her childhood had a foundation where the place that was meant to keep her safe and feel loved was the same place where her instincts told her it was unsafe.

If you think you react a certain way to things that are based on past trauma, and/or you can't distinguish your intuition from a fear response, my hope is that you can find the help you need to untangle those past events that are affecting you physically and triggering you in such a way that is possibly making you confused. If you've ever felt frustrated when people say, "Just listen to your gut," or when they ask the question, "What is your inner wisdom telling you?" and you have past trauma, I want you to know you're not broken, there's nothing wrong with you, and it's often more common than you think. Specific work in this area should help, and in the meantime, you can still work on honing your intuitive skills.

GET OUT OF YOUR HEAD

Many women tell me they are "all up in their heads, all the time," which leaves no room for anything but intellectualizing and trying to only "think" their way through playing a bigger game in their life. Now, don't get me wrong, I love a smart, well-thought-out plan as much as the next girl, but when we rely only on our heads, we leave less room for the other important parts of ourselves to help us think through things and make decisions—our hearts and bodies. I believe all are equally important and the trick is learning how to use them.

Not listening to your intuition is like some other behaviors I'll tell you about in this book—one of those behaviors you can engage in and your life is . . . "meh." You can think your way through things, ignore your inner wisdom and make mistakes, and recover from them. Many people go through life like this. But just like you don't intentionally go to a fancy restaurant to have chicken fingers and mayo to dip it in, you didn't come to this book to keep making all your important life decisions only from your head.

Not honing and listening to your intuition removes your best self from yourself. Your inner wisdom is your home, and you deserve to make your way back home to yourself.

As I mentioned earlier in this chapter, another reason we don't listen to our intuition and/or don't try to hone it is because to do so might mean we are faced with having to make difficult and life-altering decisions, and many times what goes along with that is to have hard conversations. We're constantly looking for a guarantee that we're making the right choice; that if we make "difficult decision A," it will be the right path for us that will take us to our purpose in life, all will be well, and we can go skipping along through the meadow, tossing daisies in gleeful delight.

As we're working on listening to our inner wisdom and acting on it, sometimes it feels right in our bodies, sometimes it still feels awkward or uncertain, and sometimes we feel nothing. I wish there was a little gnome that shows up on your shoulder, nods, and does a victory dance, or even a slip of paper that gets left in your mailbox that says "Yes! You made the right decision listening to your gut. All will be good and well. *Winner!*" But, alas, this doesn't happen.

Practicing and honing your intuition are the best ways to learn to hear it, as well as *trust* it. Trusting yourself is key within this topic, and in regard to your values, taking up space, asking for what you want, and your empowerment in general. When you practice and learn to trust yourself, you become the queen of your own personal existence.

The thing about intuition is this: When we don't listen to it, it will surely come back to haunt us. It becomes an elephant in the room, felt solely by us. Only this elephant has a rabid attitude, waits and waits until the time is right, and bites us in the ass. Let's dig more into that.

TOOLS

The good news (and possibly bad news) is that if you're old enough to be interested in reading this book, you most likely have had these life lessons smack you in the face. You see, one of the best ways to hone your intuition is to remember all the times you didn't listen and then life exploded.

These instances typically happen when it comes to relationships (all relationships, not limited to romantic) and career decisions. Maybe your gut told you something was up with a partner or prospective partner and, as in my example, you didn't listen. Or at work you knew you shouldn't have taken a particular job, but it looked good on your résumé, so you did it anyway. Take a moment to think about your particular situation. The decision you made that went against your intuition, even if at the time you weren't sure it was your intuition telling you to make a different decision.

I'm less interested in the specific circumstances themselves and would rather you ask yourself *why* you ignored your intuition or questioned it. Was it because you didn't trust yourself? Was it because to do what your inner wisdom said would be to do something that didn't make logical sense? For instance, if your gut told you to take the job as the middle school music teacher, but instead you took the public relations job at the record company, maybe you did so because the PR job paid better, sounded cool to your friends and family, and seemed like a "grown-up job." But your heart and soul were in teaching music to kids. This isn't about blaming and shaming yourself for decisions you regret. It's about coming face-to-face with why you make the decisions you do. Figuring out what's truly important to *your* life, so that you can have compassion for yourself and make different decisions next time.

If you're having trouble pinpointing why you make the decisions you do by going against your intuition, here are some common reasons you might have not listened to your gut or questioned it:

- Having to have a hard conversation if you listened to your instincts
- Not wanting to look bad in front of others, worried what other people will think, and concerned only with what you "should" do
- Not trusting yourself
- Not wanting to hurt other people or make them uncomfortable
- Being conditioned to believe trusting your intuition is "too emotional" and you should stick to the facts
- Overthinking what's happening
- Seeking council and advice from others when you really don't need their help
- Getting your needs met at the time even though what you were doing was going against your intuition

Regarding that last one, there may have been times when you dismissed your intuition, like I did with my addict boyfriend and perhaps even Susan has experienced. When we go through trauma, sometimes we feel desperate to get our needs met, so we stay in situations that we know aren't good for us. For me, I was so vulnerable and somewhat hopeless coming out of my divorce, I wanted a place to belong, a person to squelch the painful loneliness. My suspicions that things were worse than I saw them were there, but I was willing to ignore them in order to feel less lonely and heartbroken, even if it was just in moments throughout the day.

I tell you this because in order to feel empowered by your intuition, you must also have compassion for yourself when you look back on moments when you bypassed your inner wisdom. It's important to think about where you were in terms of headspace, what you were going through at the time, and the tools you had, which may not have been much. It's all a learning experience in order to move forward and make progress toward your best you.

FEELING GROUNDED

In order to be able to listen to your intuition, you have to feel grounded in the first place. This can be difficult with so much uncertainty in life, especially when you're the type of person who feels much better if you assume you have control. In his book *Uncertainty,* author Jonathan Fields talks about what he calls "certainty anchors." He says, "A certainty anchor is a practice or process that adds something known and reliable to your life when you may otherwise feel you're spinning off in a million different directions. Rituals and routines can function as certainty anchors; their power comes from the simple fact that they are always there. They are grounding experiences to which you can always return, no matter what's going on."

To be in the space to be able to hear your intuition, being and feeling grounded is essential. Your certainty anchors might be simple to elaborate, depending on the time and energy you have each day. Most nights as I get ready for bed, the thought crosses my mind that I'm looking forward to tomorrow morning's cup of coffee. I do love my coffee, and the routine and certainty that it brings. I have no idea what tomorrow will bring, but I do know that I will wake up, go downstairs, and pour myself a cup of coffee with a splash of cream and one Stevia packet. Every day. It's small but impactful, so that I feel rooted in the day. Some examples of certainty anchors are:

- Drinking coffee, tea, or lemon water each morning
- A short meditation
- Calling your mom or friend on the way to work each day
- Writing down your gratitudes or saying a prayer each night before bed
- Taking a walk on your lunch break

Maybe you already have a small ritual you do each day, and if so, I invite you to acknowledge the safety and groundedness it brings you. And if you don't have one, I encourage you to pick one, with the intention of it becoming your certainty anchor.

MEDITATION

If you like meditation and do it already, the only thing I'm going to say is: Keep doing it. Meditation can be the absolute best way to hone your inner wisdom. And for those of y'all who are more like me and have been a bad boyfriend/girlfriend to meditation, maybe throwing in an eye roll and an "I'll do it later," let's chat.

The only way you're doing meditation wrong is if you do the opposite and talk out loud the whole time about all your anxieties, jumping from topic to topic while filming a video for your Instagram Stories. Meditation can feel like one of those things that need to look a certain way, as well as have specific, tangible results that we can pinpoint as "hearing the voice of God, the angels, and Stevie Nicks" that told you your future during your quiet time.

In all seriousness, research shows that meditation can improve self-esteem, lower anxiety, and boost self-trust and confidence. Much of our feelings of "not enough" come from what's called "overidentification"—where we hyperfocus on our flaws, failures, and shortcomings, making them mean something negative about who we are. Meditation can help you be gentler with yourself. The research on the benefits of meditation is endless, as well as the apps to do so, so there's really no excuse not to do it. A meditation practice is not perfect; the whole point is that it's a practice. My friend Rebekah Borucki wrote a meditation book called *You Have 4 Minutes to Change Your Life* because, yes, even a mere four minutes of meditation a few times a week can change your life.

JOURNALING

Like meditation, journaling is another practice that is often met with a collective groan. People don't know what to write, it's too time-consuming, they don't have the right journal, blah, blah, blah. Listen, confusion, uncertainty, pain, and fear are also time-consuming, and those things feel like shit and keep swirling around in your head all the livelong day, so how about we try journaling for a minute or two and see if we can't make some sense of the confusion, uncertainty, pain, and fear, mmmkay?

Your intuition needs space. It can't function if it's trapped in an apartment with way too much IKEA furniture combined with a smelly fog machine. Journaling clears out the muck, and most often you will walk into your journaling session not knowing what you'll write about or what will come of it. I, too, have scoffed when given the assignment from my coach or therapist, and am often pleasantly surprised by the outcome, and I write for a living. And sometimes not much comes out of the journaling session, but I will argue it's all still important. In distance running there's a term, *junk miles*, which means that all runs should have a purpose; anything more and you're running "junk" miles, which isn't necessarily bad, and some running coaches argue it's a necessary part of training. Think of the sessions of journaling where you don't have huge epiphanies like junk miles. You still accomplished it, you still showed up, it might not seem like it was important, but you still get a gold star for doing it.

BREATH WORK

Many of the women in my community struggle with anxiety, feel high-strung, or could essentially use some help when it comes to their nervous system and relaxing. Here are two breathing techniques that will help you do that, and as you do so, you'll be strengthening your intuition muscle.

The first one is the 4-7-8 breathing technique, which is a breathing pattern developed by Dr. Andrew Weil. It's based on an ancient yogic technique called pranayama, which helps yoga practitioners gain control over their breathing. You simply breathe in for four counts, hold for seven counts, and exhale for eight counts, repeating the pattern three times. This technique can be used to help you fall asleep, too.

The other is box breathing. The technique is simple: Breathe in for four counts, hold your breath for four counts, exhale for four, hold again for four, and repeat.

Personally, I used to scoff at breath work, thinking it was too far out there and that merely breathing was not enough to change my levels of anxiety. However, after trying it for the first time in a workshop, I was blown away at how it felt like a sedative for my nervous system, and I still practice it today. Plus, I've met a few breath workers in my travels, and they all have a calmness about them that I want even one tiny piece of.

THE DIFFERENCE BETWEEN INTUITION AND FEAR

A common and great question I receive a lot when it comes to this topic is "How can I tell the difference between my intuition and fear?" I agree that sometimes it's confusing because it feels the same. Both are "feelings" we get about something or a decision we need to make. So how do we know which is our instincts speaking to us and which is a fear response?

First and foremost, if you're asking this, you're already on the right track, because that means you've spent some time stopping and listening. Part of the unlearning in every chapter of this book is noticing and listening to each behavior so you can make wiser choices that serve you better. This topic is no different.

But there are some things you can look and listen for when you're trying to discern between the two.

1. **Intuition tends to be more of a soft, gentle whisper, whereas fear is louder, more persistent.** Some people say their intuition feels more grounded, but their fear is on a loop.
2. **Intuition is often described as "I just can't explain it," and if it's fear, you'll typically have a story around it.** For instance, maybe you're stuck on whether you should apply for a job that is a level up from where you are now but you're not sure about this particular company. You might have an inexplainable feeling that you should go for it at a different company, but you can't think of anything to back it up, you

simply know. Your fear will tell you you're unqualified, it's too much trouble, or that you should stick to the job you have because you have seniority. Your fear will also highlight the worst-case scenario.

3. **Intuition tends to not have an emotional charge on it, whereas fear is very charged.** This can sometimes feel counterintuitive. For instance, in March 2020, when we were all madly to severely freaking out over the COVID-19 worldwide pandemic and unsure about the global economy, my anxiety went into overdrive for about a week or two, like most people's. As the sole breadwinner in our family, my husband had very recently left his job to be a stay-at-home dad. Logically, I should have been terrified, or so I thought. But I had an inexplainable feeling that we would be okay. I didn't know what "okay" looked like—maybe my industry would crumble, I'd lose my income, and we would lose our house and be forced to live in a shoe, but my heart told me we would be okay. There was no emotion around it, merely a knowing.

4. **Intuition lives in the present and doesn't remind you of the past or tell you all the possible future scenarios, versus fear, which is all up in the past and future like flies on dog shit.** Your fear and inner critic tend to revel in made-up nightmare scenarios and remind you of past experiences that went badly. Your inner wisdom cares only about the here and now.

5. **Fear feels restrictive and small, and intuition feels expansive and open.** Practice feeling the difference between fear and your intuition. If this is new for you, try this exercise: Close your eyes and imagine something or someone you love and trust deeply. Or imagine a big dream you have coming

true, or, better yet, imagine both of those things together. Feel the expansiveness, even if for you that feels like love, excitement, joy, or hope. Next, imagine what scares you, whether that's a person, a place, or a situation. Feel what happens to your body. Try to notice the difference in what you were feeling previously. Intuition and fear will likely feel similar in those differences, intuition feeling expansive and open, and fear feeling restrictive and small.

THE
UNLEARNING

NOTICE: Pay attention to where this chapter hit you the hardest. Perhaps it was when I talked about trauma and your intuition, or dismissing your gut feelings when you were in a relationship, or understanding the difference between your intuition and fear.

Think about times when you've ignored your intuition. What happened in the end? Are you in a situation where you're doing it now?

Notice if you have any beliefs about your intuition in general—such as that you don't have it, that it's often wrong, or anything else.

GET CURIOUS: If you struggle with listening to your intuition and/or not trusting it, why do you feel that is? Is there trauma or an old wound that confuses the wisdom that's trying to come through or your certainty of it?

If you struggle between reading what is fear and what is your intuition, what is something you're willing to do to practice and hone listening for your intuition? What feels like it's calling you to honor in terms of tools and exercises?

SELF-COMPASSION: In some cases when people realize their trauma or old wounds are holding them back, such as not being able to listen to their intuition, they can go down a rabbit hole of feeling angry or frustrated about it, feeling hopeless—like they are "broken" or there is something wrong with them, or giving up altogether on the topic, even when they know it's something that can help them.

Although intuition is considered a "sixth sense," for many, as we've explored here, it is not something that comes as naturally as your sense of sight or hearing. Sharpening your intuition will take time and practice; treat it like a new skill and cut yourself some major slack if you're struggling in this area. You can't beat yourself up into honing your intuition. In addition to time and practice, your inner wisdom will need a heavy dose of self-compassion.

KEEP THE MOMENTUM: One of the exercises I give clients as well as one I do myself is a prayer/meditation/affirmation/request. You can call it whatever you want to, but basically it encompasses a bit of surrender and asking for your intuition to come through. In addition to using the tools I've provided in this chapter for help, when you find yourself in a place where you're not sure if it's your fear talking, or you're stuck on a decision, or you're feeling unsure in general, tell yourself, "The answers are within my reach." Keep repeating this or some variation of it. ("The clues are all around me," "The clarity is coming," or "The solution is here" are also good.) This isn't about coming to an instant answer (although if that happens, hooray!), but instead telling your brain and body that you are open and listening and ready for the right answers at that time.

7

Start Building Superior Stories

A client of mine, Rachel, told me the following story. "When I was fourteen, I became obsessed with my weight, counting calories and eventually restricting food to the point where the pounds really started to come off. My dad told me I was looking much healthier. My mom said she was proud of me. I skipped a couple periods, dropped out of the school play, and did my best to hide my slightly dulling hair.

"Eventually, my mom got a little suspicious. At my yearly physical, they weighed me, and I felt pleased with myself. I sat on the exam table; my mom smiled at me and told me how different I was going to look as I lost more weight. The doctor came in, and she and my mom discussed my rapid weight loss. She congratulated me on my accomplishment. I thanked my doctor and told her I was planning to lose more. My mom then raised concern after she consistently saw me having a juice box for dinner and chewing on the straw for the rest of the night. She reviewed my BMI again and asked how much more I wanted to lose. We all just sat there awkwardly, unsure how any of us should be feeling."

Rachel goes on to recall this pivotal moment in her youth as being one where she looked to two women of authority for the answers—her mom and her doctor—neither of whom had any. She says she hadn't been conscious that what she was doing was bad for her health physically, nor was she aware that she was setting herself up to accept that her behavior of wanting to be thin at any cost was okay, and it was celebrated.

This isn't to blame and shame these women. Rachel's mother and her doctor likely got the same messaging growing up—that to be thin was an important part of being a woman, that the size and shape of her body was the key to acceptance, love, admiration, and worthiness. So it's not surprising that all three of them didn't know how to handle the situation, and the experience instilled Rachel's story further: that to be thin at any cost was good and valuable.

As Rachel learned that being thin was important in woman-hood, maybe you learned different disempowering and sometimes awful things about what it meant to be a woman. Perhaps it was that women who wore bright red lipstick were whores. Or that women who spoke up and talked back were bitches or just plain scary.

Maybe you learned that ambitious women were callous and mean. Or that wealthy women were greedy or got that way only because they were trophy wives. Or perhaps that mothers who took breaks from their families were selfish.

We all have assumptions about women, whether you know them or not. Either way, they have a massive impact on your confidence, your decisions, how you feel about yourself, and how you show up in your life every damn day.

You're reading this book because something inside you knows that all of those stories that feel like crap aren't actually true. Maybe it's only an inkling, but it's there. The stories that said you should never make waves, that you aren't good enough, that you are bad at picking partners or handling money.

Something inside of you is longing to believe more empowering things. To create personal narratives that are full of hope, possibilities, and love. Stories about yourself that are in perfect alignment with the version of yourself you're longing to become and know that you *can* become.

The truth is, you've gotten to where you are now based on the many less-than-stellar stories you've made up about yourself and that simply aren't true. And, look, that's not a bad thing—that you've come this far based on those versions. Imagine how far you can go if you change the narrative. Think of what's available to you if you become crystal clear on when you're making up disempowering stories, challenging them, and creating new ones. Think of the positive trajectory you could be on if you no longer were married to stories that kept you small and in its place had a love affair with stories that made you the star character.

You deserve so many wonderful things. In order to get them, you must do things like step out of your comfort zone, ask for what you want, hold true to your values, and sometimes set boundaries. What all of these things have in common is that it's much easier to do all of them when the story you're telling yourself is that all of these things are possible. In addition to being possible, they're deserved. Work on the story you tell yourself, and you'll be well on your way.

WHAT WE'RE TAUGHT

When I surveyed my audience on this topic, I found answers that didn't surprise me. I asked women, "As you were growing up, what did you learn a woman needed to be like?" Here's a sampling of what I got:

Sarah, a thirty-nine-year-old nurse, said, "I was taught that a woman needed to have attention from men to be valued. That a catcall was a prize. It's taken me many years to unlearn that."

Kristin, forty-four, said, "My message was that you follow/do what the men want, your opinion is of less value than theirs. Go with the flow and let them lead."

Joelle, forty-seven, said, "My mother taught us that a woman should be thin, be a stay-at-home mother, and spend her day washing, cleaning, and cooking. A woman should only have a *boy*friend, get married, and have a family. If she worked, she was self-centered; and she didn't need 'a night out' or 'girls' anything, especially if you had a husband."

Katy, a twenty-nine-year-old woman from Canada, says, "Teenage or young adult women who wear tight clothes are 'asking for it' and have no right to complain when men or other women comment on their bodies. This is what I saw and heard in high school, so I wore pajama pants for years instead of yoga pants or leggings."

Robyn, twenty-six, said, "You are a girl and therefore cannot take over the family business, because you won't carry on the family name . . . the legacy. Also, it's men's work. You'll never be strong enough, handy enough, brave enough, et cetera, for this work and be successful."

Don't get me wrong—I did hear a handful of women tell me they were explicitly taught more empowering things, like that being career-driven was a positive attribute. However, that was typically coupled with disempowering modeling around body image or relationships. Of course, no parent or caregiver is perfect, but it's clear young girls don't commonly get handed messages that enable them to rise above their limitations in all areas of their life.

This goes beyond stories we make up or are taught about what a woman should be like. We make up stories about pretty much everything, especially when we have even an inkling of uncertainty. The great news is we can change it, so let's dig in.

WHAT IT LOOKS LIKE

Making up stories in our head allows us to create structure in what can feel like chaos. Mentally and emotionally we can be unsure about something, maybe it's a stressful project at work, an upsetting situation with a family member, or questions about a parenting decision. In those situations, we can feel ungrounded, we have no concrete answers, and we want order. Making up stories gives us that—regardless of whether the story we make up is true or not.

My friend and colleague Dr. Sasha Heinz has studied human behavior in this regard.

> Human beings are meaning-making creatures and we're very good at reconstructing a narrative retrospectively. We don't create the narrative of who we are prospectively, but instead look back at all the things that have happened to us and weave some sort of narrative that makes sense. We create the story of our life based on past experiences, and often-times that story is disempowering.

We create stories based on our past experiences, what we see in the media, as well as cultural and social messaging, and most often this is all done unconsciously.

Both Sasha and I agree that the amazing and powerful thing about the human brain is that we have the autonomy to reconstruct the narrative. This is great news—that we can create a new story about who we are. So all those years of thinking we're not good enough, that we don't measure up to other people, that we need to overachieve until we're too exhausted to get out of bed in order to be valuable . . . We can eradicate that and positive-affirmation our way into a new story, correct? Well, yes and no.

THE IMPORTANT (AND OFTEN OVERLOOKED) FIRST STEP

People often assume they are going to go from thinking they aren't "something" enough or they are attached to a label put on them from a young age because of someone else's subjective opinion, like a parent or teacher, to thinking something radically different and better about themselves. When the reality is, you have to first *believe it's possible* to change the story. Then you have to start taking action, believing it might be possible that something could be different, and many times, that action, or even purely the thought of it, feels like shit.

As facilitators of change, we see this often. People get interested and excited that they can change their narrative, their story, and their thoughts. That they can embrace a new, more empowering belief system about themselves. They like the *idea* of it. But when it comes to sending an email to your boss asking to speak with them, knowing you're going to ask for a raise, which will require you to shut down or at least bypass the narrative that you don't deserve it or will never be brave enough to ask—that's where people tend to stop.

In the 1980s, Carlo C. DiClemente and J. O. Prochaska, two well-known researchers, came up with a six-stage model of change to help professionals understand their clients with addiction problems and motivate them to change. Originally the model was created for troubling behaviors such as smoking, overeating, and problem drinking, but it's widely used in such industries as fitness and personal growth. Really, anyplace you are tired of your own bullshit and want to shift things.

Let's look at the Stages of Change and how they will work with you changing your personal narratives.

1. **Precontemplation:** This is where people don't know they have disempowering stories they make up, or they know they exist, but they might be unconscious narratives. Also, this is a place of not being ready or wanting to change.

2. **Contemplation:** Here, you know you have disempowering narratives and are interested in changing them, but you feel skeptical that it can work for you, or ambivalent.

3. **Preparation/Determination:** This is where it gets juicy! At this stage, you are committed to changing the disempowering thoughts and stories you have about yourself. Enough is enough, but you still might be unclear or are considering *how* to actually do this.

4. **Action:** Here, you take action by doing things such as completing most of the journaling questions in this chapter, coming up with new narratives for yourself, noticing when you are making up stories, and maybe even talking about this topic to some of your trusted friends. You begin to feel your confidence rise, and you feel better and happier. You're on your way!

5. **Maintenance and relapse prevention:** This stage will have you keeping up with the action and using the tools when you fall back on old patterns, which will likely happen, but less and less often as time goes on.

6. **Relapse or termination:** This tends to happen when people get triggered, such as when they have a breakup or an argument with someone and negative self-talk crops back up. It's not an "if" it will happen, but a "when." I don't consider the negative self-talk to be the relapse, but your reaction to it. If you throw in the towel and say, "Forget it, this doesn't work for me," or feel that you're too broken or think you have too much baggage to continue and try again back at Step 4, that's what I want you to notice.

Changing your thoughts and thus your beliefs about yourself takes time, commitment to the process, and perseverance.

Also, it's Step 4, the action part, that tends to stop people. There might be a few reasons this happens—laziness, not making it a priority, being more comfortable in your false narratives because they're more familiar—really there are many reasons people stop here. I point this out to tell you you're normal as well as to hold your feet to the fire. We're all human and we all have fallen into this, so just notice if this is you.

And it makes sense if you've remained stuck—you've lived your life collecting evidence that your previous narrative was true, or else it wouldn't be your narrative anymore. Maybe you've always told yourself you're not athletic, and therefore you're always starting and stopping workout routines (or maybe your parents told your brother he was the athletic one and you were the funny one). Then you have "evidence" that your bumbling, unathletic self is a true story. When you try to change this workout habit, it would require lots of action, and for you to *believe* something else might be true, and then follow through with an exercise regimen that works for you.

Or you're convinced you're a "bad picker" based on your past relationships. In order to change, you'll need to believe you might be a smart picker or at the very least a smart-picker-in-progress, and perhaps even good at relationships. You'd also need to commit to working on your own issues in order to walk away when you see red flags or commit to what you will and will not tolerate in your romantic relationships. It's the action that's the hard part, and, again, many times this is where people quit.

CONFABULATIONS AND CONSPIRACIES

I am a Daring Way™ Facilitator (methodology based on the research of Dr. Brené Brown). We are trained to take people through a process in which they name their story, then "rumble" with all the feelings associated with it—perhaps for the first time ever—and then learn to create a new story in the end. We teach and encourage participants to look for confabulations and conspiracies. From our workbook: "A confabulation is defined as a lie told honestly. To confabulate is to replace missing information with something false that we believe to be true." For instance, you meet your friend for coffee and tell her, "My boss thinks I'm an idiot who can't make good decisions, so he continues to not give me the bigger projects." In this example, you aren't lying to try to get your friend to feel sorry for you. You honestly believe that your boss thinks you're an idiot. Unless your boss has explicitly told you that you can't make good decisions and are therefore an idiot, and that's the reason he won't give you bigger projects, you're telling your friend a confabulation. The only truth is that you're not getting bigger projects at work, but you're making up the rest of it. We do these things unconsciously and quickly, and we tell them convincingly to ourselves, and to others.

Conspiracies are defined as "Stories based on limited real data and plentiful imagined data, blended into a coherent, emotionally satisfying version of reality." For instance, your friend Sharon nonchalantly tells you she and a bunch of your other friends met for yoga on Sunday. You weren't invited and are instantly hurt. You spend the rest of the day assuming that you did something or said something to piss one or more of your friends off, and that they are planning on slowly pushing you out of your circle of friends. How dare they! You were friends with all of them first and were the one who introduced Sharon to the rest of them. When you finally break down and ask why you weren't invited, Sharon hugs you and says, "You told us you hated yoga after that one time we went and that guy's ass was too near your face and you said you never want to do it again. We only assumed you'd say no, but you're more than welcome to come if you want!"

The limited information you had was that they went to yoga and you weren't invited. That was it. You made up the rest, and even though it was painful to make up the story you did, it was emotionally satisfying. Our human brains love to come to conclusions, to close the loop, even if our conclusions suck.

We also look for any evidence that our conspiracy theory is true. In the example above, maybe you would remember anytime one of your friends looked at you kind of funny, or when they gossiped about someone else, and you pile that into your evidence file that it's true that they want to break up with you.

Both confabulations and conspiracy stories end up dictating how we feel, how we treat and speak to ourselves, and how we treat other people.

WHAT ARE THE CONSEQUENCES?

When you make up false narratives about who you are, how you should be, and what others are thinking about you, you are holding yourself back from living your best life. You're letting your unconscious—which many times is in cahoots with your inner critic—take the lead. Although this is common, it's also unacceptable (in my most loving, best-friend-looking-out-for-your-best-interest voice).

Let's for a moment connect the dots between your stories and the choices you're making and not making. Say you've been in your job for a while, and it's a job you really like. You've been spinning a story that because you don't have your master's degree like some of your coworkers do, you don't measure up. And maybe some of your colleagues went to prestigious schools that people ooh and ahh over. So there's a little insecurity, a lot of compare and despair, mixed in with a small side of shame.

This story and the subsequent feelings and beliefs about yourself can lead to a lack of self-confidence. Which will likely lead to you not speaking up in meetings, not making your ideas known, not asking questions you need the answers to, and not going for promotions or asking for raises.

I encourage you to get out a piece of paper or a journal and think about a negative narrative you have in regard to work, your romantic relationships, money, your friendships, your goals, really anything. Separate the areas of your life into categories, because if you think about your entire life, it can feel overwhelming. Start with one area of your life and write out the disempowering story you make up about yourself. Do you make up that you fall short in any of these areas? If so, how? Be specific.

Next, think about the small choices you make (or don't make) because of these beliefs. Do you turn down opportunities? Do you settle for crumbs? Do you procrastinate out of fear or uncertainty? These choices may seem small on their own, but they stack up on top of one another and can have a major impact on your life.

Yep, this exercise sucks to get through. But the more you know about them, and the faster you recognize them and reframe (which we'll get to soon), the better you can make choices that are on the path to what you want in life and your biggest self. Will the action be challenging? Probably. But the cost of the discomfort of taking action is *well worth* what's on the other side for you.

WHEN YOU MAKE UP STORIES ABOUT YOURSELF

My hope is that by reading this book, you're accumulating tools to use to be able to notice fairly quickly when you're acting or thinking in ways that are not helpful to you or that are simply mentally and emotionally unhealthy. The goal is not to eradicate these ways entirely, but to notice quickly when you fall into these habits, and consciously course-correct.

When we're trying to change the false and negative narrative about ourselves, the first and sometimes most difficult part of the work is noticing when you're doing it. Imagine you're driving fast down a freeway with blinders on, allowing you to see only what's directly in front of you. You're unable to pick your head up or move your eyes in any way; you can see only what's dead ahead. You have no idea where your exit is, but you know you have one that you need to take. Plus, you're in the fast lane on a five-lane highway and the exit will be on the right.

Suddenly the blinders come off, and you look up and see that you are coming up quickly on your exit. You can swerve right to make it, possibly crashing into cars on your way or turning the wheel so hard you'll flip your car over.

Wouldn't it be easier to not have the blinders on in the first place? Even better, to know how many miles ahead your exit is, or to be so familiar with the highway that you know exactly where it is? You'll prepare, get in the correct lane safely, and won't miss your exit and die in a fiery inferno.

This metaphor might be dramatic, but this can be what it's like to be blind to your biggest triggers, to allow things to happen and be unaware when you're making up stories about yourself. Instead of waiting until you've already made up a false narrative about yourself, plus had challenging emotions because of it and maybe made decisions not in your best interest because of that narrative, let's try to look up, see what's in front of you in terms of when and how these happen in the first place, so you can be prepared.

In addition to being prepared rather than blindsided by disempowering narratives, let's go through a process of challenging and changing these stories. I want to highlight that sometimes these are deep wounds that might need more work and attention in therapy, and some narratives may be a simple reframe. What the following exercise will focus on is simply the reframe.

THE REFRAME

For this exercise, you'll need a journal. I prefer pen and paper, but you're welcome to use a computer or your phone. You can

download an accompanying workbook for free at andreaowen
.com/msn.

1. Take Note

Let's start with some questions. Jot down the first thing that comes
to mind:

What, generally speaking, were you taught about what it means
to be a "good woman"? Do any of those descriptions go against
what you believe to be true now?

How do you think you have measured up to what you were
taught—even if what you were taught isn't what you believe now?
When you answer that, is it your inner critic speaking?

Is there anyone or anything that specifically triggers you (e.g.,
outspoken or ambitious women)? If so, what about that (or them)
makes you uncomfortable, judge them, or something else?

Is there a certain story you have about what women should be
like that you want to let go of and/or change? If so, what is that?

Is there a certain story you have about who you are in other
areas of your life that you want to let go of and/or change (e.g., relationships, finances, career, your future, etc.)? If so, what are they?

Who benefits or profits (if anyone) from these false narratives?
For instance, if you believe that you're not beautiful enough as you
are, and have spent years, perhaps decades, trying to lose weight
when you are otherwise a physically healthy person, is only the diet
industry benefiting and not you?

If you're on a roll and know there are more internal stories about
you that you want to challenge, feel free to keep writing. These can
be big, heavy topics, so take the time and space you need to answer
them.

2. Why and Says Who?

Take one of the disempowering narratives you came up with from the preceding prompts. For example, maybe you're convinced you are a bad picker in relationships. Perhaps you've had a series of unsuccessful relationships, or a bad breakup or divorce, and are certain you're either too difficult to get along with or that you *always* choose partners who are terrible for you.

First, why do you believe this? Sure, it may be true that you've had a series of failed relationships, but is that the only fact? If so, and you believe that you're doomed to be alone forever or always choose badly, you're making up a conspiracy. For this part of the reframe, we're investigating the why.

You can also dig further into this by asking yourself, "Says who?" Sometimes, when asked this question, we are quick to reply, "Everyone," and wallow in our self-pity. Hey, self-pity is fine for a bit, but once you pull yourself out, take a moment to think about *who* it is that's on board with your negative narrative. Perhaps your friends have casually joked about your choice of dating partners, or you've been reprimanded by a passive-aggressive boss, which is creating the story that there are in fact others who can attest to your disempowering self-talk. However, you get to decide what your story is. See number 4 (What Do You Want It to Be?) for new, more empowering narratives, but before we get there, it's worth repeating—*you get to decide what you believe to be true about yourself.* You have the power to retrain your brain into recognizing crap stories, challenging and questioning them, and creating new, more dynamic ones that will put you back on the path to being your most powerful self. No one else can do that but you.

This step can also help you clarify the "why" by asking, "Where did this come from?" Which brings us to the next step . . .

3. What Is Your Truth Versus Your Conditioning?

Was this disempowering narrative, messaging, or conditioning passed down to you from your family or culture? For instance, let's look at Robyn's example in the first section of this chapter about being a woman (girl, as she put it, which is telling), and therefore she could not carry on the family business. She was told this, so it's obvious this was her conditioning, given to her from her family, but I'd also be curious how much of this she believes, as well as if she feels this is bleeding into other parts of her life. By being told by her parents that she isn't as valuable to the family business as her brother is, has she adopted any other beliefs about herself as a woman? Perhaps if she wanted to start her own business, that she wouldn't be as successful, say, as her brother or any other man?

Let's think about common narratives that women are encouraged to buy into with regard to how we "should" be. Here's one: In order to be accepted and loved, we need to be nice, quiet, pretty, and selfless. Certainly, the narratives can be culture-dependent to varying degrees, but I am guessing you can fairly easily tell me what you've been socialized to believe here.

If you could snap your fingers and change this, if you could magically erase that narrative and define what is true for *you*—what would that be? The way you were born, the way you naturally move around this life, and what was miraculously and perfectly embedded in your DNA—*This* is your Truth. It's not everyone's truth, just yours.

4. What Do You Want It to Be?

Now that you're clear on what your disempowering stories are, how they got there, and what your actual truth is versus your conditioning, the million-dollar question is, *What do you want your narrative to be?* The amazing thing is not only do you get to pick, but it can be anything. It can be big and broad, like "I can be anything I want" or "I don't need anyone's permission anymore except my own." Or it can be specific, like creating new stories about what you will and won't tolerate, your athletic or artistic ability or other talents, or that you can in fact get to a place where you can afford your own home.

I encourage you to get specific here. You aren't here to play games with your life and gloss over shitty stories that leave you in the dust. If you're struggling to come up with new narratives over your old ones, here are some examples for you to take your pick from:

That you're a boss-ass bitch (you define exactly what this means to you).

That you're constantly improving yourself, no matter what pace you're at.

That every relationship that doesn't work out gets you closer to the one that will.

That it's your duty to fulfill your natural personality—whether you're more introverted and contemplative or extroverted and boisterous.

That you are talented, and the world needs your talents.

That you are powerful and have full autonomy in your life.

That you have the capacity to create change.

5. What Action Needs to Be Taken?

As you'll hear me repeat, all personal development, including building superior stories, relies on you taking action. You can't wish it into existence, unfortunately.

The previous steps in the reframe are actually huge. Never underestimate the power of reflection, answering powerful questions, and challenging your previous beliefs and assumptions. You can't change without doing those steps.

If you haven't taken the time to do those steps, I invite you to add them to your calendar. Think about all the other things you have in your calendar or day planner—workouts, errands, meetings, dinners out with friends, your therapist appointments, and getting your nails done. If you want to change your life, add on that time to retrain your brain into thinking better thoughts and stories that will cannonball you into your best life. Sure, a fantastic manicure is great, but have you tried thinking you're a total and complete badass?

Or perhaps your action is to replace your negative narrative with a positive or even a neutral mantra. For instance, say you lost your job and have been looking for a new one. Prospects look slim and you've been telling yourself, "There're no good jobs available; I'm either overqualified for low-paying jobs or underqualified for my dream job. I'm going to be unemployed for years." Yes, you are probably stressed. Yes, you're frustrated looking at job websites every day. But if there's only one fact (you are looking for a job) and you're filling in the rest of the story, you have the ability to change the rest of the story with more positive possibilities. This isn't about being blissfully airy-fairy and ignoring reality, unless you want to. If it feels amazing to tell yourself, "The right job is out there waiting for me!" Then knock yourself out. But you can also choose to be more neutral. What if you tell yourself, "If not this, then something better," or, "This is hard and I'm resilient and made for this," instead of, "There are no good jobs available," or, "I'll be unemployed for years"?

If nothing else, take action around reflecting on the question "What is my conditioning versus what is my truth?" Allow that question to pop up when you're feeling afraid, procrastinating, comparing yourself to other people, or just generally feeling down. You might be surprised what you find there, and the ball will continue to roll in the direction of more positive stories.

The goal is that you get to know the disempowering stories so well that you can act as if they are no longer available for use. Gone like your favorite lipstick that got discontinued in 2012. You felt lost without it. You thought, "How will I find another shade that suits me so well?" And you managed. Make those disempowering stories ones you recognize immediately for what they are, challenge them, do the work you need to do, and let them go.

HAVE THE CONVERSATION

Part of the action piece might be about having a conversation with someone. This topic is a great opportunity for you to talk about the stories you make up with the people who are affected by them. For instance, if you come to the conclusion that you have unconsciously bought into gender stereotypes that say that women should do the bulk of the housework and household duties while the man can relax, be the "fun parent" if you have children, and otherwise have a vacation kind of life, it's time to have a conversation with your partner about it. Not blaming him and making him responsible for all the stress you've been under for all of your adult life, but sitting down and saying, "What do you think about this?" or, "I'm just realizing I was raised this way and it's not working for me anymore. Can we discuss this and work on it together, so it doesn't become a problem later?"

Or the conversation might be with your trusted girlfriends. If you all go out for brunch and start to commiserate about how much weight you've all gained over the holidays, try interjecting and saying, "So, I read this book and it talked about how we make up stories in our heads about who we are. I love you all and I'm so over this conversation that tells us we aren't awesome if we've gained a few pounds, you know?" Be that friend.

Conversations with others might be a work in progress; if anything, I'd rather have you start with yourself and your own personal stories. Remember, you weren't born thinking you weren't good enough, you don't measure up, or whatever other disempowering beliefs you have. You were conditioned to think this way and believe those things, and you have the power to flip the script.

THE
UNLEARNING

NOTICE: A good way to catch yourself when you are making up a story is to take note when you're beating yourself up about something. Some examples: If you're being hard on yourself for being late for a client meeting, what do you conclude about yourself? Typically, it's not that you're employee of the month, but it's that you're stupid and the client thinks you're unprofessional. Or if you find that you're comparing yourself as you innocently scroll through social media, what is the result? That you're just as successful, beautiful, and happy as everyone else? Or, more likely, you're thinking everyone else has their life together but you. Notice if you're making up a story about who you are in those moments, which might be more often than you think.

GET CURIOUS: Dig around with the following questions:

What is the story you're making up about who you need to be as a woman/daughter/mother/sister/employee/wife/partner/fill in the blank with any of the various roles you fulfill?

Then ask yourself: "Is that true? Is that helpful to me or anyone else?" For instance, if you're making up that you need to be a mom who volunteers at your kids' school, plus works full-time, plus engages in all your hobbies to show your kids what it means to put yourself first, as well as work your side-hustle business, that very well may be too much for one human, and there's a reason you have insomnia and anxiety. Who are you making up that you need to be? Is it realistic? And who benefits the most from this? Is it you or someone/something else? In addition, poke at the question of *why*. Why do you have all these disempowering narratives? What is their origin story? Pay close attention to where they came from so you can challenge that root—because most likely it's a made-up story that has roots in your culture and/or family that ends up being baseless and out of alignment with who you really are.

SELF-COMPASSION: If after reading this chapter you're aghast at all the disempowering and self-defeating stories you've been making up most of your life, take a beat. You're definitely in good company; probably 99 percent of the women reading this book can relate. Take a moment to feel however you feel about it, then try to practice some self-compassion. It's normal to make up stories in your head, and you've also been raised in a culture that sets women up to be fundamentally insecure. Do the math, and you get what you get. The fantastic news is that now you know, and you have some tools to change.

KEEP THE MOMENTUM: In addition, know that creating new, more influential stories is a lifelong process and does get better as you practice. Yes, you will likely "fall off the wagon" and find yourself in a pit of feeling not good enough or comparing yourself to others and coming up short, but I assure you that with practice you'll notice more quickly, have compassion for yourself, and be able to challenge and/or change the narrative.

You are awesome, smart, and resourceful. Remember, you've created stories about yourself all of your life, which means you have the absolute power to create new ones. One step at a time, one story at a time, and you're well on your way to shining more brightly, taking up the space you deserve, and being the badass mofo you know deep inside that you are.

8

Start Riding It Out and Practicing Resilience

Rebecca had had the worst year of her life. Her father had been diagnosed with a terminal illness that would be a long and painful journey. The relationship with her live-in boyfriend had ended, and being in her late thirties, she was extra upset about this, thinking this would have been the relationship that would signal her getting married and having children. To make matters much worse, her ex-boyfriend began harassing and stalking her, as well as not relinquishing some of her personal belongings—things that belonged to her ailing father. She questioned whether she should get the police involved, but worried that that wouldn't help and would in fact make matters worse.

Rebecca had a demanding job working with special-needs children and, to add insult to injury, she was being undermined at work by a senior coworker. She was at the end of her rope. Rebecca had decided to get sober a few months prior, something she was initially excited about, but now it felt futile and she wanted a drink. She came to a call with me and began sobbing, "When will all this end? It just keeps getting worse! What can I do to turn things around?" During our call she kept saying she had worked on herself so much, read so many personal-development books—there had to be a way for her to get out of this mess.

My heart broke for Rebecca. I know this place well, and it's likely that you do, too. This place where you can see no out. Where everything feels like it's on fire, including you. She knew how important it was to work on herself; she had been doing it for years, and she felt like now was the time she had been working and planning for. She wanted a tool. She wanted *something*, a life hack, a five-step process, a hat she could pull a rabbit out of, anything to get out of where she was at.

The answer is there is no one tool. When you're going through an extremely difficult time, there is no switch you can flip that will change your circumstances or how you feel in the short term. The fantastic news here is that our human brains were made for change and resilience. Not for staying stuck, but for growing, learning, and bouncing back from miserable situations. You have to persevere, you have to put one foot in front of the other, even if it's merely a shuffle in your slippers.

In many ways, our culture tells us that the goal is to always be happy, on a positive trajectory, and successful. Needless to say, those aren't bad things, they're what we all want. And to get there, we all go through hard and sometimes miserable times. What I'm wanting you to look at is your judgment of it, your resistance and avoidance of it, and if in any way you hide these struggles. Just as the sun rises and sets, you're guaranteed to have times in your life when the sun is setting and rising, or in other, nonmetaphorical words, you're guaranteed to have shitty times in your life and great non-shitty times, too.

I promise you, the harder you resist that place, the more it will kick your ass. The more frantic you are when you're there, the longer you will stay there. The more you make yourself wrong for even being there in the first place, the more you will feel like an epic failure. The point of life and for making it outstanding isn't to avoid these troublesome places, it's to stumble into them, trudge through, and come out more badass for having gone through it in the first place.

You came here to make some noise in your life. You came here not to be the most fragile of flowers, but to be the type of flower that can weather the storm, survive the winter, and even perhaps survive being stomped on in a zombie apocalypse. You came here to be persistent and powerful. Let's begin.

WHY WE ARE SO DESPERATE TO GET OUT

Allow me to start with the most obvious reason we frantically grab at something, anything, to get us out of our lousy circumstances, and that is that being in a place of lousy circumstances is the fucking worst. It hurts, it's painful, and there might be other feelings layered on like fear, shame, embarrassment, or loneliness.

You might also feel like everyone around you has their life together but you. It never fails; when we are down and out or even just feeling down and out, we get wedding or baby shower invitations in the mail, or someone posts on social media about their epic vacation, their super-successful business, or their happy and secure retirement plans. These things happen for people on the regular, but when you're feeling like a failure, they seem to be louder and more in your face.

You might also compare your circumstances, as well as your resiliency, to other people's. Maybe Shannon also got passed up for a promotion at work by some guy with less experience, but ended up getting a raise, and you got passed up for a promotion and never got a raise. Or you hear about someone who went on a silent meditation retreat and came back feeling totally renewed and healed and you kind of want to punch them in the face. Where is your break-through? When do you get to win?

We understand logically the wisdom that "you have to face the dark in order to appreciate the light" and "if you're going through hell, keep going," but when we are actually in the midst of our dark hell, all these platitudes can feel like personal attacks. There are very few people who are at peace with their dark night of the soul when they're at the bottom of it.

Although there's no arguing how much these instances suck, let's look at why resilience is imperative to your life and ways to pick yourself up and move in the direction of getting out.

WHY IT MATTERS

You know what futility feels like. If you've ever tried to calm a toddler having a tantrum and they're past the point of no return or if you've ever tried to argue politics with strangers on social media, you understand the feeling of pushing against something. At first, we feel like we can make a change, then realize we can't, and hope-fully understand that by walking away and letting things go, we're actually happier and the difficulties of it can diminish faster.

That last part is what I want to point out. When we push against our challenges, when we try and try to change things that we can't, we end up causing more harm to ourselves sometimes than if we had let it go and walked away. Clichés are clichés because they're true and universal, and the cliché "pick your battles" is one that is necessary for you to remember and implement, especially during dif-ficult times. Whatever you're resisting and fighting against, maybe your body has been telling you it's time to face your traumatic childhood and you don't want to because you know it's going to be a hard journey. The resistance—is that a battle you're willing to fight until the end? Or is it better to surrender to what it is, accept its challenges, and move forward? Bottom line: Get clear on what's important to you—*really* important to you—face those obstacles, and leave the rest behind.

In addition, when you choose to ride out life's challenges contrary to desperately seeking to control them, this is the definition of building your resilience muscle. Some wise person once said, "All wisdom comes from healed pain," and I'm a firm believer in this. Of course, you can get wisdom from things that don't hurt, but when you ride through life's hard times, you have a certain respect for the challenge, a kind of "I see you over there kicking my ass up and down the street, and I honor the lessons that came with it."

It can also give you the feeling of balance, since there's no such thing as perfect *life* balance; but building resilience can create more harmony in your life. When you encounter difficult situations, it won't hurt any less, but you'll know with certainty that you'll get through them stronger on the other side.

Your earned wisdom will be metaphorical trophies, badges, gold stars, and medallions. They will make you the bomb-ass wise woman that you are and will continue to be.

TOOLS

Control

Sometimes when we're in struggle, we can keep spinning instead of feeling grounded because we're trying to control things we have no control over. This is one of those lessons many of us have to learn over and over again, because for some strange reason we seem to forget we can't control everything, and we need to relearn the lesson when hard things crop up.

So get *very* clear on what you can control versus what you can't. Not just know this abstractly, but make a list, either on paper or in your head.

Research shows that we retain more information if we write things out by hand, so I encourage you to get out a piece of paper and draw a line down the center of the page. On one side are things you can control, such as your thoughts; who you reach out to; what and how much you read or listen to; if you exercise or eat well; and your perspective. On the other side is what you can't control, like the weather, the past, and other people's feelings and behaviors.

For instance, in March 2020, I was working with a client, Samantha. In one session, she was panicked as the onslaught of COVID-19 was happening and schools started to close. As a single mom, Samantha didn't have a lot of support. She told me, "It feels like we're all running around in circles and no one knows what's happening or what is to come." Because she was a business owner, her income was uncertain, which made her anxious and sick with worry, and desperately searching for answers. In order for her to even start to ride out the pandemic, we came up with a mantra. When she felt her anxiety rising, she told herself, "Two feet on the ground." She'd place her feet flat on the ground wherever she was, close her eyes, and repeat it. It was her baseline, bringing her back to the start of what she could control in that moment—with two feet on the ground. This is an example of taking control of your thoughts. I encourage you to start there when you're feeling helpless and desperate for control.

From there, really think about your list and what you can

manage. This list might be short, but it's mighty, because it's all about you.

Perspective

Perspective reminds me of being at a buffet. So many choices, some of which I won't try because they're new and I like to stick to what I know and like. I like fried chicken, but as I've gotten older sometimes when I eat it, I swell up like the Pillsbury Doughboy, and not in the yummy, cute, buttery way. But I still continue to pick at the buffet because it's familiar.

Like with greasy-fingers-and-swollen-face-inducing fried chicken, sometimes we can get used to picking the familiar but uncomfortable perspective of being the victim. For instance, many women grew up believing (often unconsciously) the "damsel-in-distress" persona was a valuable and useful way for others to perceive them. They are taught that it's better to be passive, helpless, and typically finding themselves in some kind of trouble—physically, financially, logistically—and needing to be rescued, usually by a man. These types of stereotypes seep into our minds and can make us feel like the victim, when really this is a role that was presented to us that we accepted and, without any fault of our own, robs us of our power.

Let me be clear, sometimes you rightfully *are* the victim. And in other instances, staying in the perspective of victim can feel disempowering and keep you stuck. So in place of picking the fried chicken/victim perspective, what do you want to pick? Choose a word that feels empowering, and that you can get on board with.

Let's use Rebecca's example in that you've had a shit year and it doesn't look like it will end soon. Say you're stuck in the perspective of "sufferer," because yeah, you're suffering. The thing is, you can feel like you're both suffering *and* something else. You can be more than one thing, have more than one feeling about where you are and who you are. Perhaps in addition to sufferer, it's:

Fighter
Scrapper
Phoenix rising
Expansive
Intentional woman
Conscious creator
Weathering the storm

Once you pick one (or more), define what that label means to your life. An intentional woman looks at life very differently than a sufferer does. What does this look like for you? You probably treat your days differently if you tell yourself you are a phoenix rising and *feel* like one rather than like a victim. My hope is that your empowering perspective will take more of a front seat than your disempowering one. It's a simple exercise, but one that has the power to change the way you think, feel, and act.

Support

Lean on people who inspire you, but not if you compare yourself to them or hero-worship them. This is an important caveat, because when you're in a shitstorm period of your life, you can be vulnerable to assuming therapists, online influencers, authors, and other experts are the pinnacle of happiness and success. You might want to be like them or, at the very least, be best friends forever with them, and it can take away from your own growth. To be inspired and motivated by them is one thing; to worship them is another. The difference is if you hero-worship, you put those people on a pedestal, you make up that they never or very rarely have bad days or months, or you "cancel" them for a minor infraction or for strictly being human. Leaders are fallible just like you. They travel a similar path to you, but they might be in a different place on that path and/or have different opportunities or resources than you have.

Back to leaning on people who inspire you. Look at your imaginary Board of Directors you put together in chapter 1. Or maybe it's a mentor or manager at work who has proved to be supportive in a work role, and a personal one as well. Or maybe it's authors, podcast hosts, or even your therapist. Ask yourself, What is it about this person that I find inspiring? When you interact with this person, what about them motivates you and removes you from the place you're in that you don't want to be? Try not to focus on wanting to be more like them, but alternatively on what the attributes or values they have or seem to have that you want to emulate and make happen in your own life are. Maybe you follow a personal-development speaker who has been through a similar experience as you and they talk candidly about it. Is it their resilience? Their courage to do the work it took to heal? Think about what it is that *you* want that you also believe you can do in your own life. Simply admiring what they did does nothing for *you*.

Pace Yourself

Next, make sure you're not trying to get a sip of water from a fire hose. You may be going through your difficult chapter in your life and signed up for two retreats, downloaded three new meditation apps, and signed up for SoulCycle because you are ready to Change! Your! Life! Obviously, I'm here cheering for you, and at the same time, slow down, woman. Many times we feel like we're changing our life by buying the books and subscribing to the podcasts, but the real work happens in your real life. Knowledge is great, but take it in sips, not giant gulps.

What is the *one* thing you need to work on right now? Maybe it's nothing but getting through each day. Maybe it's not drinking booze or binge-eating, so it's important to focus on your recovery at this time and nothing else (not that that's a small feat, by any means). For instance, if you're focusing on your first ninety days of sobriety, maybe now is not the time to dive into your romantic relationships or a new entrepreneurial pursuit. Using Rebecca's example, when I was working with her, her only assignments were to lean on the people who brought her the most support and to practice self-compassion.

Mercy

Which brings me to my next bit of advice—self-compassion. Yes, I mention this in every chapter as a necessary part of unlearning old conditioning and habits, but it deserves to be pointed out here. When you're going through your extraordinarily challenging time, it's easy to beat yourself up. For how you got there, for the mistakes you made, for the time you "wasted," for not being where you thought you'd be at whatever age you're at, for not being as far along as you "should" be. The list is long, mean, and seems to be the never-ending story when it comes to regret and ways to berate yourself. You may be so used to living in the land of self-bullying, especially during hard times, it might feel alien to do it any other way. If it does, keep going. You may very well have to redirect yourself one thousand times throughout the day. The path to feeling better and healing does not have "beating yourself up" on it. It's not on the menu of enlightenment, so don't order it.

If and when it does come up, notice, and take an action that will redirect, or what I like to call course-correct, you. Get up and take a lap around your office or home; have a mantra in your back pocket you use, like "I'm not here for this"; or even, if it works for you, use an affirmation like "This is tough, but so am I." Last, if it were your best friend or someone else you love and care about and they were going through an extremely difficult time, you would not beat them up for it. You would not be mean and cruel, and I know this isn't the first time you've heard this advice. So if you're looking for a sign to actually take this advice to heart and treat yourself like you would someone you love and care about, honey, I'm waving this sign right in front of your beautiful face.

ONE HOUR AT A TIME

When things are especially difficult, sometimes one day at a time feels like too much. In 2006, I went through one of the roughest times of my life. I was going through a brutal divorce, and everything I knew to be true and safe had been taken away. When I would drag my ass out of bed each morning, I couldn't imagine taking it one day at a time. Making it all the way through the workday, then slogging through the evening, then being alone each night felt monumental. Depression had sunk in and it was all too much. So I told myself, "One hour at a time." I would get up and tell myself, "Just get ready for work and get in the car." Then I'd make it to work and tell myself, "Just make it to lunch. Do what you need to do to make it to lunch." And so on. I got a Sharpie and would cross days off as they went by for a visual so I could see time passing. I would see a bunch of X's on my calendar and use that as evidence that time does in fact go on and that I was making it through day after day.

YOU WERE MADE FOR THIS

Allow me to get spiritual with you for a moment. Whether you believe me or not, you have fire in your soul. Your mother's mother's mother and on until the beginning of time from the motherland—all of those women have experienced strife, challenges beyond our imagination, and somehow made it long enough to have a daughter. Thousands of years and countless generations later, here you are.

Your ancestors have traveled (and not in first-class on a passenger airplane), sometimes against their will, weathered literal storms with possibly not the best shelter, dealt with pandemics, other illnesses, various traumas, and probably endless joy and happiness as well. Being resourceful and resilient and riding out hard times *is in your blood*. You were born with everything you need. It's part of the human experience, and sometimes remembering that can help you get through the challenging time, get through the day, or get through the hour.

THE
UNLEARNING

NOTICE: You might be in a difficult situation right now, or you have very likely been in one in the past. If you're in one right now, think about how you're reacting to it. Do you surrender to it (I'll talk more about surrender in chapter 11, which is about checking out), or do you fight it tooth and nail? Is there a particular way you deal with things, for instance stay in denial at first or get angry, then try to control other people in order to feel better? The point is not to label yourself as wrong for how you handle hard struggles, but to pay attention to how you handle them.

GET CURIOUS: Do you judge yourself for hard times and struggles you've had in the past? If so, why? Do you feel that struggles are meant to be kept to yourself or to get support with? If you feel the need to keep them to yourself, why do you think it's okay for others to ask for help but not you? When you think of the hardest thing you've ever faced, how do you think it's made you a better/stronger/wiser person?

SELF-COMPASSION: Compassion is going to be your best ally here and, at the same time, might be a real challenge to put into action when you're feeling especially low. Without compassion, you'll stay stuck at best, and at worst, go backward. Remember: Not only have you survived all of your challenging struggles thus far, but they've shaped and prepared you for further ones you'll face now and in the future. With self-compassion—which is a key component of resilience—you'll be able to make your way through your difficult time with more grace and ease.

If you struggle with self-compassion, check the Recommended Reading section of this book and dive into the topic, because, again, self-compassion is going to be your catalyst for change and betterment.

KEEP THE MOMENTUM: The great news is that if you're reading this, you've survived a global pandemic. It was one of the biggest fears of most, and you've walked the path. When you're going through another difficult time, I encourage you to do one small thing for yourself every day. Whether it's practicing self-compassion after you've noticed your inner critic taking hold, reaching out to a friend, noticing and getting curious about any unhealthy coping mechanisms you're using, changing your perspective, or journaling, just one of those things for even a few minutes per day can allow you to gain momentum and continue to ride out your difficult situation.

PART 2

SHIT TO
STOP DOING

9

Stop Allowing the Brainwashing to Make You Small

Once when I was a sophomore in high school, I was over at my best friend's house and her stepfather said to me, "I saw you walking the other day when I was driving; I honked at you to say hello and you flipped me off!" He was laughing about it, but I could tell he was surprised it had happened. Feeling embarrassed, I mumbled an apology and told him I didn't know it was him. When the truth was that because of regular street harassment starting at about age fourteen, anytime a man in a car honked at me, I held up my middle finger. I knew well the sound of a car slowing, seeing men hang out of the car window in my peripheral vision, or even merely feeling the stare. Just out of childhood, when you're regularly told, "Nice tits!" or "Sit on my face!" or when you have a tongue flicked at you by men old enough to be your father, it's disgusting and frightening. The only thing I knew how to do was not make eye contact and give them the finger, and sometimes, if I was feeling especially brave, I would yell, "FUCK YOU!" Which I quickly learned actually elicited more aggressive and sexual responses from the men.

I was ashamed that I had done this to my friend's stepdad, who was not, as far as I could tell, trying to sexually harass me. His laughter told me he was more confused than anything, and, looking back at our short conversation about it, I know he had no idea why on earth I would do this. Why this nice young lady would make such a gesture even though at the time he honked at me, I thought he was a stranger.

At the same time how on earth could I, barely a teenager, explain to him that it had become a reflex, born from rage at feeling like my body, my appearance, and my existence were open season for men to comment about, yell at, harass, and in some instances grope? How could I explain how demoralizing and dehumanizing it felt—that my body felt like public property? How could I explain that through my anger, I still felt like it was somehow my fault?

As I got older and spent years in the workforce, how could I express that behind my rage was the fact that I had been sexually harassed at nearly every job I'd ever had except the ones where I worked only with women?

How could I explain that behind my seething anger was the truth that I had been physically and sexually assaulted and felt that it really didn't matter? That it was just something that happened to women and girls and that now, I simply had something in common with more women and girls?

It was impossible to explain any of it to anyone, because at the time it was happening, I thought it was all normal. I couldn't name it because I didn't have the words for it. This intense ferocity I felt for myself, and for other girls and women as I witnessed it. The confusion I felt watching other women laugh it off and seem to flirt back with these men who were saying such crude things to them. And if I dared complain I was either dismissed or told to take it as a compliment?

I didn't understand any of it until I sat in one particular college class when I was thirty-one years old, sixteen years after that awkward conversation with my friend's stepdad.

It was during my last semester of college, and I had to take a women's studies class in order to satisfy a requirement for my bachelor's degree in exercise physiology. The class was called "Men and Masculinity," and I rolled my eyes on the first day of class when the young woman next to me told me she was a feminist. Back then I didn't identify as one, nor did I like feminists, for the simple fact that I *didn't know what that was*.

I wasn't raised with women in my life who talked about Gloria Steinem or Audre Lorde. I didn't know anyone who'd marched in women's movements or voted for or even spoke of equality.

I grew up in a church that taught me sex before marriage was very, very bad and that abortion was even worse. Molded by a culture that told me girls who speak their minds are not nice. As a young adult in the nineties I was told by the people I chose to have company with that feminists were man-hating, hairy-legged lesbians who were against motherhood and against any woman who chose to stay home instead of work outside the home. That they were against femininity of any kind, like lipstick or high heels, and spent a lot of time burning their bras while smoking Virginia Slims and looking for ways to trash men.

This is embarrassing to talk about and admit, but when you have no other lessons and you love and trust the people who are teaching you, as well as are never taught to be objective, think critically, or ever question the source, you believe what you're being taught as fact.

I was always a "front-row student" in my college courses, ready to speak up to ask questions and give my opinion. But in that particular class, as I sat pregnant with my own daughter, I listened much, much more than I spoke.

A couple of weeks into the semester, I had a sinking feeling in my stomach. "This is the thing I've been enraged about my whole life and I didn't know what it was," I thought.

I was reckoning with everything I'd been taught about men, women, masculinity, femininity, and feminism. I felt a combination of shame, disgust at myself for what I had believed and points I had argued against feminism, and excitement that the things I had been so angry at had a name: patriarchy, misogyny, and sexism.

This absolutely does not mean that everything changed at once and I was on my way to being the Best Feminist. I'm still unlearning all the ways I was and still actively am participating in patriarchy and even my own internalized misogyny and sexism. How I was brought up to unconsciously believe that our value as girls and women was based on our appearance, how attractive we were judged to be by men, how sweet and accommodating we were, and, as adults, how productive we are. To let go of female stereotypes that branch off into class, race, ability, body size, and sexual orientation.

You may or may not have been brought up with similar ideologies. Maybe you have been a feminist since you were young, or maybe you don't identify as one now. Maybe you grew up with strict religious philosophies, or maybe your family never went to church. Either way, I firmly believe no woman can deny her life would be different, and in many ways better, if she didn't ever have to think, worry, or try to change her appearance or her weight, or have to feel like so much of her worth depended on that or being attractive (especially to men). If she didn't have to think or worry about being sexually harassed or worry about her safety in most situations. If she didn't grow up having to learn how to not have a roofie slipped in her drink or how to not get raped.

My wish is for all that energy to get replaced with girls and women looking in the mirror and smiling at themselves as a substitute for immediately frowning at body parts they wish were different. Or, worse, feeling self-loathing when they see their reflection. I wish for all that energy to be replaced by learning what's important to them, what their values are, how they want to make the world a better place. For all that energy to be replaced with unconditional self-acceptance, self-trust, and self-love. For them to be able to articulate what that means and looks like in their life, embody it, and pass it on.

Yes, we have come a long way. And there is still so much work to be done.

PUNISHMENT VS. REWARD

When it came to writing about women's empowerment, and being two books in—I couldn't write another book and not talk about all of this. It felt like ignoring a giant elephant in the room to continue to teach about self-worth, self-trust, and reaching out for help to other women when the reality was that we've been taught that we are valuable only if we are beautiful, quiet, nice, and have the perfect figure. That we are most valuable when we are vastly productive and carry most, if not all, of the mental and emotional labor. We've been taught to often question ourselves because confidence and self-assuredness are rarely something we learn growing up. We've been fed a message that women are catty and backstabbers.

You may be thinking, "I hear you, but I was never explicitly taught that." Maybe you had people in your life who openly taught you differently, but if you grew up identifying as a girl or as a woman, then these are unconscious and implicit lessons we all learned. The definition of conditioning is: the process of training or accustoming a person or animal to behave in a certain way or to accept certain circumstances. Let's face it—we all grew up being trained to behave a certain way, and to accept certain circumstances. Whether the people who raised us knew it or not.

During the #MeToo movement in 2017, founded by activist Tarana Burke, as women shared their stories of being sexually assaulted or harassed, we all heard the argument, "Why are women just speaking out about this now? Why didn't you say something then?" Some of us knew why and some of us didn't. In my grief and anger during that time, I wrote and wrote, mostly for myself to process and heal. One of the epiphanies that came of that writing was that early on, around my teen years, I began to understand the "rules."

When we speak up for injustices like sexual harassment, when we whistle-blow, when we make a scene, when we do things like choose not to have children but instead focus on a career, when we do anything that is out of the narrow definition of what it means to "be a good woman," we are punished. We are punished with shame, humiliation, threats of or actual violence, being ostracized, or our safety being taken away.

On the flip side, when we stay quiet, "stay in our lane," when we "know our place," when we sacrifice ourselves and become martyrs for our families and our communities, we are rewarded. In other words, when we follow the rules, we are safe. Rewarded with the label of "good mother," or "good woman," and the extra icing of reward on that cake is protection and acceptance from men.

So, in essence, the reward ends up not being a reward after all when we become conscious of what's really happening. When we realize our spirit is being suffocated.

WOMEN'S EMPOWERMENT + SELF-HELP

So what does this have to do with self-help? Can't women's empowerment just be women's empowerment and we learn boundaries, positive self-talk, and letting go of things like perfectionism? It's interesting—when women initially learn about the work I do, and get curious about it, they then sometimes ask the question, "Where did this come from?" They wonder what the origin is of their inner critic, the fact that they don't trust themselves, and their feelings of "not good enough."

My reply is that the source is one or a combination of three things:

1. Sometimes it's your family of origin (messages you got growing up about who you are and how you should behave).
2. Sometimes it's simply habitual (coping mechanisms that you've learned).
3. And sometimes—and in my opinion this is the main reason—it's our jacked-up culture that raises us to feel fundamentally insecure, never enough, and that we have to do it all perfectly (with just the right shade of lipstick and no cellulite, please) in order to be valued. And that if it *is* numbers 1 or 2, your family of origin or merely habits that have been created, they were born from number 3—the same culture.

Early on in my career as a women's empowerment coach, one of the things I quickly realized is that when we're talking about women's empowerment, we're talking about feminism. But we also can't deny that if we're talking about feminism, we're talking about patriarchy—the power structure that makes feminism necessary. I don't think anyone who remotely understands feminism would deny this.

And I can't not mention, if we're talking about patriarchy, we're talking about white supremacy. This is where I get some pushback, but only from white women in my audience.

I've always been a bit obsessed with getting to the root of the problem. When I first started out as a life coach, I talked a lot about the inner critic, also known as negative self-talk. I talked and taught about this for a couple of years, and in my research and experience, I came to understand that at the root of negative self-talk was shame—the fear of not wanting to be perceived poorly by others, past shame trauma, and the fear of failure and success, among other examples. I couldn't in good conscience know that by talking only about managing negative thoughts I was essentially telling people to slap a Band-Aid on a bleeding wound that required a lot more care. So I got trained in shame work and went on my merry way.

When I took a giant step back to investigate the root of the problem in terms of women's empowerment, what it comes down to is patriarchy and whiteness.

The fact is that the people at the top—the people with the most power—are disproportionately white men. So when it comes to shining bright, asking for what you want, self-confidence, and taking up space, women struggle with this more because of the power structures put into place from the birth of a patriarchal culture. This isn't to say men don't have their struggles; they do. But women, especially Black women and other women of color, struggle more in terms of getting ahead. Take into consideration age, physical and mental ability, sexual orientation, class, and other ways women can be oppressed. So, no, women's empowerment can't just be women's empowerment. The fact that we even all know the term *women's empowerment* means that we don't have power in the first place. Therefore, it's all related and we must look at the "rules" we learned in order to unlearn them.

III

Speaking of men, this isn't about blaming them. No one man is responsible for this. Patriarchy, generally speaking, is a system that gives men the most power and has women largely excluded from that power. And, yes, we have come a long way from women not being able to get credit cards without a man's signature and even not being able to vote. But we, as women, still are discriminated against regularly, are not taken as seriously as our male counterparts, and make less money. We still have a long way to go. Not to mention, patriarchy is the same system that teaches men their emotions are weak and make them less of a man and that violence is the way to solve problems. I'm guessing that intimacy and happiness are important to you in your relationships with men—whether those relationships are romantic or not—and a man who was raised to participate in a patriarchal culture (most every man) will have a nearly impossible time with intimacy and, many times, true happiness. Unless he also faces it, educates himself, participates in his own unlearning, and pushes back on patriarchy.

Men grew up with the same conditioning women did, but their rules looked different. Their punishments and rewards looked different, too. The tie-in is that it all works together in a system and cycle, leaving very little, if any, room for emotional literacy or emotional intelligence. Which leads to a lot of disconnection and loneliness.

When patriarchy is at the wheel, no one can truly be themselves. We're all playing the game, men included.

WE DO IT, TOO

One of the topics I teach regularly is around negative self-talk, or the inner critic. Everyone, not just women, struggles with this, but typically for women the negative self-talk is around not feeling like we measure up to other women and fear that we will be judged and criticized if we put ourselves out there. My friend and colleague Makenna Held is a leadership coach and a perfect example of this. At age thirty-one, Makenna made a bold and courageous move by fulfilling a lifelong dream: She purchased Julia Child's summer home and started offering cooking classes out of it. When the public found out about this, she received messages that she deserved to die, ought to be killed, and that Julia Child should come back from the dead to "take care of her." She's even been called a prostitute in her social media ads for showing a moderate amount of cleavage. Makenna showed me screenshots of these messages and, sadly, most of them were from women.

It's not a huge surprise that women receive rude and sexual comments from men—often anonymously online. But a few years ago I began to notice more and more comments online from women criticizing and being hateful to other women. We keep hearing that we all need to support other women and lift one another up, and I couldn't agree more. However, if we're truly going to do this—and I mean go whole hog on being one another's hype women—we need to also understand, unpack, and heal from our own internalized sexism and misogyny (and while we're at it, any other internalized oppression that we have).

Internalized sexism manifests as sexist beliefs, behaviors, and attitudes that we women do to ourselves or other women and girls. Things like chronic dieting, body-shaming yourself and other women, slut-shaming, routinely seeing other women as adversaries or competitors at work (especially those with great potential or in high leadership positions), seeing other women as adversaries or competitors in social or family situations (especially for the approval of men), and playing into stereotypes like women are bad at math or bad drivers; the list goes on and on.

Until we see and understand what we are doing, why we are doing it, and who benefits from it (because it's not us), try our best to stop doing it, and heal from it, sadly we're just spinning on the self-help hamster wheel and will stay small in our lives.

VISIBILITY

I work with a fair number of women who want to be writers, life coaches, or do some kind of hobby or career that requires them to be in the public eye to some degree. It might be writing a blog or a book, offering their services, or even giving their opinion on social media. Over and over again, many of these women struggle with what we call in the industry "visibility." Absolutely, most people struggle somewhat with being vulnerable in front of others—there is endless research on this, and books written about it. But there is extra fear for women. Maybe it's generational trauma from our great-great-great-grandmothers being burned at the stake, domestic violence they've experienced, or being a woman plus being a member of another marginalized group. Maybe it's the fear of see-ing comments online hurled at other women like what happened to Makenna—death threats, threats of rape, or criticizing the shape of one's body. Fear of the punishment for putting yourself out there. It's obvious why a woman would struggle immensely with visibil-ity. When everything inside of her tells her it's safer to stay quiet. That she is protected only when she is invisible, she is secure by stay-ing quiet, and she is rewarded if she joins in to hurl insults, harsh judgment, and criticism.

INDOCTRINATION

Starting in fifth grade, I became obsessed with the fictional series of books Sweet Valley High. The series centered on twins, Jessica and Elizabeth Wakefield, and to sum it up, they were perfect (by U.S. standards), and I aspired to be just like them. Now, I am not a very sentimental person; I've thrown away most of my kid's art projects and don't have a shoebox full of memories. But for some reason, throughout many, many moves in my life, two marriages, and managing to lose things that really matter to me, I have somehow held on to a box that contains more than fifty of these books. Nos-talgia is a powerful emotion, and I had high hopes that my daughter would read them.

I recently dragged out the wallpaper-wrapped box that con-tained the books (my mom, the consummate decorator, took my childhood wallpaper and decorated the box) and pulled them out as I came to terms with the fact that my recently-turned-eleven-year-old daughter was not in fact interested in my "old books with brown pages," as she called them as she wrinkled her nose. I sighed, pick-ing up book #10 in the series, titled *Wrong Kind of Girl*. As I read the back of the book, my heart sank. The plot surrounded a girl, Annie, who'd been nicknamed "Easy Annie" by Jessica Wakefield because she was rumored to have had many boyfriends (not had sex, mind you, only had boyfriends, which was apparently bad enough and not to mention the same as Jessica herself). To make a long, dramatic teenage story short, Annie has a difficult time making the cheerleading team because of Jessica, attempts suicide, and is saved from this and her depression by Jessica and a boy, the end.

As I stared at the cover of this book as a woman in my mid-forties, I thought of my ten-year-old self reading this book. Learning important things like how to be a teenager, what was important in order to be accepted, and how to treat other girls.

I had pledged allegiance to the culture that raised me; that told me that in order to be "good," I had to fit in a box whose walls were held up by virtues of quiet, pretty, nice, accommodating, nurturing, and selfless. Not to mention pure and wholesome.

I had believed my religion when it told me girls who have sex before they are married are whores. I had villainized and dehumanized prostitutes, strippers, and adult film actresses. Because to not do so, to embrace women who were sex workers and to be okay with young women who confidently had sex with whom they wanted to, and when they wanted to, would fly in the face of everything I knew. I would have been punished by others—questioned as to why I would support those women, punished for going against the grain, or worse, been categorized as one of *them*.

In order to truly embrace my own empowerment, I had to notice and sit in the discomfort of my own participation in the trampling of women. I made amends where I could and continued the perhaps never-ending process of unlearning.

When we are noticing, we are simply paying attention to things we do out of habit that you probably think are totally normal. One way to start is by noticing when you have a reaction to another woman. When she "rubs you the wrong way" or you feel triggered; if you immediately label her as things like opportunistic, aggressive, an "attention whore," greedy, or "mouthy." I'm not at all encouraging you to accept all behaviors from women regardless of outcomes, but this is solely about noticing.

Where are you putting labels on certain women when if they were men, you might not? Looking back on all the women I've encountered in my life—more specifically, the ones I didn't like—I wonder if the reason I came to such a conclusion was because she didn't fit into the "box" I had been conditioned to create. The box that held what a woman should be like.

TOOLS

Living in the Brainwashing While Trying to Change It

I'll be frank. Going for broke in your own personal development or even in your activism isn't going to change the culture or the world in the next few months. It's going to take a massive upheaval and possibly several generations for all women to be on the same playing field and have complete empowerment, including women of color, disabled, queer, trans, poor, and really all marginalized women. So it can feel like your work is a fart in a hurricane, hardly noticeable. But it actually does matter. It's true what they say about the ripple effect, how your empowerment gives other women power and permission to seek out and claim their own. After the 2016 U.S. presidential election revealed that it was somehow okay to speak to women as mere objects that could be grabbed by men whenever they felt like it, therapists saw an uptick of female clients, and in the sobriety and recovery world, we saw a lot of women relapse. Women are hurting, and seeking out ways to help themselves; these ways are not always healthy.

So what do we do in the meantime as we're working on ourselves, helping others, and maybe diving further into fighting the good fight? How do we simultaneously confront and interrupt the culture that is the root of our struggle, and at the same time live in it and stay healthy both mentally and emotionally? The following is a list of tools that require you to think, unlearn, learn, and take action. As with everything, take what you want and leave the rest, and know this work takes continuing effort and is in honor of you and women everywhere.

UNDERSTAND AND ACCEPT THAT THERE IS NOTHING WRONG WITH YOU

Generally speaking, there are two stories I hear from women who become interested in personal development. Some women feel that they have a good life and just want to improve. Maybe they want to learn how to set boundaries, squelch their limiting beliefs, and conquer their goals.

Then there are women who feel like something is inherently wrong with them. "I can't stop being so hard on myself," they say, or, "I don't know why I got this promotion. I feel like such a fraud." It could be a multitude of examples, but the feelings, thoughts, and beliefs that are in common is that it puts the blame squarely on *you*. That the way you feel must be your fault. Plus, they follow some personal-growth advice that tells them they need to be more disciplined, work on their mindset more, and just think positively, which isn't working, so they feel worse about themselves, thus further believing they are at fault and hopelessly broken.

If you feel you fall into that camp, let me assure you that you're not broken, and there is nothing wrong with you.

Now, I am all for taking responsibility where it needs to be taken; in fact, "responsibility" is one of my personal values. And yes, there may be mistakes you've made along the way that were necessary to change direction and perhaps clean up, but we can't ignore the impact that our culture has had on us as it pertains to and is directly related to personal development.

This is the first step: taking a big, deep breath and accepting that even though you might currently have feelings of inadequacy and that you have a lot of work to do on yourself, you have not failed as a human being.

Embody and release. If you're reading this, you're a smart woman (or man or nonbinary, hi!). And smart women, or at least the ones who come to me for coaching or talk to me at book or speaking events, admit that they spend a lot of time overthinking and generally stay up in their heads. We'll dive more into this relief in chapter 11, but like any good empowerment pusher, I want to give you tools to help you.

Your personal power relies not only on your brain and the thoughts and beliefs that flow through it but also on your body and the energy that flows through that. It's your body that tells you when it's time to go to the bathroom, if you're sick, tired, aroused, nervous, and who's "good," and who's "bad." If you don't get the frustration, anger, rage, pain, exasperation, and whatever else is in your body *out,* it will highjack you, keep you stuck and spinning.

These feelings are heavy and loaded, so even five minutes of intentional action can do you worlds of good. A walk around the block, sun salutations, your favorite exercise, or my favorite: ecstatic dance.

Put on your headphones and your favorite music, grab some privacy if you need it, and like the memes tell you to, dance like no one is watching. Research shows that dance improves health, so shake your moneymaker when you're feeling overwhelmed with the pressure of life.

Bottom line: Move the energy that's stuck in your body through your body and out in the form of a physical activity.

Notice your behavior when pressured. The common question of "How are you?" seemed to take on a new meaning during the pandemic. It was typically met with a heavy sigh and the answer began with "All things considered . . ." The collective energy had been rising well before 2020, no one could deny feeling it. And many times, when we would feel the pressure from work, family, or simply humanity, we'd lose our tempers with people we cared about, overwork, overthink, lose our sense of humor, drown in news stories that further fueled our anxiety, and just all-around feel like shit.

We've all done it. The key is to notice when you're in it and have handy not a bag of Flamin' Hot Cheetos, but on the contrary a phrase, a breathing technique, a short energy meditation, or a friend to text, or, if you can, take a nap. During the beginning of the pandemic, I kept repeating, "Every storm runs out of rain," which is a quote from the late, great Maya Angelou.

Never underestimate the power of a small action to your aid when feeling pressure. It's about interrupting the pattern and the narrative going on in your mind. (See the section on breathing techniques in chapter 6.)

Give people the dignity of their own process. I'm in a

large Facebook group that is dedicated to a particular piece of workout equipment that I own, and this group is only for women in their forties. The topics range from working out, to parenting, to career. Once every few weeks, someone asks a question about fillers, chemical peels, and, yes, Botox. And inevitably, there are a few commenters who say things like "Don't do it, age gracefully instead" or "Aging is a gift not given to everyone, be grateful and embrace it instead of fighting it." I understand their sentiment. Patriarchy has created ideal beauty standards that, once we reach our forties, tend to disappear if we had them in the first place. When we do things to fight the aging process, we are seen by some as a victim of patriarchy, falling in line with trying to meet these beauty and youth standards. I've also heard the argument, if we all stop falling prey to these standards, things will change. If we stopped doing all the things like wearing Spanx, wearing makeup, using antiaging creams, and dyeing our hair, we could flip beauty standards on their head and society would change.

The argument of who or what sets beauty standards is layered in capitalism, imperialism, racism, sexism, culture, and even science. If you want to carry the torch to undo that, then by all means, lead the way. But please give women the dignity of their own process.

We are screwed either way. If we take on the fight against impossible beauty standards and don't do anything to "beautify" ourselves, we are more quickly categorized as unattractive and irrelevant, and this could affect us socially and economically. But when we do what we can to fall in line with beauty ideals, we are then chastised by other women? My point is not to convince you one way or another; my point is to allow women to go in either direction and not tell them they are wrong for doing so. I want you to feel empowered either way or the other, and at the same time be aware of what you're doing.

Accept that sometimes you're going to be a hypocrite. Speaking of injectables, I got Botox for the first time in early 2020, when I was forty-four years old. I put it off, feeling like a "bad feminist" if I caved and spent money trying to look younger, trying to hang on to any shred of my youth. I should age gracefully, I told myself, even though I was still trying to define what that actually means to me (versus what it means to the commercials of the fifty-year-old stunning models who talk about aging gracefully, who are always slim and have skin like a thirty-year-old's). Aging can be confusing and complicated for women, because we've been taught from an early age that beauty is currency for us and our most valuable measure of currency. Both sexes have advantages when deemed attractive, but case in point: Women's salaries plateau at age thirty-nine, as men's continue to soar for another decade. In fact, in one study, for women who were not considered conventionally attractive, the boost in salary between the well groomed and the poorly groomed was one and a half times that of their male counterparts.

So would I be labeled a hypocrite by the sisterhood for admitting to Botox? By some, yes. I also shave my legs and armpits, sometimes wear makeup, get my hair done, and get manicures here and there. Does that mean I can't write books and speak on stages about women's empowerment? Am I playing into the trope that older, less attractive women aren't as relevant?

After many guilt-laden talks with myself, my therapist, and my wise girlfriends, I've come to this conclusion: The uncomfortable truth is that women are seen as more relevant when they are attractive, well groomed, and younger. If that means both that I'm making a bargain with the patriarchy and that more people are listening to my messages, so be it.

No one is perfect and no one walks an immaculately straight line of their beliefs. You can still push against societal rules while following them. Like anything, picking your battles will be your way of life here.

Notice when you participate in it, and don't blame yourself. Growing up, we all typically followed the narrative handed to us without question. It may have varied depending on if your family was really sunk deep into sexism, or maybe your family was a little more progressive, but there was really only one option in terms of what was modeled for us and the messaging we received.

You might have a lot of mixed feelings when you start to pay attention to your own internalized oppression. Shock, sadness, guilt, shame, anger, and more. None of them are wrong. You've been doing what you were taught; it's what humans do to survive in a community and/or family.

When I was in my twenties I had two different jobs where I had bosses who were women. Both of them were assertive, powerful, and tough, and I did not like either of them. I found them intimidating, mean, and controlling. Looking back, they were by no means perfect bosses, but had they acted the same way and been men, I would not have judged them so harshly.

I invite you to think about similar situations in your life where you might have done the same thing. Take inventory of female leadership and what you thought of it. This isn't about letting women off the hook who truly could have used some improvement, but for you to look at where you may have judged or currently judge women in positions of power and leadership.

Name it when it comes up in yourself. We must interrupt

internalized sexism. This may be a huge ask if you're just starting to see where this shows up in your own life, and especially if you're unpacking old, deep-seated views from your family or from former partners. Start with the people closest to you whom you trust enough to be open to this conversation. Talking with family members who vehemently disagree with more progressive views may not be the best place to start, especially if you're wanting to have a mutual conversation and understanding about a topic such as internalized sexism and misogyny.

When you find yourself judging another woman because you don't like what she's wearing, ask yourself, What if it's none of my business what she wears? What if it has nothing to do with me? What if I can believe her outfit has no bearing on my opinions? Try sticking to neutrality if you find it hard to switch to a "You go, girl!" when you find yourself wanting to make fun of a woman's clothing choices.

Call people in who are being misogynistic and sexist. My friend and diversity and inclusion educator Dr. Tee Williams says, "Only call people *out* who are unwilling to be called *in*." Calling in is a form of educating, typically done in private. Always done in a kind and graceful way, and never from a place of contempt. In other words, tell someone when they've said something misogynistic or sexist, or that falls into a stereotype, such as, "Women are always too emotional." Tell them in a polite way and don't be an asshole about it. No one wants to listen if they feel they are being chastised or they think you feel you're better than they are for pointing out their mistake. You might say, "Hey, I know I do this, too, some-times, and it's something I'm trying to work on. Not sure if you noticed your statement about women being too emotional is a ste-reotype and a generalization. I'm trying to do better noticing when I say things like that and would appreciate it if someone kindly pointed it out to me because we tend to do it unconsciously. Happy to discuss it with you as we both learn. What do you think?" This example opens it up for conversation in place of telling them where they're "wrong" and then shutting it down. If we really want things to change, it starts with conversation.

Ask to be held accountable. If we really want to shift things, if we really want to do our best to interrupt the brainwashing that we all got, part of the process is asking those we trust the most to point out where we also participate in internalized oppression. These can be obvious things like slut-shaming or making a disparaging comment about another woman's body, or they could be more covert, like starting many of your statements with "I could be wrong here, but . . ." That last example is not splitting hairs; these small moments where we undermine ourselves tend to be unconscious and point to a bigger problem—that we feel inferior and not enough. To state our thoughts or opinions without prefacing them with how we could be wrong is bold for many women. And we need more bold.

Be intentional about your environment. Pay attention if you surround yourself with coworkers who gossip about the other women at work or say disparaging things about celebrities. Take inventory of the shows you watch on TV. Is your "continue watching" tab on Netflix full of reality shows where women constantly fight and betray one another? Yes, mindless TV can be a form of self-care, but are you balancing it out with media that is full of empowerment?

Last, look at who you follow on social media. We live in a wonderful time when more and more women of all generations are working to normalize things like cellulite, poochy bellies, and bodies of all sizes and abilities, and just plain supporting one another. This is not about supporting all women no matter what their views, but about finding your own values system and sticking to that.

As I've stated before that's worth repeating, this is a lifelong journey. True women's empowerment begins at a culture and society level and involves us all at a personal level as well. Look internally, be kind to yourself, find women who support you and other women, and keep putting one foot in front of the other, whether you're in stiletto heels, sneakers, boots, or barefoot.

THE
UNLEARNING

NOTICE: When I was young, I played soccer. My mom would come to our games and run up and down the sidelines, whistling and cheering for me and my whole team, yelling our names and encouraging us as we would sweat out on the field. Her yells and whistles were mortifying to me back then. I was so embarrassed that my mom was relentless in this way.

Looking back, would I have been so embarrassed if it were my dad? Somewhat, but not nearly as much. It would have been more socially acceptable to have my father, a man with a deep voice, more "soccer coach–like," running up and down the field. But my nine-year-old self just wanted my mom to sit down and watch like the other moms. Maybe some clapping when appropriate, but much quieter.

If we want to change the way we treat ourselves, we have to change the way we treat other women. And if we want to change the way we treat other women, we have to notice when we're labeling and having reactions to women in the first place. This topic is all about getting to the root of the problem—the real reason you feel like you don't measure up and perhaps blame yourself for it.

I've given you a lot to notice in this chapter, and if I had to distill it: Take inventory of the "rules" you were taught, either that were expressed or silently known. Write them down and keep noticing as you go about your day-to-day life. Then try to be conscious of any internalized sexism and misogyny you have, even if you think you don't have any. In the beginning, just notice before you move into bigger action, as there might be feelings to move through.

GET CURIOUS: Once you start noticing what I've pointed out in this chapter and getting curious about it, I'm not by any means saying you need to let all women off the hook for their behavior. This is about you noticing *your* thoughts, judgments, assumptions, and perceptions. Here are some questions to ask yourself:

Looking at the "rules" I grew up with, how do I feel about them?

Have these "rules" held me back? If so, how?

What feelings do I have about it?

That's interesting that I'm judging her. I wonder what that's about?

Would I have the same reaction if a man had said that to me?

What is it exactly that I don't like about her and why? Is there a deeper reason?

Why am I so triggered by her? Is it at all about me?

Is it her behavior I don't like or her as a person? Can I see the difference?

SELF-COMPASSION: You may be at varying places on the spectrum when it comes to realizing the "rules" that have been handed to you. Perhaps you have long known this, or you are recently starting to see things more clearly. In addition, recognizing your own internalized sexism and misogyny can be jarring and bewildering, among other feelings.

The truth for many is there is an element of grief involved. For some, it can make you feel disillusioned—coming to terms with the fact that what you thought was true and good actually isn't. If this is you, your grief is normal—or whatever feelings you have, for that matter. Guilt and shame might make an appearance, too, but they do not serve you. Self-compassion will be key here. As I mentioned in the Letter to Readers section of this book, women's empowerment in many ways is an act of rebellion because it forces us to act against the standard "norm," and to simultaneously "play the game." Without showing yourself some grace, you'll likely spin yourself into a tizzy.

KEEP THE MOMENTUM: My friend Nicole runs ultramarathons, which are one-hundred-mile races. They last an ungodly number of hours, and she runs through the night, having to poop in the woods (and sometimes in front of strangers), takes breaks here and there (but not to sleep), loses toenails, and insists it's all a mind game. She talks about these races with such passion and enthusiasm, she has on more than one occasion almost talked me into doing one with her.

I see this topic not as a marathon, but as an ultramarathon. It's absolutely playing the long game, painful, bewildering, but enormously rewarding. In the unraveling of old patterns and beliefs, you are not healing and learning a new, more powerful way of being just for you, you're doing it for the women who've come before you and the women who will come after you. It may at times feel like "Why bother?" and like you're trying to push a boulder uphill, and yes, it also may be that you take two steps forward only to take three steps back while simultaneously losing a toenail. Perseverance is crucial. Your life and your power that comes with it are determined by your values, your beliefs, and the actions that stem from them. But once you are clear on what has held you back in the past, you can more easily move forward with a new truth that will propel you onward.

10

Stop Waiting for Confidence
to Smack You in the Face

My favorite character in the movie *Grease* was Charlene "Cha-Cha" DiGregorio. You may have loved Sandy, Rizzo, or Frenchy, but to me, Cha-Cha was everything.

Let's break down Cha-Cha for a moment. We don't know much about her; as a character she has very few scenes and lines. However, in her first appearance, as she's introduced to new people by Kenickie, he says, "Hey, there's someone I'd like you to meet. This is Charlene DiGregorio." To which she replies, "They call me Cha-Cha, because I'm the best dancer at St. Bernadette's." Most of us remember she then gets slut-shamed by Frenchy in the next line, but that aside, can we focus on the fact that she tells people *she just met* that she's the best dancer at her school?

Can you imagine meeting someone from another department at work, introducing yourself, and telling them you're the best sales-person this side of the Mississippi? Or introducing yourself at a PTA meeting as, "Hi, I'm Emma and I'm the best Rice Krispies treat maker for class birthday parties this district has ever known." With a confident smile on your face, unflinching.

This is what Cha-Cha does. She stalks Danny in the school gym when the dance contest is going on, knowing full well that she needs a great dance partner to win. She steals him away from Sandy the first chance she gets (as Sandy throws her arms up in the air and storms out, not putting up any kind of fight). Then Cha-Cha proceeds to dance her heart out, which doesn't even begin to describe the passion and ferocity she puts into her dancing. She and Danny win the contest, and instead of waiting to be handed the trophy, she snatches it out of the teacher's hand and waves it in the air triumphantly in a "See, losers! I *told* you I was the best dancer!" style. It would not have been weird at all for her to have added a "mad scientist" type of laugh.

When people *clearly* don't like her, she gives exactly zero fucks about it. Most women feel completely crippled when we know we aren't liked. When Frenchy mentions Cha-Cha's "worst reputation," it looks like the gym will light on fire with the glare Cha-Cha shoots her. She could burst into tears, she could chase the Pink Ladies around trying to be friends, she could apologize to Sandy for stealing her date at the dance, but she does none of those things. She's not there to make friends, she's there to have a good time and get what she wants.

Of course, I'm not encouraging you to act like you don't give a shit about other people's feelings, take people's dates, or not act graciously when given an award. Obviously, Cha-Cha is a fictional character, but if we look at this strictly as symbolism, Cha-Cha sees what she wants and goes after it. She's not concerned if she hurts someone's feelings, nor does she feel responsible for them. She doesn't care about "playing nice." She saw an opportunity and went after it. Can we all stop for a moment to breathe in the confidence that she inhabits?

Where in your life have you passed up opportunities because

you didn't think you were qualified enough, smart enough—basically not good enough? Probably somewhere. Would Cha-Cha pass up that opportunity for a promotion? Nope. Would she not speak up in a meeting because she felt other people wouldn't like her ideas? Nope again. She knows she deserves it, and if it doesn't work out? Meh, there's always next time. There will always be a next time in her mind.

Cha-Cha inhabits a certain confidence that we can all use a little more of and is the epitome of making noise. But confidence can feel like one of those things that needs to look a certain way (maybe it's not your style to brag out loud to new friends about your accomplishments, and that's okay). When people think of confidence, they might think the reason they don't have it is because there's one thing they're not doing, or that to create more of it in your life the process needs to be linear. It can feel confusing to many, so let's break it down so you understand how a lack of confidence might show up in sneaky ways in your life, as well as give you tools to make building confidence a lifelong practice.

THE STRUGGLE

In many of these chapters I've been talking to you about what happens if you don't create the change in your life. I've expressed to you what it looks like when you walk around believing disempowering stories, or what happens when you don't ask for what you want. And now that we're on the topic of confidence, I'm going to give you the absolute benefit of the doubt that you totally and unequivocally understand what a lack of confidence in your life is like, because you've probably lived it.

But sometimes we don't see our lack of confidence. It becomes so embedded in our thoughts, unconscious beliefs, and everyday actions (or inactions), we simply don't know. For those of you who might not see how a lack of confidence can hold you back, here are some examples:

- **You wait to start something until you're "ready."** This can be going to the gym, dating again, selling your art, applying for the job you want, or finally writing your novel. You feel like there must be more steps to take, degrees or certifications to attain, or you're not even sure what else there is to be done, but you're sure you aren't ready yet.
- **You have difficulty speaking up and prioritizing your own wants and needs, as well as not trusting that your own wants and needs matter.** Perhaps you don't see this in your life because you've made your identity as the nurturer or caretaker in your life, or the "operations manager" of your household. You categorize putting yourself first as selfish, or don't want to be perceived as selfish if you do put yourself first. Which then turns into settling for less and accepting crumbs. This can happen at home, at work, with your family of origin, and in your friendships.
- **You find it difficult to come to a decision and make your own choices.** You seek out the counsel of all your friends, your psychic, and online quizzes. Either you feel like you won't make the correct choice, or even if you do, you're worried you won't be able to follow through and succeed with the choice you made.
- **You have poor boundaries.** Let's be honest about this one, I don't think there ever has been a person who's picked up a self-help book who's been a pro at boundaries. Lacking

self-confidence makes us have insufficient skills to set healthy boundaries, and also the inability to follow through with the boundaries once they're set.

- **You talk to yourself negatively and compare yourself to others, where the conclusion is that you don't measure up.** Beating yourself up for the smallest mistake and then believing the conclusions those thought processes bring you to. For example, if you drop the ball with a client at work, then tell yourself, "I'm so stupid, how could I have forgotten that meeting? They think I'm an idiot." Then you subsequently believe that you truly are a stupid idiot. Everyone has negative self-talk from time to time, but if yours is chronic and your feelings and actions come from this place, it can become a huge problem.

Speaking of negative self-talk, if after reading this list you can relate to some or all of these bullet points and are beating yourself up for it, please back up and know that you are normal. They don't teach self-confidence in schools, and probably your mother and her mother struggled here, and it was unintentionally passed down to you.

Studies show that young school-aged girls are rewarded for being quiet and calm. So the skills we need to build confidence at an early age—like risk-taking and making mistakes—are things we actively avoid. On the other hand, boys are expected to tease and rough-house, which are things that build both resilience and confidence.

When we grow up and enter the workplace, traits like self-promotion, jumping at opportunities, speaking up, sharing ideas, and offering advice to more senior staff—these are all things that are attributed to getting ahead and promoted—and tend to be attributed to men. And when women embody these traits, they are more often than not seen as bitchy and disliked by both men *and* women. This fear, whether conscious or not, is enough to make women overly cautious and hold themselves back. All that to say, it's not our fault.

Awareness is the first step in change, and it's important that you're clear on where your lack of confidence might be showing up in your everyday life and choices. So if this feels heavy, take a deep breath, give yourself a hug, and let's dig in.

WHY IT MATTERS

Self-confidence is an umbrella topic that covers all of the rest of the topics you're reading in this book. Without a little confidence, you can't start stepping into taking up more space, asking for what you want, and setting boundaries. You don't need to completely get to confidence first to do those things, but you'll need the understanding of where you get tripped up so that you can catch it when it happens rather than not knowing and letting things slide beyond your control.

For instance, if you consistently have the same issue with one particular friend and seem to go around in circles with it, that's likely a boundary issue. If you don't have the knowledge and tools *plus* the confidence to have the conversation that will allow you to stand up for your yourself and stand up for your friendship, you'll keep going around in circles.

MYTHS OF CONFIDENCE

As much as I still love Cha-Cha DiGregorio and continue to fantasize about what it would be like to be her, I wish it were actually easier to emulate her in real life. If confidence were easy to come by, it would have been bottled a long time ago by Big Pharma and somebody would have more money than God right now because of it.

As I've taught this topic for more than a decade now, there are some powerful myths about self-confidence that I'd like to squash. See if you fall into any of these. They are:

Myth #1: You are born with confidence and it's in your genes. People who believe this myth typically feel like it must be true because they weren't born with it. I used to believe this, too, and wished that I'd been bestowed this gene.

Myth #2: You can gain confidence by using the fake-it-till-you-make-it technique. This myth convinces you that you can achieve confidence by acting like you're the shit when you really do *not* think you're the shit. All this does is make you *feel* like shit as well as a big ol' phony. This myth also includes the "if you can't beat 'em, join 'em" mentality, which encourages women to act like men in order to get ahead, which only makes us act inauthentically, and also many times we wind up being disliked by other women for acting that way.

Myth #3: You can just wait until you're older to finally get confidence, like it comes with social security payments or something. Because we all know how much confidence Blanche Devereaux had in *The Golden Girls*. However, no one wants to wait until they're a Golden Girl.

Confidence is not something you're born with, something you get by faking it, or something you automatically gain in middle age. It's something that's built piece by piece over time. It's something you try, mess up, try again and again until you see progress, and then keep practicing the process for the rest of your life. The goal being that it eventually becomes second nature and you forget that there was even a time when you didn't have it.

Self-confidence has a foundation in courage. The dictionary defines courage as "mental or moral strength to venture, persevere, and withstand danger, fear, or difficulty." Practicing courage is about doing things that are out of your comfort zone that are all different levels of frightening. Personally, I disagree with the common personal-empowerment advice of "do one thing every day that scares you," because, quite frankly, while I'm all for audacious goals and catapulting out of one's comfort zone, people's nervous systems need a break once in a while and I don't want anyone feeling burned out and fried from the need to constantly scare themselves into betterment. Pace yourself, and the trick is to know the scary/excited/nervous/thrilling feeling of trying something new that you will move toward instead of away from, which will feel courageous.

Examples of big, courageous things are starting a new business, dating again after a difficult breakup, and setting up a meeting to ask your boss for a raise. Smaller things are signing up for a new class you're interested in (even if it's online), volunteering, and taking a nap in the middle of the day when you've always felt the need to overachieve. And examples of courage that may be big or small for you, depending on your experience, are not letting racist or sexist comments slide, leaving an unhealthy relationship, and even the courage to challenge your stories, like you read about in chapter 7.

Courage can look like many different things. It doesn't require big, sweeping events that shake you to your core with fear. Even practicing small acts of courage will likely evoke fear in you, but all of them add up to a courageous, confident *you*. I want you to answer the door when discomfort knocks. Because that discomfort is your courage, your bravery, your greatness.

TOOLS

Truth vs. Conditioning

Before we get into tools for how to start to practice more courage and confidence in your life, it's important, as always, to look into what you've been socialized and conditioned to believe and how to behave when it comes to confidence. Ask yourself the following questions:

Growing up, what did you believe confidence looked like in women? Was it spoken about in a positive or negative light from your primary caregivers? Or not at all?

What did you assume about confidence? For instance, looking at the myths described, did you assume it wasn't for you? Anything else?

Did you ever assume you had to do certain things in order to gain confidence? Such as a certain amount of success, weight loss, friends in your circle, or money?

Did you see women in movies, TV shows, or books who seemed confident? Did you think that was something you could attain? Why or why not?

After you answer those questions, look at your answers and think about your Truth. Notice any assumptions growing up that you *now* know aren't true. For instance, maybe you used to believe that to attain confidence you had to accomplish a certain financial point. Or perhaps you saw confident women in movies, but would also describe them as bossy, backstabbing, and show-offs. It's important to make these distinctions, to extrapolate what you grew up believing, even if the clarity of what your family or culture taught you has come in hindsight.

If you're struggling to find your Truth, start by challenging your answers to the preceding questions that you know seem wrong. Logically, you might know that confidence cannot be found by a number on the scale or that you have to be conniving. But these beliefs might be embedded deep inside of you and will take some unlearning in order to challenge, question, and accept new beliefs about what it means to be confident.

My hope is that your Truth becomes this: Confidence is learned, and it can and will be learned by you. Confident women practice courage and resilience. They ask for support in their struggles, understand their fears, and take action anyway. They embrace their inherent strengths and work on themselves.

You get to finish that description and define your own confidence, and I encourage you to get clear on any and all falsities that you have carried around that don't match up with being what a confident woman means to you.

WHEN TO START

The thing women who have self-confidence have in common is that they take action before they're ready. Studies show that the key to self-confidence is through experience that creates mastery of a skill. I want you to write "start before you're ready" on your bathroom mirror in lipstick, have it printed on a T-shirt, and get it tattooed on the top of your foot so every time you look down in disappointment or fear, you see those four words: Start before you're ready. Because guess what? I wasn't perfectly ready when I wrote my first book. I wasn't ready when I started my business, got married for the second time, or got up on stage to deliver a keynote to thousands. I wanted what was on the other side—to have done the thing, to know that I could do it, learn from it, do better the next time (except the marriage—I want this one to be my last), and slowly but surely gain confidence. This is how it works, my friends, experiences that create mastery.

If you wait until you're ready, you'll be waiting for a very, very long time, or possibly forever. Please allow me to stand up for this next part, and know that I'm clapping and stomping my feet as I say this: THIS CANNOT HAPPEN. I'm all for you going on the exact journey you need to go on, to give you the dignity of your process, but woman, when it comes to starting before you're ready, when it comes to consciously jumping into things that bring you joy and will take you to where you want to be, please, I beg you, be brave.

As much as I can tell you to run toward your best life and cheer you on as loudly as you can imagine, I don't want you to feel left out in the cold without more to think about to help get you there. So, while you're starting before you're ready, let's discuss things for you to focus on to kick your confidence up a notch.

KNOW YOUR VALUES

Call it your "golden rule," your North Star, Nitty Gritty, I don't care what you call it as long as you know what's important to you and the way you live your life. If you picked up and are this far into this book, my guess is that your values revolve around self-improvement, courage, and love. Just a hunch, you know your-self much better than I do, but when you know your values, name them, and describe them, you're well on your way to acting on them. And acting on them will involve being brave and living your life like you give a damn (because you do). Your values make up your identity—the woman you want to be.

Before you skip this exercise because you think it's unsexy, or you think you can't possibly write down such amazing things like courage on your list of values because you can't remember the last time you did something courageous, listen up. Many, if not all, of your top values may be what we call "aspired" values. They're the values you're going after, the ones you seek. So consider this your invitation to think about and write down the values and life you want to have—the ways in which you want to behave. It doesn't matter if you feel far from it and need to course-correct every single day. That's the whole point—to move in the direction of your better life, and that's what matters.

It matters because you didn't come here to play games. You didn't come here for some half-assed dress rehearsal. Woman, no. You came here to step, stomp, or sashay into your ideal identity. The woman you chose this book for. The woman the people who love you the most know you are.

Once you're clear on your values, you can then decide what it is you need to take action on (and I use the word *need* intentionally here). If authenticity is on your list of values, are you opening up to friends? Are you setting boundaries? Are you asking for what you want? Taking action on these things may be scary, but they both honor your values and take courage to do, and by doing so you'll gain confidence. Even if you make mistakes, you'll build resilience along the way.

GROWTH VS. FIXED MINDSET

In her research and subsequent book *Mindset: The New Psychology of Success*, Dr. Carol Dweck makes the argument for what she has called a growth versus fixed mindset. If a person has a fixed mindset, they typically believe their failures limit them and define what is possible in their lives, as if their potential is limited and predetermined. A person with a fixed mindset takes feedback and especially criticism personally, and recoils at the mere thought of being challenged.

Having a growth mindset means that you see failures and challenges as opportunities for growth, know your perspective and level of effort determine your abilities, see feedback as constructive and helpful to your growth, and see others' success as inspiring and motivating.

According to Dweck's research, we are not born with a fixed or growth mindset, we learn it. It's also important to note that people don't easily have one or the other. Dweck says, "Everyone is a mixture of fixed and growth mindsets. You could have a predominant growth mindset in an area but there can still be things that trigger you into a fixed mindset trait. Something really challenging and outside your comfort zone can trigger it, or, if you encounter someone who is much better than you at something you pride yourself on, you can think 'Oh, that person has ability, not me.'"

Simply put, a growth mindset focuses on the learning process, not the outcome. So the goal is not to get to a place of all successes and achievements, the goal is to gain confidence through accepting challenges, trying new things, accepting feedback as useful, and paying attention to your attitude, self-talk, and how you feel along the way. Yes, it will be uncomfortable, but a growth mindset and the subsequent confidence that comes with it will not only be worth it but can change your life.

DECIDE

No, I'm not saying you just decide to have confidence and then you have it. If this were possible, this would be a very short chapter. I'm also not telling you to decide something and that's the end, the final thing on your to-do list. The decision is essentially that, a decision.

But making a conscious, intentional decision holds power. You might not be ready, but you're deciding anyway.

A UK study found that setting an intention will make you much more likely to accomplish your goals. So if your goal is to be more confident and you know the route to get there is to take action, decide when and how you will take action. When will you sit down and create a case to ask for a salary increase? How will you work on changing your mindset from fixed to growth? What day this week will you make a list of your values and define what they look like in your life?

IDENTITY

In coaching, one of the principles is asking powerful questions, and one of my favorite questions is *Who do you need to be to get to where you want to go?* In other words, the identity you've been in might not be what you need it to be to get from point A to point B. You might have all the motivation and inspiration you can accumulate, you might have made all the goals and put them in your calendar waiting to be crossed off and then posted them on social media, but if you still have the core belief that you're the opposite of what you're trying to achieve, it will feel like climbing out of quicksand with concrete shoes. And in the end, you feel even shittier about yourself.

My friend Candace was about to turn fifty and she told me, "I've been thinking a lot about turning fifty and I decided I want to be the kind of older person who is healthy—you know, in my seventies and eighties speed-walking and being an active old lady. So then I decided if I want that twenty to thirty years from now, I need to be a healthy person *now*."

The intention is not to create giant goals to conquer and slay all day, especially if you're not even close to those goals. If you're wanting to slightly or even very much change your life, small, baby steps are required. Candace started walking just twice a week and also started flossing her teeth—something she'd been wanting to do for years but never did.

These small steps affirmed to Candace that she could in fact be on her way to being a healthy senior citizen, by doing it now.

James Clear discusses this in his book *Atomic Habits*, where he says, "In order to believe a new identity, we have to prove it to ourselves." Which means that you're going to need evidence that you can be the person who attains the goals, whether you're trying to work out more, get promoted, or run for congress. Not necessarily the end game, but pint-sized steps like working out for twenty minutes twice a week, having a conversation with someone at work who can possibly help you get promoted, or checking with your state board of elections to see how to get your name on the ballot.

So if you want to be a confident woman, start from the beginning, define it, and first ask yourself the question, What is a confident woman to me?

Is it someone who shines as much as she has inside her, noticing when she's uncomfortable but doing it anyway?

Is it someone who takes up space with her body, her voice, and her opinions?

Is it someone who asks for what she wants, even when she's nervous?

Is it someone who practices listening to her built-in wisdom?

Is it someone who is resilient, even when life hands her a shit sandwich?

Is it someone who confronts and interrupts sexism, misogyny, and other social injustices?

Is it someone who doesn't blame other people for her circumstances, but instead forgives people, takes responsibility when necessary, and moves forward?

Is it someone who notices when she's checking out of her life, loves herself along the way, and decides conversely to face life head-on?

Is it someone who works on intentionally creating nurturing friendships with other women and learns to trust them in order to get the support she needs?

Is it someone who kicks the door down when she feels fear?

You get to decide. What is a confident woman to *you*? Feel free to use my list and make your own adjustments or add descriptions. There is no wrong way—it all depends on the vision you have for yourself, what's important about the way you live your life, and who you were meant to be. Neither I nor anyone else can decide that for you, nor should it be that way. You are in control here.

Next, ask yourself, Who do I need to be in order to be a confident woman?

Maybe you tell yourself:

I am a woman who starts before she's ready.

I am a woman who does small courageous things.

I am a woman who exercises her right to voice her opinion.

I am a woman who asks for what she wants, even if she's afraid.

I am a woman who listens for and trusts her gut.

I am a woman who takes small action on the solution instead of complaining about the problem.

I am a woman who is resilient and built for getting back up when I fall down.

I am a woman who knows her worth.

I am a woman who is always working on herself; even if the progress is small, it is mighty.

I am a woman who pushes against cultural stereotypes and interrupts oppression.

I am a woman who has hard conversations that I know will benefit me and everyone else involved.

From there, you'll make small choices and take small action in order to prove to yourself that you are, in fact, this woman. And, hey, if you want to take big action, by all means, my hat is off to you and we are cheering you on! Just know that the point is to prove to yourself that you can create a new identity, an identity built around confidence.

YOUR ALTER EGO

In 2012, I worked past my own fear and tried out for my local Roller Derby league. Never would I have identified as an athlete, but I was drawn to the aggression of the sport, the diversity and inclusivity of the team members, and the challenge of learning something new. In Roller Derby most players pick their "derby name" (some players skate under their real names, arguing that derby names bastardize the sport, and I can see their point). For those who pick a derby name, many times it becomes their alter ego. Tonya Walker isn't scary in real life, but Killa Patra very much will hip-check you and you didn't even see her coming, plus she won't apologize, because that's how the game is played (hat tip to my former teammate).

So when it came to picking my own derby name, I thought about middle school. Remember how as young girls, especially around middle-school age, one of the worst things to be labeled as and called was "conceited"? The girl who brushed her hair in the bathroom mirror at school a few seconds too long was conceited, the girl who put effort into her appearance was conceited, and the girl who admitted she had boys who liked her was conceited, right? I wanted to convey with my derby name that it was okay to be conceited, to take back that word. I wanted my alter ego to give zero fucks, like Cha-Cha DiGregorio about how she was the best dancer . . . so "Veronica Vain" was born. Veronica Vain cared about only two things: kicking ass on the track and looking amazing while doing it.

Creating an alter ego for yourself isn't something new; Beyoncé famously did it as Sasha Fierce, and Christina Aguilera as Xtina. If you're new to the term, clearly put, an alter ego is a different version of yourself. An easy way to create your alter ego is to imagine your best, highest self, amplified. If you choose to do this exercise, I encourage you to use the following steps to create your alter ego:

Step #1. Determine the purpose of your alter ego. Why do you need it and what will you use it for? Is it to have more confidence when you're faced with hard conversations? For when you find yourself getting caught up in listening to your inner critic? Perhaps you have some audacious goals on your vision board, and they seem impossible. Or you feel you've never had the confidence you want and are willing to try this exercise. Maybe it's specific instances you'll use it for, or maybe it's being able to raise your level of confidence in general. Whatever the purpose, it's uniquely yours and important to establish.

Step #2. Why does it matter? In addition to thinking about the purpose of your alter ego, think about your emotional resonance to your goals you just named—the places you'll use your alter ego. For example, say you want to speak up more in meetings at work. You think of good ideas or have questions, or generally want to contribute to the conversations. The words get struck in your throat and you can't seem to speak up. It's gone on for months, and now it's normal for meetings to happen where you don't contribute at all. Ask yourself, Why does speaking up matter to you? More specifically, what feelings does it bring up when you think about not speaking up versus speaking up?

It's not enough to feel like you "should." In this example, I would bet that it's more than the act of having your ideas heard, it's about being heard in general. Perhaps it's about contributing and working as a team. And whatever the reason, what does that mean to you, and how does it make you feel? With every meeting that passes that you are silent, the meeting ends, and you walk back to your desk, do you feel small, inferior, and like you don't matter? Do you beat yourself up and wish you could just get unstuck?

This step is about connecting to what it is you want on an emotional level. The thing you would look back on with significant regret at the end of your life if you didn't do it. Make the thing that you want to do mean so much to you that its actions would have their own montage set to music and could become a viral video everyone cries to. *That* is what your alter ego is going to help you accomplish.

Step #3. Create your alter ego's beliefs, personality, and attitudes. What strengths does she have? What is her mindset? What does she believe to be true that you have a hard time sticking to? For example, maybe she fully embraces criticism and failure, knowing it's a clear sign she's on the right track as well as using it as fuel to keep her persistent. Be specific here; perhaps she has a badass theme song or entire playlist. Remember, this is your ideal self, you get to make your persona exactly what you need her to be in order to fulfill the wants and needs of your ideal real life.

Step #4. Call on your alter ego when needed. Not sure how to respond to an email where you need to say no but the people-pleaser in you is hovering over the keys, about to type, "Sure!"? As a substitute, pause and ask, "What would (insert your alter ego's name) do?" Many times, that needs to be the only question you ask. Tap into the emotion if you need to, gather up twenty seconds of courage, and type out "Thanks for asking, but I won't be able to do that."

This is about building new, empowering habits around confidence. Again, in order to keep the momentum and build more confidence, you need to prove to yourself that you can in fact exit your comfort zone. That you can do things that you never thought you could do, or that you thought only "other people" did. Small steps equal big shifts to your inner identity. It's about finding those bits of identity through tools like the alter ego that will build and make up the you that has always been there.

THE
UNLEARNING

NOTICE: Pay attention to where you lack confidence. You may be confident at work, but when it comes to relationships, it's a bit messy. Maybe it's in all areas of your life, or just one. Or it might ebb and flow depending on the season of your life. You're a new mom? Being a new parent is hard, so that may be your biggest area where you could use some self-assuredness; plus, you might gain confidence in one area, only to have it slip back because you have a setback. Perfectly normal, just get used to noticing.

GET CURIOUS: Even if you know what your new version of confidence is, get crystal clear on what you grew up believing confident women looked like and acted like, if you thought you could ever have it, and what was modeled for you growing up. It's important to ask questions like:

Who were your earliest teachers of confidence and what were the lessons? Was that empowering or not?

Have there been any myths about confidence that you now know aren't true? Where did you hear those myths, or did you make any up?

Can you distinguish between your conditioning and your Truth when it comes to confidence? If yes, what is the difference? If not, what work do you need to do to become clearer on separating the two?

What's important about the way you live your life, and how does that translate into your personal values? If you're not engaging with those values now, what do you need to do to get there? Do you have resistance to that, and if so, what's that about?

How can having an alter ego help you?

What are you willing to let go of that is holding you back from having more confidence?

What is one thing you can take from this chapter to make movement toward more confidence?

SELF-COMPASSION: If you're feeling less than outstanding about your level of confidence, and especially if you're feeling worse about yourself after reading this chapter, thinking, "There's no hope for me!" Let me remind you: Our culture has made it enormously difficult for you to be comfortable being courageous, which is the necessary ingredient for confidence. It's an uphill battle. If I asked you if you've been hard on yourself because you haven't been able to scale Mount Everest in a few hours, you'd say no. That's ridiculous, right? That's an impossible task for anyone, so there's no point.

No one uses beating themselves up as a path to having more confidence. It is not your fault if you lack in this area. So know that you were brought up to feel fundamentally insecure and second-guess yourself, even if you have the best-intentioned parents and caregivers. The time is now to show yourself some grace, use the tools, and take it one step at a time in the direction of more courage and more confidence.

KEEP THE MOMENTUM: I want to make it very clear that self-confidence, like any personal-development topic, is a process. Something you learn about it, notice how it shows up uniquely in *your* life, and learn how to make small but strong changes. Then you take action—sometimes it works out and sometimes it doesn't. You move forward or tumble back, occasionally both at the same time.

Working on your self-assuredness will affect all areas of your life—work, relationships, parenting, hobbies, big future goals, and even how you think about your past. Never underestimate the power of your thoughts and how you feel about yourself, as well as your inherent power that's inside you.

Life is but a series of choices we make every day. Those days turn into months, which turn into years. What if *today* was the day you decided to take action to create more confidence, even if staying the same feels easier? What if today was the day you said yes to you? You were meant for big things, a bold and fulfilling life, and it's yours for the taking.

11

Stop Checking Out of Your Life

At one time in my past I had a treasure trove of behaviors I'd choose from at any given moment to check out. I'd open it up and choose . . . What shall I do today to aid in the running away from my life? What can I do to avoid being drenched in feelings?

For a decent period of time it was relationships. Every weekend I'd get all dressed up to go out with my girlfriends, go to a bar or club and scan the room, looking for a man to make eye contact with who'd become my source of self-esteem and a temporary obsession. The chase would begin. For some reason I had an ounce of morality to tell them I did have a boyfriend—perhaps it was an effort to keep a kind of boundary around my heart. We'd have some sort of relationship for a handful of weeks or months, sneaking around to meet up, me ping-ponging back and forth from feelings of euphoria and the thrill of it to shame and self-loathing. When the shame became too much, I'd break off the relationship, vowing to stop and be better. I would promise myself I'd be good. Then I'd be back where I started, believing the way I felt about myself was too much to deal with, so I needed relief. And I'd get all dressed up to go out with my girlfriends again.

Mixed in with my love addiction was disordered eating and exercise, which I know is the way so many of us check out. It was easier for me to obsess on and control the size of my body, the food I ate (or didn't eat), and the amount of punishment I put my body through in the name of "fitness." This was something I felt in control of, since sometimes my life and always my relationships felt out of control. Growing up in a culture that worships thinness, youth, and beauty, it was easy for me to fall into this trap. If I could just have a flat stomach, if I could just get into smaller-size jeans, if I could just cut out a meal or two a day, then my life would be good. *I* would finally be good. I'd have shame that I wasn't thin enough or that I'd broken down and eaten an entire pizza by myself in one sitting, need relief, and find it momentarily by restricting calories, sometimes purging, and monitoring how much I burned off. And the cycle would continue.

It took me years to realize the true underlying reason for these addictive and obsessive behaviors. It wasn't the face-value takeaway of knocking boots with hot guys and wanting to look like a bikini model. My behaviors were a manifestation of the depths of what it means to be human. I had shame I didn't even know was there about my past, myself, my relationships, sex, merely walking around feeling the raw nakedness of being alive. Like most people, I had a crippling fear of abandonment, which revealed itself through my love addiction. Apparently, it was hidden away like a vibrator in a bedside table, not wanting to be out in the open, but very much there. To be human is to have shame, and I didn't know this. All I knew was that something hurt, and I wanted to get away from it. I didn't want to talk about the pain, I just wanted it gone. So I found that relief in fits and starts. Unfortunately, because the relief was so sporadic and short-lived, my unhealthy habits picked up speed and branched out into drinking, drugs, shopping, and really anything that could take me out of how I was feeling at any given moment.

And it's not always definitive behaviors we use to check out. Sometimes it's disconnecting altogether. I've been told I'm great in a crisis—most recently, someone said this to me while on the way to pick up my father's ashes from the morgue. It had been only about ten days since he'd died; I had not broken down in front of anyone, and instead I took charge of the many details regarding his service. Maybe it's my personality, maybe it's classic overfunctioning in times of tragedy, or maybe it's because I've mastered it from years of practice, but I can easily shut down my emotions, compartmentalize them, and focus on what needs to be done.

Several years ago, my daughter, who was five at the time, needed an emergency appendectomy for a ruptured appendix. I stayed levelheaded and almost stoic the whole time we were in the ER, when they told us she needed to be admitted to surgery right away, and the four days we stayed at the hospital. My ability to remove myself emotionally from any situation almost comes second nature to me.

Or take Erica, thirty-six, in Ontario, Canada:

"My feelings will arise and say 'surprise,' and if I am startled by it or feel like it is too much to handle, I try to dismiss them. Needless to say, this never does the trick and my feelings start to multiply. Starting to feel overwhelmed, my mind goes into overdrive, throwing all facts, knowledge, and logic right out the window. My inner critic takes center stage and my body responds in tandem with my new mindset. I feel the anxiety rush throughout my entire body, and it paralyzes me: My arms start to tingle, my stomach gets tied up in knots, I start sweating, my breaths get shallower, and my chest feels like it is closing in on itself. When this happens and I am around others, I plaster a fake smile on my face and tell myself, 'Not here, not now, think happy thoughts.' I do everything in my power to suppress my feelings and emotions by ensuring they do not rise to the surface. This takes everything out of me and is absolutely exhausting. Within minutes the feelings start to subside and go away. I fool myself into thinking these feelings are gone, when the truth is I was never in control and it is guaranteed that my feelings will resurface later, and with a vengeance. The more I try to suppress my feelings and emotions, the harder my body and mind work to make them reappear and resurface."

Disconnecting can be a great skill to have in difficult times. When my daughter got sick, I would have been no help to my husband or son, not to mention the surgeon and nurses taking care of her, if I had been having a meltdown. In regard to Erica, if she's under pressure at work, disconnecting can help her get something done in high-stress moments. However, some of us spend most of our days in this state. Something challenging, hurtful, or messy comes our way and we immediately become a beaver building a dam. Nothing can get in and nothing can get out.

WHO CARES?

You might be thinking, "What does it really matter? So what if I take mini–emotional vacations? Would it make that much of a difference if I stopped checking out when things get hard?"

Or maybe you're convinced your disconnection is what keeps you safe. You've been hurt too many times to count, and your checking out is fine and none of anyone's business.

My honest answer is most certainly you can still live a good life and continue to check out. You can live, love, laugh all day long. You can still have relationships, get promoted, and feel happy. But, having been on both sides of this and after a decade-plus in recovery (and let it be known that we're all recovering from something), I know your true strength as a person, your absolute best self, is you as a woman who let in *all of herself.* When you can face your life head-on, you are simultaneously stepping into your power. I also know that you can't truly be the boss of your life if you're consistently running away from it by numbing out and disconnecting.

To be powerful is to be present. To be self-expressive requires you to know yourself fully. So many women come to me wanting more self-confidence (see chapter 10), but you can't practice and have more self-confidence if you're standing outside of yourself. Maybe you see yourself in some of these examples:

Tracie, fifty, said, "When the pandemic hit, I had two teenagers at home who were miserable without seeing their friends, I had chronic work stress, dreading my job, and found myself racing for the glass of wine at five o'clock many nights of the week. It's really been my go-to for as long as I can remember, to 'take the edge off.'

"I do healthy things as well, but for certain, the thing I'm doing consistently (and my awareness around this not being the best thing in the world) which has definitely heightened over the past couple of years, is looking forward to the glass of wine after my workday. 'Time to destress, unwind, take the edge off.' Everyone does it, boasts about it; it's socially and culturally acceptable, and even encouraged."

Anais, twenty-eight, said, "After an extremely hard relationship I totally lost touch with my feelings. Before that, I had always been qualified as very sensitive, emotional; I could cry about anything, I was moved easily.

"But suddenly I felt like I was in a box, almost like I was protecting myself against feeling anything again. I didn't recognize myself anymore, it was a struggle. I got on a plane and did not shed tears saying goodbye to my friends and family. My heart was buried somewhere.

"When difficulties arise in my new relationship, when things get hard, my feelings shut down. I feel nothing. I am engaged and in love with the man of my dreams now, but this 'protection,' the 'wall,' sometimes comes back when I am scared or hurt . . . It is more than a 'strong face,' it is out of my control and I feel nothing."

To check out of your life means to give away your sovereignty. To disconnect from yourself is to abandon yourself. I know this may be all you know, and that your habits may have been born from trauma and loss and fear, but I am here to tell you that we need you to heal. We need you to wake up, be conscious, and understand that your potential and true talents lie in your presence.

You are stronger than the things you're running away from, I promise you that. The pain, grief, loneliness, uncertainty, or whatever it is you're pushing down *will not kill you.* What will slowly be your demise is the constant checking out. The numbing away of your soul, your spirit, your power, your life.

THE EDGE

We all know the phrase *take the edge off,* right? You're looking for ease, to reduce the tension and intensity you feel. I work with a lot of people who struggle with anxiety, myself included, so I understand that life can feel like you've been personally victimized by it and that it's constantly happening *to* us.

Taking the edge off can look like a glass of wine, an intense workout, watching a few hours of TV, really anything to distract yourself and what I like to call taking a mini-vacation away from whatever it is that's causing the stress. And sometimes that's exactly what you need. In the personal-growth world, we call that self-care.

But what happens when the "edge" fills in most of your life? What happens when you find yourself taking the edge off or taking mini-vacations and it's not just self-care? When it's become how you cope, and you've become so masterful at the ways to remove yourself from life that you could add it to your LinkedIn profile?

You probably know the obvious ones, like eating, overexercising, calorie restricting, shopping, sex, pills, our phones, and working. Many women also use control, planning, gossip, obsessively taking care of others—anything that allows you to not be in your pain or discomfort.

Our culture tells us pain is bad. And I don't entirely disagree—I mean, pain sucks. Physical pain, mental anguish, and emotional distress are all things I'd rather not dance with, either. We all disconnect and numb out to some degree.

Check in with yourself when you're regularly feeling like you need to "take the edge off." Get honest with yourself and ask, What is the edge, really? Is it work stress, where you're overloaded and haven't told your boss? Is it a relationship that you have where you're avoiding having a hard conversation? Are you constantly worried about the future and unable to cope with that worry without having something to take it away temporarily?

My point here is that "taking the edge off" has the ability to be "fine." And by "fine," I mean not harmful and not removing you from your life. But I feel that for many of you reading this, "taking the edge off" is actually extracting you from being present, erasing you from your ability to fully show up and shine. We, collectively, need this to be unacceptable. When it goes beyond self-care into

the abyss of believing we are not equipped to handle hard things—
that notion needs to be something we do not tolerate.

PAIN = POWER

It's not new that pain has the ability to become someone's power.
That a woman has rebuilt her life from the blood, sweat, and tears
of her experiences. We've seen the memes on social media and read
the stories from our favorite authors with quotes like "A strong
woman is one who can rebuild her life from the bricks others have
thrown at her." How the worst parts of our lives end up being our
most treasured lessons and help us grow the most. We know this,
and yet . . . in many ways we still try to run from our pain.

I wrote at length about how to feel your feelings in my last
book, *How to Stop Feeling Like Shit*, because after talking to women,
I noticed many of them were telling me they weren't sure what that
looks like. For now, I'm going to offer a perspective that has the
potential to help you when you find yourself disconnecting from
unwanted feelings.

But first we need to start from the beginning: noticing when in
fact you are disconnecting. Some of you may think, "Oh, yeah, I
know I do," without a moment's hesitation, but others might not be
so sure.

So ask yourself some questions:

- What do you do when you feel overwhelmed, uncertain, or
  stressed? When work is getting the best of you, when you have
  financial uncertainty, when you get into a big argument with
  your partner, what do you do?

- When your kids start disconnecting from you or are too much to handle, when your beloved pet or human dies, when you find out someone less qualified at work got a promotion, what do you do?
- When they "find something" in your mammogram and you have to wait for a follow-up appointment, when there's a virus spreading throughout the world, when politics is making you crazy, what do you do?
- Do you do breathing exercises, call a trusted friend, or cry it out? Or do you have an extra glass (or bottle) of wine, eat loads of carbs (or start obsessively counting calories on your favorite app), or scroll for hours on your phone? (Maybe you do a mix of all those things, but probably you lean toward one.)

In the life-coaching world, we have the term *holding space*. It's become a bit of a cliché, but at its core, it's a beautiful skill that is essentially creating a metaphorical container for someone else to be vulnerable in. Making sure your body language, and the timing of your responses, facial expressions, and words tell the other person they are safe, they are welcome to tell their truth and to show all of their humanness with no judgment, criticism, opinions, or rushing. It's a skill that is learned and mastered with time and practice.

The thing about holding space—whether you're a helping professional or simply holding space for a friend—is that it's really hard to do if you can't hold space for yourself. If you are constantly judging your own feelings and your own experience, you are setting the stage for what it means to have challenging feelings and struggling times. I'm not saying you can't be kind and compassionate to others if you aren't kind and compassionate to yourself first. You can.

However, truly kicking ass in your life requires you to be present and accept all of yourself. And in order to do that, you can't cut off parts of yourself that are uncomfortable or that you judge unacceptable.

So if you need to work on this, how can you hold space for yourself a little better than you do now? How can you trust your humanity, your shadow side (we all have one), and love your woundedness?

It might start with *believing* it's possible to do. Because it absolutely is. It's possible to sit in the ache and uneasiness of pain without turning to a behavior that will take you further away from who you really are. It starts with believing, then finding the tools that work for you.

SURRENDER

After my father passed away in 2016 the grief I grappled with was unlike anything I'd ever felt before. At one point I was alone in my kitchen, about three weeks after he'd passed. My husband had gone back to work and my kids were at school. Life, as I understood it, was supposed to be back to normal.

As I unloaded the dishwasher, I was swept away with a wave of grief that felt like it would kill me. Clutching the counter, I let out a wail that was more like a scream and a roar. I was sad, as well as angry. Angry that he was gone, angry that I couldn't accept that he was missing from my life, angry that I had to do normal life things like empty the dishwasher. None of it made sense and I was furious.

As I fell to the kitchen floor in a heap, I thought, "I would love a bottle of wine right now." Not a glass, mind you, a bottle. The thought continued: "No one would know. It's early enough. It would make all of this go away."

As someone who had years of sobriety and recovery, I immediately knew these thoughts were dangerous for me. Being alone with intense feelings, wanting to change these feelings, and having conscious thoughts of drinking is a perfect storm for a relapse. Thankfully, I called and texted a couple of friends who talked me off the ledge. I didn't drink that day.

The truth is, a bottle of wine would have made it all go away for a while. Maybe I could have staved off the grief and anger for a few hours. However, I would have woken up the next morning with a hangover and the intense shame of what I had done, and I would have altogether postponed my grief. Moved it over for another time where it lies in wait, in some ways gaining momentum.

Not long after that day in the kitchen, I got the word *surrender* tattooed on my forearm in my own handwriting. It's a reminder that to surrender is not at all about giving up. Quite the opposite, actually.

To surrender is to allow whatever pain, discomfort, fear, disappointment, anger, loneliness, all the more difficult emotions to enter me. To surrender means to let them in and trust that in doing this, I am not afraid of the feelings themselves. They are information, my body processing what events have recently taken place, and sometimes what stories my mind is making up.

To surrender is to allow the process to unfold. To allow instead of push to control or change something. To trust my body and my heart and to know, with no hesitation, that I was made for this. For love, happiness, success, confidence, contentment, and fulfillment. For grief, sorrow, rage, despair, confusion, and everything in between.

To surrender means when I let all of it in, I allow myself to be free. I allow myself to truly step into my immense power. In the years I've been practicing this, this power has seeped into my creativity, into the love I feel for the people I'm closest to, into the confidence I feel about everything. This power in many ways feels like home. The home that I truly feel is the natural state for all women.

The wail/roar/scream I bellowed that day felt like a primal part of my soul that needed to be released. It was the song of grief. The song that so many of us are needing to sing.

Maybe for you it's not grief, but a stew of sorts mixed with all kinds of different pain. Maybe it's your wounds from childhood, from your teen years, or from yesterday. Maybe it's your broken heart, your disappointment, frustration, or uncertainty. Your insecurity. Whether it's been hanging out with you for what feels like your whole life or it's new to you, I am here to tell you none of it, not a single feeling, is wrong.

Your pain, dear reader, is the door to your power. It's always been open to you, for you just need to step in.

CHANGE YOUR VIEWPOINT

Another tool we use in life coaching is offering other perspectives. We get stuck in certain perspectives—stories we tell ourselves—and understand them as truth. For instance, you might have the perspective that certain feelings are difficult and should be avoided. Anger, grief, loneliness—all the more challenging emotions get in the way. This seems to be the common perspective that most people have adopted. The problem is not that you have this perspective, the problem is that it's the only one you have.

My best friend, Amy Smith, offered another perspective many years ago when I first got sober, in terms of feeling emotions. I was struggling to wade through an especially difficult time and knew I no longer could reach for a gigantic glass of wine to take this particular edge off. It felt impossible, these feelings. My mind swam with thoughts of "I can't do this sober. This is stupid. One glass of wine is fine." I began to feel panic over not being able to run away emotionally somehow.

Over the phone she said, "What if our feelings were just our body's way of taking care of itself?"

"What the hell does that mean?" I asked.

She explained this new perspective as follows: We accept that our body sweats, sneezes, pees, burps, and does other normal and sometimes gross things to expel what it's processed and doesn't need anymore. It fights off viruses and fevers; essentially it does its best to take care of us physically. We don't question these things.

She was challenging me to adopt the perspective of trusting that my body knew what it was doing. The breakdown was:

1. I received information (a challenging time with my family).
2. Knowing that information made me automatically feel fear, sadness, and uncertainty.
3. My body responded with crying and anxiety.

"Would you do everything you could not to sweat during an outdoor workout in the summer?" she asked.

"Obviously not," I responded.

She continued, "What if you look at it in the same light? Sweating isn't the most comfortable thing, but you get through it. You know that's what your body needs to do to cool off. You let it happen and then it's over. What if you could look at what you're going through as the same?"

That perspective may seem preposterous. You may wonder how you can compare sweating from a CrossFit workout to bawling over a breakup or someone you love dying. I'm not saying you need to simplify or downplay your circumstances, but rather have faith that your physical body is merely processing the information you've been given, and once it does, you'll be okay. More than okay—you'll have honored yourself and be able to walk forward with more power, confidence, and clarity than you would have if you'd disconnected and numbed it all away.

FEELINGS ARE NOT THE ENEMY

If you're down with any of the thoughts

I don't have time to feel my feelings
I'm better off not learning how to feel my feelings
I've tried and I'd rather just drink wine and shop online
I don't even know where to begin
This is seriously all a bunch of bullshit,

then you're exactly where you need to be. To start, I'm going to break this down into bite-size pieces.

My friend and colleague Rebecca Ching, psychotherapist and Certified Leadership Coach, says this about feelings:

"Feelings are data, and as such, they don't form our identity, but they are also energy. And emotions call our attention to parts of our life and story that need to be acknowledged and listened to. Now this work is not efficient at first glance because it can be a windy, uncertain road. But getting curious about our emotions and doing the long haul to really understand them is deeply efficient. We can protect ourselves from our emotions through numbing, avoiding, minimizing, denying, and rationalizing. But unaddressed emotions are stored in our body—and the body will get loud if we do not pay attention to them. In addition, if we do not pay attention to and befriend our emotions, we lose our ability and capacity to lead them and they end up leading us—taking us out physically, emotionally, spiritually, and relationally."

If you're in a place where you're pretty far removed from leaning in to your feelings, or you still haven't bought into the necessity of embracing them to fully step into your power, I'm going to make one request: Create a truce with the feelings you don't like.

Let's look at it as that coworker who's always annoying. We'll call her Susan. Susan shows up late, eats granola loudly with her mouth open at her desk, and constantly talks about herself. At the holiday party she bumped into you and her lit cigarette singed your hair. The final straw came when you both ended up in the HR office over an argument that started when she kept trying to get the perfect selfie while the two of you were supposed to be brainstorming on a new project. It seems the two of you can't quite manage to get along.

I would never tell you that you need to be friends with Susan. I would never tell you that you need to pretend what she did didn't actually happen. But what if you could call a truce with her? Tell her how you feel in a kind and gracious way, and accept and surrender to the fact that she's pretty much the worst and she's going to stick around. Maybe try to have some compassion for her, because clearly she needs some help in her life. What I'm asking is for you to make peace with Susan.

Truth is, the vast majority of us put our feelings into two categories:

good and bad. You know and love the good ones—happiness, fulfillment, contentment, etc. And the others—anger, sadness, disappointment, etc.—are the bad.

I'm sure you're thinking I'm going to ask you to categorize *all* your feelings into good or neutral—that would be ideal, and if you can, go for it—but what I'm going to ask you to do is pause and think about how your life would change if you could implement that, in addition to the other tools I have written about in this chapter.

How would your life change if you actually *believed* that your pain was your power? Would you stop avoiding it and gather the tools to help you move through it easier? How would your life change if you accepted that grief and sadness were just your body's way of taking care of itself, and that once it made its way through your body, you could not only move on with your life, but have gained strength?

How would your life change if you could no longer use huge amounts of energy to cut off challenging feelings, but rather let them pass like someone trying to merge in traffic? To know you don't gain anything by pretending you don't see them and not letting them through?

Once you see and experience your own resilience through difficult and sometimes heartbreaking times, you will gain self-confidence. You'll start to see your patterns and where you can improve. You'll start to notice your own bullshit and create personal boundaries with yourself, deciding what you will and will not tolerate anymore.

Pain and your wounds are power when you can learn not to fear them, but instead to know you were made for them; it's where your greatest learning is and it's where you'll find your greatest growth.

THE
UNLEARNING

NOTICE: Pay attention to when you're numbing or checking out. Do your best to pinpoint when and how you do it the most. Remember, this is about noticing, not judging, not trying to fix, not categorizing anything as good or bad. You're simply taking inventory of your behavior. Then get honest with yourself. Are you ready to look at this? If not, why not?

Is there anything that was particularly triggering about this chapter? If so, that's good information. If you're triggered or resistant, that's a place to start.

GET CURIOUS: Dovetailing off your noticing, if there was a particular section of the chapter that either triggered or spoke to you, why is that? What's underneath? Is there a particular method of numbing out (such as drinking, work, or exercise) that you know in your gut isn't working for you or is harmful? If you think that feelings are the enemy, do you think you can work on making peace with them? If no, why not?

SELF-COMPASSION: If you do have less-than-healthy behaviors that cause you to numb out and are feeling guilty, ashamed, or embarrassed about it, listen up. Those behaviors, for a period of time, worked for you. They allowed you to feel safe and gave you what you needed. If it feels right, you may want to thank this part of you—the part that figured out that the way to feel secure was to escape, at least temporarily. It was doing what it needed to do.

And now it's time to find other ways of coping, other ways of living. To do that, you'll need to speak to yourself in the most loving way possible. If you've been running away from your feelings for what seems like forever, then work on this by feeling your feelings. Being kind to yourself will need to be a priority.

You can start small here. If you notice that you're beating yourself

up, make your next thought "Maybe I don't have to think that way today." If you need to keep repeating that when the negative thoughts
continue popping up, continue practicing.

KEEP THE MOMENTUM: It's normal to want to escape pain,
or even what we perceive as pain. Know that you're not wrong for
doing it. And just when you think you've done it—you've walked
through something especially hard and not drunk, eaten, or shopped
your way away from it, and you're celebrating . . . you might find
yourself back at square one. Something difficult happens again and
you find yourself at the bottom of a pint of Ben and Jerry's or thir-
teen hours into old seasons of *The Bachelor.*

Sometimes we *do* backslide. That's life. It's not always about
kicking ass all the time. I don't say this to give you an out or to
let you off the hook to numb out every day. I say this for you to be
able to recognize that you're doing the best you can, and as I've re-
minded you before, you were meant for hard times. Keep getting up,
keep knowing your feelings are merely information and your body's
way of taking care of you, and keep loving yourself along the way.

12

Stop Complaining if You Plan on Doing Nothing About It

During the height of the #MeToo movement in 2017, I wrote a spoken-word poem called *My Resignation* and read it on my podcast. It was about saying no to the culture that raised me, the culture that had put me in a box, where I had accepted the demand that I be accommodating to all, "a lady," and placid. In the poem, I reveal three anecdotes about young men who hurt me in the past, starting with a high school encounter with a boy who I'll refer to as David.

David and I went out on one date toward the end of our sophomore year. As we were making out, things progressed more quickly than I wanted them to, and I said no, to which he replied, "I thought this was what you wanted." I told him that yes, eventually, but not all at once on the first date. Our evening ended there. There was no anger or animosity, just some undeniable awkwardness.

On Monday at school during lunch, I heard, "*Prick tease!*" being yelled nearby. David and all his friends were laughing and pointing at me, and since we were all part of the same circle of friends, I played along, all the while feeling humiliated. This razzing went on for months, mostly by his friends. It was the first time I realized that if I said no to boys, there would be consequences.

About a year after I wrote my poem, twenty-seven years after this happened in high school, I saw I had a private message on Facebook from David. I had forgotten we were even friends there, as we'd had no communication at all, nor had I even seen so much as a status update from him. At first I panicked, thinking he'd heard or read my poem and knew I was referring to him. Determining that this was close to impossible, I opened his message. It was a typical Facebook message you'd get from someone you haven't seen or spoken to in years. He congratulated me on my success, acknowledged that we hadn't spoken in decades, and then asked if I had time to do him a small favor. Essentially, he was asking if I'd give some advice to someone he knew who was interested in writing a book.

My immediate response was visceral. "*Fuck no,*" I thought. He wanted a favor from me after he'd made me a joke in tenth grade? He wanted me to accommodate him now after the incident that he probably thought was nothing, but that helped shape the way I thought about and acted toward men? I sat staring at his message for several moments, and after a surge of unexpected courage, I replied:

Hi David,
Sure, I'll talk to your friend. And I'd love to have a conversation with you if you're open to it.

To my surprise, he replied almost immediately that he was available that afternoon.

I immediately panicked. What was I thinking? Why had I asked that? What if I promptly reverted to my young self and cried when

I talked to him? What if he was dismissive, rude, or defensive? What if he told me that's not what happened?

Then I questioned myself. Had I made the whole thing up in my head? I texted my friend Shelby; we'd been best friends all through high school. I told her the story and said, "Do you remember that? Am I remembering everything correctly? Is that what happened?" She replied, "Yes, I do, and you're remembering everything correctly because I was there and that's what happened." I even went and dug up my high school yearbook from the attic, and there in the back David had signed my yearbook—his message with misogynistic undertones made me cringe. There it was in black and white, validation that I hadn't imagined it.

I also went back and forth trying to convince myself that I was overreacting. It was just high school stuff. People experience much, much worse, and I was being too sensitive and the whole thing was stupid. But there was no denying that no matter how much my head tried to put together the words that I was overreacting, my body said otherwise. My body still felt the shame, humiliation, anger, and hurt. Not only for me, but for girls and women everywhere.

However, the anxiety that filled me up when thinking about talking to him wrecked me. I called two of my dear friends, Amy and Kate. Amy lovingly told me that yes, I might cry, and that was because this mattered to me. That the sixteen-year-old girl inside me was still rightfully angry and hurt. And that under no circumstances was it my responsibility to take care of his feelings. If he was uncomfortable, so be it. After all, she pointed out, he had made me very uncomfortable.

Then I tried to back out. I told Amy and Kate, "It's not like he and I are friends. We never went out again after that, we haven't spoken in almost thirty years, plus, we've been Facebook friends for years and have never communicated before now. It's fine, I'll just let it go."

"Obviously you're good enough friends for him to message you and ask you for a favor and you're good enough friends to have made out in high school. This matters to you, Andrea, or you wouldn't have brought it up to us," Amy said, passionately.

To which Kate added, "Listen, we, as women, need to stop only complaining in our circles to each other about this kind of behavior. This doesn't change things. We have to ask the men in our lives who've behaved this way probably unknowingly to have conversations with us. You deserve to have him hear about your experience."

In that moment I knew they were both absolutely right, and what Kate said struck me the most. It did me or the collective of women no good at all for me to stay silent and complain only to my friends.

Remember in chapter 4 when I talked to you about accepting life's challenges as invitations? This was one of those moments when I couldn't accept that this was a fluke. No, the Universe had handed this to me as an invitation. Like, "Hey, babe! We know you're still upset about this shitty thing that happened to you in 1991. And look! One of the boys who hurt you has suddenly and coincidentally reached out to you even though you haven't spoken to him in forever. Imagine that! Your call with what you want to do here."

That afternoon I was faced with the choice to keep complaining about it to my friends, keep trying to convince myself it was no big deal—just some teasing in school—or to take action in getting on the phone with him, showing up as my best and most brave self, and telling him my story. No matter how he responded, at least I knew

I was taking action on something gigantic for me—giving voice to something more than just a time when I was hurt, but speaking up for so many women who've been humiliated in the same way.

David and I spoke that afternoon. After some small talk I awkwardly told him my experience, and he listened. He said he didn't remember those details, but remembers our one date, and believed my story. He said, "I remember you were mad at me for months at school after our date, and I never knew why. I knew I had blown it with you, but I didn't know what I had done."

I told him that I only wanted him to know that to him it was probably innocuous "locker-room talk," but for me what happened had created a belief that if I said no to boys, this was the price. That what I wanted now more than anything was for him to say something to other men when he heard things like this.

He was remorseful and thoughtful in his responses. He apologized without casting blame at me or anything else, and I do think that he heard me completely. We ended the conversation with me making one request. I asked that as they became the appropriate age, he would talk to his children about this—especially his son. I believe the mistakes we make can be used as teaching moments, no matter how ashamed or embarrassed we are to have made them. We carry wisdom, experience, and insight as adults when it comes to our regrets, and it can be invaluable to talk to a young person about what happened and how you were able to clean it up.

I understand this situation went as well as it could have. I was hoping for that, but was not at all expecting it. But I knew even if he was defensive or dismissive, even if I got angry after his response, I had the tools to be resilient (see the tools on resilience in chapter 8). If you're gearing up to have a conversation like this one,

I recommend setting your intentions for how *you* want to show up. Do you want to be brave and clear? Do you want to share your message or experience with what my friend Amy always says, grace and kindness? You're free to want what you want in terms of outcomes, but don't let the success of the conversation depend on that. You taking action in the first place is what matters.

In my situation I knew I could walk away having taken action and been proud of how I showed up. I would preferred to have walked away having said something regarding an important event in my life than stayed quiet and complained only to the women in my circle. Because I know absolutely nothing will change if I did that. In terms of our biggest complaints, we need to be part of the solution rather than just talking about the problem. Is it unfair that I had to do the heavy lifting? Is it typically women (or any other marginalized group) who tend to carry the emotional labor in these situations? Yes, to both. But that doesn't mean we bow out when given the opportunity to speak up.

When we complain and do nothing at all about big, meaningful things such as the story I just told you—especially when we're given the opportunity to do something about it like I had—we're giving away our power. We're essentially saying, "This problem is hurting me, but it's the deal I've been handed and it's permanent, there's absolutely nothing I can do. I am the victim here and this is the way it will always be." I am here to tell you that 99 percent of the time, we *can* do something about it. We can use our voices, stand up for ourselves, invite people to have conversations, or educate ourselves and others on the topic at hand.

The most important thing I want you to take away from this chapter is not so much complaints such as commenting that you're cold when you notice the thermostat is turned down to

67 degrees. What's imperative is that you stop and think about the things you complain about that are preventing you from going out and seriously kicking ass in your life. The things that when you think about taking action on them, you might throw up a little in your mouth. The things that you want to be known for taking action on, the things that you have to truly dig deep on your courage for.

I also think it's imperative to add that I, as a straight, white, cisgender, able-bodied woman, have an enormous amount of privilege in this situation and in life in general. I wasn't risking a whole lot by speaking up to David. Sure, he could have been hateful and maybe said something untrue about me on social media to try to harm my reputation, but my risk was still low. I want to acknowledge there is a much higher risk for, say, a Black or Brown woman speaking up in her workplace about big, messy topics like racism and sexism. She, depending on the circumstance, faces at the very least economic risk by trying to claim her power.

As I mentioned, more than anything else, I want you to be conscious about your complaining, know you have more power than you probably think, plus have some tools for how to tackle your biggest gripes. Onward!

MAKE YOUR COMPLAINTS WORK FOR YOU

About ten years ago I came across a "no complaining for thirty days" challenge on social media. "It will change your life!" it promised me. At first, I rolled my eyes and balked at this. How dare someone challenge me to get rid of something that feels like a necessary limb? Don't they understand that my complaints are unavoidable? That lamenting about the unfairness or idiocy of people that make my life more difficult is the way I feel like I'm doing something about it?

I decided not to participate in the challenge. Not because I wanted to keep complaining; I do understand that complaining isn't great for us—even science tells us that. I declined the challenge because I don't think those challenges are helpful. Sure, they can help you see how much you complain, but usually it looks something like this:

Day one: You notice how much you complain. Ugh, it must sound so annoying to other people.

Day two: Feel bad about yourself for all your complaining, tell yourself you're hopeless and will never get it right, look for jobs cleaning out Porta-Potties with a traveling carnival because you feel like complaining is all you can do right.

Day three: Go back to complaining.

No, thanks.

When I decided to not participate in the challenge, I also decided to make my complaining work for me. Your complaints can be windows into what's important to you and the way you live your life. When I notice that I'm complaining about something, I use that as an opportunity to understand what it is that I want. At first it might be obvious. If someone won't email you back at work about a project you are both working on and you find yourself complaining about it, it's clear you want them to email you back so you don't have to follow up or check your email every hour to see if they've responded yet.

In this example, you could have a conversation with this person at work. Politely ask them, "Hey, I notice that it takes a couple of days to get a response to my emails and it seems to be holding up the progress of this project. How can we make this work better?"

Typically, when we're complaining about someone doing something we don't like and/or we want something to change, the solution will require us first to have a conversation about it. Many people would prefer to keep complaining, be passive-aggressive to this person to try to get their point across, or get teeth pulled by a drunk dentist with rusty pliers rather than have a hard and uncomfortable conversation. But until people read minds and then from there give you what you want, kind communication is key to getting a solution to your complaints.

Earlier in the year I had a client named Linda who owned a business with her husband. She was covering a management position she didn't want to cover; nor was she any good at it. There were constant interpersonal problems she hated dealing with, boundaries being crossed, and she was being bulldozed and taken advantage of by her employees. She and her husband weren't hiring someone to cover that position because it wasn't part of their original business plan, even though they could afford it.

Yet week after week, Linda and I would get on the phone, and she would spend fifteen minutes or more complaining about how difficult the people she had to manage were being, how much anxiety it was bringing her, as well as how much it was affecting her entire life. After about five weeks of this I said, "Listen, Linda, I'll be honest with you. I'm tired of hearing you complain about this, so I know *you've* got to be tired of hearing it come out of your mouth. How bad does it have to get before you take a leap and hire someone? Is this pain worth the money you're saving? How much of your life will be negatively affected before you put your foot down and give this job to someone who's qualified for it so you can do what *you're* really great at?"

What Linda needed to do was have a hard conversation with her husband about it. It took her getting to the end of her rope and holding on with sweaty palms for dear life to finally break down, get clear on her limits, and tell him that she could no longer do this anymore—that if she had applied for this job as an outside employee instead of taking it by default, she would have quit months ago. Her line in the sand was that they needed to hire someone for her well-being, for the sake of their marriage and business partnership.

Her husband had not known the severity of her mental and emotional state. He knew she didn't love covering that job, but she had backed down when he insisted they wait it out. She felt her only "solution" was to complain to her friends and to me about it. Suffice to say, they hired someone to take the management position, and almost immediately she saw a change. "My stress level has diminished," she told me only a couple of weeks later.

WHAT IF THE SOLUTION ISN'T THAT EASY?

What if Linda and her husband really could *not* afford to hire someone and she had to stay in that position? What then? Businesses many times require sacrifice, and with anything, sometimes we *have to* travel through difficult jobs, people, or situations. Or, with my earlier example, what if your coworker continues to take her sweet time emailing you back, even after you've asked her to reply like a courteous, normal person?

In those circumstances, you must ask yourself what you're willing to put up with in order to get to the end goal or results you want in regard to your complaint. The question you must ask yourself is: *Is this worth it?* Because sometimes it is, and sometimes it isn't.

If it's worth it—say, a promotion is within your reach and you're willing to put up with ten-hour workdays and your boss's bad breath—if you're willing to sometimes have hard conversations to ask for what you want and deserve, what you're leaning in to is acceptance.

Acceptance can be extraordinarily helpful when you're conscious about what you're accepting (in this case, sacrifice, hard work, and kindly offering breath mints, in exchange for the promotion). Acceptance is *not* giving your power away, but knowing where you're going, knowing what you need to do to get there, and knowing you can't control absolutely everything from here to there.

Was I willing to accept walking away from having a conversation with David? Was Linda willing to accept the mental and emotional breakdowns she was having from not hiring someone to help her? No on both. But each situation is unique and nuanced. What I want from you is to be clear on what you can and cannot try to change, what you are and aren't willing to do to try to change it, and to be at peace with yourself in regard to what you choose.

LET YOUR COMPLAINTS RIP

I don't want you to walk away from this chapter thinking that when you catch yourself complaining about how small the parking spaces are at Trader Joe's, it's your duty to cause a riot and start a petition to have the spaces widened. But let yourself off the hook when you truly are "venting," or what I like to call conscious complaining.

My dear friend Amy and I voice-message each other often. When we have a catalog of complaints, we preface our message by saying, "I'm going to tell you all the things I'm mad at . . ." and we rattle them off, one by one. Some of the complaints are small and humorous, like "Mercury is in retrograde and I can't post to Instagram Stories, plus I started my period and ruined my favorite pair of underwear." In these moments we just let each other complain, as these are normal, mostly trivial, everyday gripes.

Then there are complaints that are bigger, where we ourselves might not see where we could take responsibility for our complaints by taking action on them. Amy and I have an agreement that when we see this in each other, we call it out. In an effort to make some noise in our lives, to hold each other to a higher standard, to show our love for each other by encouraging one another to take action on our biggest complaints (or stop complaining about them), we are showing up as the women we aspire to be.

Remember when I told my client Linda that I was tired of hearing her complain about her situation, and that I was sure she was tired of hearing herself complain about it? It was a risk for me to say that, but people don't hire me to get on the phone so they can complain incessantly. I want this to be the same with your trusted friend or friends. Maybe it's one friend, but have an agreement that if they ever hear you complaining about the same thing week after week, they will lovingly call you out on it. Because like the fact that people don't hire me to listen to them complain week after week, you weren't born to bitch and moan on the constant and hope things change. No, ma'am! You were born to see things that are hard that you don't like, that you need to try to change, and take appropriate action on it. Massive change may or may not happen, but the point is to take responsibility for your desires, ask for what you want, and make a point that what you want matters.

THE
UNLEARNING

NOTICE: Start by recognizing your complaints. Sure, you'll have the usual "I'm tired; this show is too boring; my thighs are chafing." But really start recognizing the bigger complaints: "My partner won't hear me when I tell her we're getting into too much credit card debt; I'm so tired of the family joke being that I've decided I'm not going to have kids; my boss said something incredibly sexist on a conference call today and no one said anything." These are the complaints that butt up against your values, the things that aren't only bothersome, they make you feel angry and hurt.

Pay attention to your options—you could not say or do anything about those complaints, and nothing will likely change. What will that cost you? Both options are difficult—saying something and having it be uncomfortable or even not getting your way, the other option saying and doing nothing. But which one is more in alignment with who you want to be?

GET CURIOUS: The thing I want you to get the most curious about is the complaints you have that you don't or won't take action on. Why? What is the risk? Is the possibility of the worst-case scenario happening if you take action worse than not taking action at all? This isn't about making a concrete decision about what to do; it's about weighing out your options and what's at stake both literally and in accordance with what's important to you.

I also want you to let go of any thinking that taking action on your complaints is either good or bad. For the sake of this exercise, I want you to get curious and clear on the why.

In addition, inquire within yourself: What are you getting out of complaining? Are you getting validation from someone else? Or feeling righteous in your anger? Do you feel like you're getting something done with your complaining? Any of these things are fine; it gets you closer to understanding yourself better.

SELF-COMPASSION: As you're digging in, thinking about your biggest complaints, and maybe coming to the realization that you don't in fact take action on many (or any) or them, watch out for the mean voice in your head that tells you you're wrong for that. Remember, our culture does not encourage us to speak up about the things that bother us and the things we want changed. Reading this chapter, answering the questions, and thinking about what you want to speak up about are the first steps in taking action. That is something to be proud of!

KEEP THE MOMENTUM: If nothing else, it would be a win if every time you complained, you asked yourself, "Do I plan on doing anything about this?"

You can accept what you're getting or choose to focus on the solution. My hope is that you start to think about how much you have power over.

This also might be a great topic to talk to your friends about. Pick your battles here—your buddies might throw a drink in your face if you're constantly saying, "Let's focus on the solution over complaining about it, ladies!" every time someone complains about spin class being canceled or slow Wi-Fi.

Use your complaints as information, just as you would your emotions. What comes out of your mouth as grievances are telling you something, especially about the significant things.

13

Stop Pointing the (Middle) Finger at Your Parents

Sit down with a new therapist to talk about your life history, and they'll likely smile, press their fingertips together, and say, "Tell me about your parents."

The way we grow up shapes us. Your childhood matters. Everything from the way you manage your finances, to your politics (or lack thereof), to how you see and react to your romantic relationships—so much of how you behave and think—has been shaped by your primary caregivers. The self-help aisle is bursting with books on how to heal your inner child, your mother wound, and your daddy issues.

And it's not just our parents who shape us. Maybe it was a mentor you had, a sibling, an intimate partner in your twenties, anyone who had an impact on you. The vast majority of us have had someone in our life who's played an important role, and it's likely that someone has impacted us in a negative way at least somewhere along the line that we tend to blame for how we are today.

My friend Laura's parents split up when she was a toddler and her brother was in high school. Her dad was in and out of her life until one day he was simply out. Her brother enlisted in the military when she was still very young and, from what she remembers, hardly visited. Her mom had about a half dozen boyfriends throughout Lauren's childhood, several of whom she became close to, but all of whom she eventually had to see walk out the door (you know where this is going, right?).

When Laura and I became friends, she was married and in her late thirties. "Every man I've ever loved and trusted has left me. Most of the time I'm waiting for my husband to leave, even though he gives me no evidence that he will." She said they would get into raging fights, her accusing him of flirting with someone on Facebook, her calling him names, and basically her projecting all her pain onto her husband. She knew what she was doing wasn't helping, and when I asked her what she had done to remedy it, she said, "I'm just this way. I can't help it, this is all I saw growing up, men leaving me."

Laura's story of her broken heart is not at all uncommon. Most of us have a painful story of our past caregivers, but the circumstances might be different. Maybe it's not your parents, but *someone*, and perhaps some event, has paved out the path for you. Sometimes you haven't quite connected the dots yet.

The more you're aware of this, and the more you know what or who you might be blaming for your patterns of thought and behavior, the more you can take responsibility for and control of your life, and that's where your power is.

WELL, THIS IS AWKWARD

Over the course of this book I've been telling you to look at your family of origin and your past so you can hope to see the full picture of what was modeled for you and the messaging you received, as well as how our culture has shaped you. This is so you can get to the source of the issue to understand why you think, react, and behave in certain ways, challenge the messaging you receive, and create new beliefs and behaviors.

More and more people are getting in touch with their feelings, reading books on spirituality and personal growth, and following mental health experts online, which is a great thing. And sometimes a side effect of this new awareness is using it as an excuse to not take responsibility for their own shortcomings and their life. To duck out and make excuses for unhealthy behavior. Looking at your family of origin and your parents' shortcomings is not so you can blame them. That would be the easy way out.

Let me be clear—they may have done things that are incredibly egregious. They may continue to do such things. And (not but) if this is your experience, we get to a point in our lives when we need to accept that although you may have not been dealt the best hand when it comes to being parented, when you are well into adulthood, it's time to take responsibility and accountability for your life going forward. You are bigger and better than blame.

WHY WE DO IT

Like your favorite dessert, blame can be the absolute best. There are many reasons we do it, and like I've mentioned in this book several times, the first reason is because we're human. Blame is as natural as a sloth sleeping fifteen hours a day, seriously.

But unlike the sloth's sleep being good for them, part of who they are, and what makes them cute . . . not so much for people-blaming.

To start, blame can feel like a hot, steamy love affair. It gives us relief, puts all the responsibility on someone else, and allows us to be the noble victim. How dare they hurt us! Don't they know what they've done? *The horror.*

By avoiding our own flaws, mistakes, and hard things we don't want to look at, we get a false sense of power. A feeling of control. We don't have to change or even be vulnerable at all.

When I was twenty-two years old, I had my first Big Girl Job working as an assistant buyer for a company that owned and operated forty-two retail stores. The VP of the company, Morgan (who was also the owner's wife), was a scary Miranda Priestly type, whom I both looked up to as a boss lady I wanted to become and feared at any moment would set me on fire with just a raised eyebrow in my direction.

One day she called me into her enormous office and proceeded to berate me for a mistake I had made. She pulled a calculator out of her desk and calculated how much money I had cost the company, to the tune of $10,000, which in retrospect was a stretch of a calculation, and if it were true, it was a drop in the bucket to them. But back then, considering the fact that I made $27,000 a year, making a mistake that cost nearly a third of my annual salary felt like an enormous snafu. Morgan set her calculator down and stared at me, waiting for my response. What did I have to say for wasting her money, time, and apparently, by the look on her face, her life?

I was flooded with shame. This was my first "real" job, and at that time I wanted nothing more than to climb the ladder and one day be like her. I had let everyone down. When the truth of it was, the task I had been assigned that I had screwed up I had no idea how to do when it was assigned to me. My boss had handed it over in a rush, and when I asked her for more direction, she said, "Figure it out and wing it."

So I did, and clearly my winging went wonky.

The reality was I hadn't been trained. I had asked for better direction on a task I had no idea how to do and had not been given help. If Morgan had wanted me to not waste $10,000 of company money, she might have asked during my scolding how this could have been avoided. But I was in such deep shame at that moment of being blamed, I couldn't defend myself. In retrospect, that's exactly what she was wanting—me to have no defense and to take the blame.

Blaming makes people feel powerful, which I have no doubt Morgan felt in that moment. I was wrong, she was right, it was all my fault, she was the victim. Obviously, I was all up in my feelings about it and she had total control. There was a winner and a loser.

While many people use blame to sit in the Throne of Victim, sometimes blame also gives some people a sense of superiority, which my example shows as well. We all compare ourselves to others, and sometimes blame can be position-seeking. In other words, we're looking to be on top in some way, and blaming can be that quick fix.

We also love blame because taking responsibility is vulnerable, and we typically treat that like a hot potato. Once I got drunk at a party (many of my most cringeworthy stories start with this line) and mouthed off about a friend who was there at the party. Not only there, but listening, and I knew it. I was going on and on, teasing her, but I could tell by the look on her face that her feelings were hurt, that I should promptly shut my piehole, but I did no such thing. It was awkward afterward, I knew I should apologize, but instead I chalked it up to being drunk. I blamed the alcohol and my being "boisterous" and "lively." When, in truth, I had been a complete asshole and she deserved an apology. But for me to do that, for me to come to her and tell her I had made a mistake and was truly sorry, was too vulnerable for me to bear at that time. It would require my looking at my own shame of hurting her, having her see me stripped down, and risking her not receiving it well. I opted out and continued to blame the booze.

When it comes to deeper issues like letting go of blaming our parents, looking past their behavior and parenting and looking at our own wounds can be remarkably painful. At first glance it really is a no-brainer to point the finger at Mom and Dad—easier than it is to excavate the agony that includes getting a handle on your past that you've been dragging around like your carry-on luggage at the airport.

Blame also unloads jammed-up feelings. Oh, how we like to bury our feelings and expect them to die, right? If we can ignore them and suffocate them enough, surely they'll go away. But they don't (trust me, I've tried).

Therefore, when we're in a situation that gets our goat, spewing out blame like projectile vomit can feel like the cure to all our ailments.

Last, it's difficult to accept that others are different than we want them to be. Especially parents, siblings, and partners. It's easier to hold out hope that they could change. We blame them for making our lives (and sometimes their own) miserable, and sometimes we blame them for damn near everything. We have standards and expectations, which they fail to meet. Therefore, we remain disappointed and heartbroken.

My hope is that you can connect the dots as to why you blame, and know that you're normal, and now let's get down to business and reconstruct.

FORGIVENESS

Let's start with the Mother of All Personal Development Devotions: Forgiveness. The truth is forgiveness can be complicated, and shrouded in heaps of anger, trauma, and just plain lousy circumstances. Forgiveness is a process that can take years for some, and for many is a process that needs to be revisited sometimes as soon as we think we've forgiven.

Before you even begin the process of forgiveness, ask yourself, Do I even want to forgive? Forgiveness is a deeply personal undertaking, one that cannot be forced or prescribed. Your emotions still might need to be processed, you might still need to sit in your anger or grief, or maybe you don't know what needs to be done first, but you know it's not forgiveness yet. That's okay. You can still work through your trauma with a professional; you can still live your life. Forgiveness is one way to move away from blame and into your own empowerment, but it's not the *only* way.

For those of you who are ready, understand that you're an adult, maybe what your parents, your ex, or your UPS guy did was atrocious, but now it's time for you to take control of your life and move forward. Let me remind you that you are deserving of reconciling the hurt that has taken up too much space until now. It's understandable that you've carried around the wound like a child carries around her worn-out teddy bear, but I can assure you that not forgiving, by not even beginning the path that may very well be your path to freedom, is stifling you and quite possibly blocking you from living your biggest, most powerful life.

Forgiving people from our past can feel like digging up dead bodies that have been long buried. The problem is we leave them there hoping the more distance we put between us and them, the more they'll go away, along with all the hard feelings that accompany them. Unfortunately, there are no trophies given out for "Buried Feelings, Resentments, and Anger," so those stashed convictions are best risen from the dead and faced.

A common obstacle around forgiveness is the belief that by forgiving, you are condoning that person's behavior, letting them off the hook, and giving them a giant, flashy permission slip to hurt you again. *This is not true.* Forgiveness can be for you and only you. The other person doesn't have to apologize, express remorse, or turn around and be the next Mother Teresa. They don't even have to know you're working on forgiving them. It's for your healing and your betterment alone. You matter, and your heart matters the most in this.

Forgiveness work can also very much be about setting boundaries. If someone has harmed you, continues to harm you, has taken no steps toward making things right, and is making it near impossible to be in their vicinity, then guess what? *You don't have to be around them.* When it's a parent, a sibling, an adult child—these can be the most heart-wrenching boundaries to set in place and require a metric shit-ton of self-compassion and a support system.

So how do you know when you've forgiven someone? There are some telltale signs that you've moved forward and are in the process of forgiving or have forgiven:

1. You can talk about what happened and it no longer has a charge around it. In other words, you speak about it as an event that happened, and it might make you a bit sad, but it won't take you out. It won't hit you with emotions that linger or make you say, "Those motherfuckers can rot in hell for all I care."

2. You can wish good things for the person you've forgiven. You don't wish them harm, or to enact revenge, or, as you make a wish blowing out your birthday candles, hope they perpetually get an Achilles blister with every pair of shoes they wear. On the other hand, you can truly hope for the best for that person.

3. You can acknowledge the lesson you've walked away with. It doesn't have to be this major spiritual experience, or the biggest lesson of your lifetime, but perhaps it's as simple as "That was my teacher who showed me what I can no longer tolerate." Or maybe you learned to trust your inner wisdom.

WHAT ABOUT OBLIGATION?

Obligation comes up over and over again when I work with women who are setting boundaries, especially when it comes to family. They say, "I can't *not* speak to my brother, he's my brother," or, "My mother expects me to call her every Sunday. I'm a bad daughter if I don't." They accept the story that they owe their time and emotional space to people who continue to treat them like shit. As if somewhere etched in stone is "Herein Lies the List of How to Be a Good Daughter" and anything less than checking off all the boxes damns you to a fiery inferno in hell. I know it may not seem like it sometimes, but just because you're in the same family as someone else doesn't mean you owe them anything. If you have tried your best, shown up as the greatest version of yourself, and held true to your values, and you still can't be around this person, setting boundaries will be the saving grace to liberate yourself.

Spend some time here and think about if and where this affects you. In doing research for this book, a friend told me that she recently noticed that when people tell her she's being "selfish," it's often because she's not doing something they want her to do. That her father told her this all the time growing up and she has heard it from her ex-husband as well as her current partner. She started noticing a pattern that when she doesn't do what the men in her life want—put them first and put her own needs and desires aside for them—they view it as her being selfish. When in reality, she's simply putting herself first.

I won't lie—this work may be some of the hardest you'll do. Neither I nor anyone else can pump you up and cheer for you hard enough to make it any less uncomfortable and painful. What I can do is continue to remind you that you are an adult, capable of making decisions that are best for your emotional and mental well-being. Just because you have set boundaries with people who continue to hurt you does not under any circumstances make you a bad person. It makes you a healthy individual and in charge of your life. It makes you someone who loves herself enough to draw a line in the sand and say, "I can still love you from over here. What's best for me are these limits."

YOU'RE IN CHARGE

I'm about to tell you something that might seem obvious, but hear me out. You *cannot* heal your childhood/young adult wounds through your adult partner, your friendships, your rescue dog, or anyone else. You might be thinking, "Now, why on earth would I do that?" complete with an eye roll. But, listen, we do it often. Jerry Maguire made us all swoon with his romantic "You complete me." We unconsciously create expectations of our friends and partners that are unattainable for them and then blame them when they fail.

We want a hero. Many of us want saving, even though we'd never admit it.

The remedy is to take a good, hard look at where you're seeking someone else to fill any voids you have. Some of them run deep—such as the coincidental way many of us end up with partners who are suspiciously like our parents. Or the way we cling to certain friendships that are no longer good for us. We sell our souls and are blinded by our own natural wanting to create fulfillment, when the truth is that the creation of that fulfillment belongs to no one else but ourselves.

Of course, validation, love, and a cure for loneliness are all important. I'm not saying they aren't. But there comes a time to look where you've crossed the line from what's healthy love and fulfillment over into the black hole of grasping at straws. When we do this, we give all our power to the other person, keeping none of it for ourselves. Most of us will learn this lesson the hard way, and to be honest, I wonder if it's the best way to learn it. Sometimes seeing and feeling how powerless it is to experience this causes your eyes to be flung open so the real healing can begin.

SEE YOUR PART

An additional way to let go of blaming and claim your power is to find your part in the matter. I like to call these blame boundaries—the noticing of what's yours and what's theirs. This can be tricky because I don't want you to take on everything yourself and put all the blame on your shoulders. Maybe it's helpful for you to acknowledge that you've been holding on to this hurt because you've refused to forgive the other person. Or that you've been holding steadfast to expectations that that person has repeatedly failed to meet.

As much as I think you're awesome, the truth of it is the world doesn't revolve around you. You know this logically and probably have the self-awareness and maturity to understand that. But many times, when we're holding on to blame, we feel so wronged that we believe it's completely the other person's fault, and our self-righteousness is being the party host, serving up drinks and greeting all the guests. When we hold on to blame and never look at our part in it, we're assuming the world does in fact revolve around us.

For example, say it's your ex. You're a single parent because they decided to be a complete asshole during your relationship and you couldn't stay together. But your life is harder being a single parent, and you find yourself a bit resentful toward your friends who have kids *and* a partner, plus you find yourself thinking, "If they had just acted like a grown-up even half the time we were together, my life would be so much easier." You find yourself feeling like the victim, having an enormous pity party for yourself, and it's all your ex's fault.

The question to ask yourself here is, How is this situation affecting how I show up in other areas of my life? For example, are you sometimes passive-aggressive toward friends because they're partnered, do you roll your eyes when someone else vents about their life, or maybe you find yourself being a jerk to your ex for no reason (other than it's *all their fault*)? If so, you're letting this situation/resentment/blame take the driver's seat.

You may in fact have difficult circumstances. Someone may very well be incredibly shitty to you. And at the same time, you are always in charge of how you react to this.

I want to leave you with this: Know and believe that this is where your strength is. I can't emphasize this enough. You, as an adult, taking responsibility for your hurt. It doesn't mean the other person or people weren't assholes, and it doesn't mean all the pain goes away. It means that *you* get to decide what you let be in charge. It means *you* get to decide what's next for you. It means you understand and give a damn about expanding your life and your personal power. *Do not* let anyone else be responsible for that. I beg you to know in your bones that you are worth healing, you are worth accepting and loving yourself, no matter where you are and what you've experienced.

THE
UNLEARNING

NOTICE: Recognize where you place blame, even if you start to see it's a tool you use not necessarily in regard to big things in your life, but in smaller instances, like blaming your partner for forgetting to remind you of something, when you could take responsibility as well. This is a tricky balance, but one I want you to notice.

Or perhaps where you blame your parents and are stuck or refusing to change because you're convinced you were molded a certain way and that's that.

Bottom line—pay attention to where you use blame as a tool to avoid being held accountable, especially when it involves being accountable for your own shortcomings and hurts that need to be healed.

CURIOUS: Where do you place blame and, more important, why do you do it? What about blaming are you using as "armor" that you feel keeps you safe, such as dodging accountability or seeking to "be on top" of a situation?

Is there anyone you feel it's important to work on forgiving? And if so, are you ready?

Do you place too much blame on yourself? If so, would it be helpful for you to work on understanding the difference between healthy accountability for your wrongs and unnecessarily burdening yourself?

Is there anything you're trying to heal through your relationships (this one might take some real introspection)? If so, what do you need to do to shift that?

Where can you do better about seeing your part in things, without unnecessarily blaming yourself?

SELF-COMPASSION: Reconciling blame can be a complicated task because it becomes a delicate balance of taking responsibility for your behaviors and actions and at the same time being kind to yourself. Both can exist, but you need to be very self-aware of your process and thoughts along the way.

While you're working on taking responsibility for things you're not proud of, remember that you did the best you could at the time with the tools you had. Even if you knew better and didn't do better, there was a reason you still behaved in a way you're not proud of that typically involves unconscious patterns. Be kind to yourself as you navigate this complicated path.

KEEP THE MOMENTUM: I want to repeat something I said earlier in this chapter: You are bigger and better than blame. You may have spent years either consciously or unconsciously using it as a defense mechanism, and maybe it's worked . . . up until now. Surely, there will be times when someone or something other than you is at fault for things, but there will be times when you need to look at where you need to take ownership. This is one of the most mature and healthy things you can do in any relationship, and the health of your relationships is in direct correlation to your happiness and fulfillment. This is why you're bigger and better than blame.

14

Stop Acting Like a Lonely Only

Fuck your feelings.

Feelings are weak, they don't give you the upper hand, they certainly don't solve problems, and they are a waste of time.

At least that's what much of society believes.

A huge obstacle for many women is their inability to tell the truth about the way they feel. To articulate that they are unhappy, that they didn't know life was going to be like this. To express that they feel frustrated that they are the last priority with their partner or with their family. Or that they are constantly trying to meet expectations of making everyone comfortable and happy at work, and there becomes no room for their wants and needs.

My friend Dr. Sasha Heinz calls this point in a woman's life the "dampening of the human spirit." Not clinical depression (although that happens, too), but a general malaise about life. A cynical outlook. And to create relief from that, women engage in gossip, wine-o'clock, workaholism, perfectionism, becoming obsessed with their children's lives, scrolling mindlessly through their phones, and relating to funny memes about how hard life is and sharing them on social media because *that* makes them feel an inkling of connection to others. But what they really need is real connection and to find and fulfill their own hopes and dreams. Instead, what happens is a slow march through an unfulfilled life where they're helping others fulfill *their* dreams, never asking for help, but rather spending their time getting everyone a snack or obsessively checking their work email from their phone.

The phrase *asking for help* gets thrown around a lot in personal-growth conversation, so let me give you a list of examples of what a situation might look like where someone could use support from others. It can range from seemingly minor problems to major issues.

- You have a health scare and need to go to the doctor for further testing, such as a biopsy or more blood work.
- You or your partner lost a job.
- Your child just got a special-needs diagnosis, they are struggling with their mental health, or they are acting out at school and home.
- You have an ailing parent and are unsure of what their long-term care will look like, or your own aging process is taking its toll on you.
- Your anxiety or depression has crept up and you're having a difficult time navigating each day.
- You're contemplating or are going through a divorce or breakup.
- You're being treated poorly at work and are not sure what to do.

As you can see, these situations are different from situations when you need someone to meet up with and vent to. You probably already have that friend, but this friend is the one who can do more than just commiserate with you about lazy coworkers.

WHY WE KEEP THINGS TO OURSELVES

Every time I encounter a woman who struggles to ask for help and I ask her if she thinks her friends also shouldn't ask her for help when they need it, she quickly says no. Undoubtedly, she wants her friends to lean on her for support, so why does she—or maybe even you—think it's not okay when it's the other way around?

The answers are many. First, we have cultural and societal myths that hold us back and encourage us to keep quiet. These are typically the first thought we have when we consider reaching out for help. The myths are:

1. **That we're a burden if we tell someone our problems and/or ask for help.** Most women don't want others to perceive them as "needy." I use quotation marks because in reality everyone is needy. If we don't have our needs met, we'll die, plain and simple. In relationships, having needs met must be reciprocal, or the person who's feeling not reciprocated will be unhappy. However, culturally, many women are so afraid of looking "needy"—in other words, the type of woman who demands attention and is desperate for love—that we recoil at the thought of it and don't reach out at all.

2. **That our problems are worse than others', and that triggers our shame response.** When we're deep in our pain and problems, we tend to rank our struggle. Our inner critic gets its feathers all ruffled and tells us our stories are too

embarrassing, too shameful, and that no one else struggles like this.

3. **That our problems are not as bad as others'.** On the flip side, sometimes we do the opposite and rank our problems low on the list of what is worthy of someone's time and space. We make our problems look like a molehill compared to someone else's mountain.

4. **That we'll look weak, stupid, incompetent, like an asshole, etc.** Telling someone else our problems is vulnerable, and so is asking for help. Again, our shame trigger responds when we think about someone categorizing us as anything but ideal.

5. **That we'll be judged or dismissed.** Since the majority of us have had this happen sometime in our life, many times it still stings so much that we automatically assume we will be judged ("OMG, how could you have let that happen?") or dismissed ("Oh, you're surely blowing it out of proportion. It couldn't be that bad"). We know what it feels like, and we never want to risk returning there.

6. **That's it's more badass to be independent and power through any challenge.** We live in a culture that idealizes hyperindependence. Hey, I'll sing along to Kelly Clarkson's "Miss Independent" right along with you, but people who buy into this myth tend to not want to believe we all need our people.

7. **That we don't trust women or we feel we need to compete with them.** This might be a lot to unpack. Your mistrust of women might be rooted in real experiences of being hurt, and you might have a competitive personality, which is healthy. But I urge you to do some thinking about

how much of those behaviors are your own internalized misogyny. The vast majority of us grew up hearing and believing sexist stereotypes about women—that we are not to be trusted, are too emotional, are backstabbers, etc.

8. **We might have a mother wound or a history of being hurt by women.** Like internalized misogyny and sexism, this can be a lot to unpack as well. Mother wounds are aplenty (as are father wounds). How did your mom show up for you growing up? What does your relationship with your mother look like now? In addition, you may have very real experiences of being disappointed, hurt, or betrayed in past friendships. These types of wounds could be the reason you steer clear of female friendships.

Now, listen. I'm not going to pretend none of these things will happen if you do reach out for help or that these things don't matter. The person you confide in might feel burdened if they have a ton of hard things happening in their life, too, when you reach out to them. Or you tell someone about your less-than-stellar yearly review at work and they tell you they recently got laid off. Naturally, these things happen, but it's not black or white. Just because you can't control how you'll be received, or really anything else, for that matter, that does not mean you should pull up the drawbridge and shut everyone out forever and ever.

I want to also point out two other reasons you might have a history of holding on to your struggles. These particular defenses might hide out a little more in your subconscious and may be harder to spot.

You might have chronic depression. Having depression and hearing that the remedy to your problems is reaching out for help can feel like an unhelpful solution for two reasons. One, depression can tell you that no one wants to hear your problems. I know I mentioned this already, but when depression is active, you might have the fears previously mentioned, and in addition, many times there isn't anything to pinpoint that this actually is the "problem." Maybe you have a good job, are in good physical health, and are financially stable and still feel sad and lonely. It feels futile to reach out and tell someone you feel sad for no reason.

Second, if you do reach out for help and someone offers good advice, it can feel like a monumental task to take action on their suggestion. I understand there are times when the job of catching up on your email or taking a walk around the block can feel exhausting.

You don't actually want to change. I know, I know, you're reading a self-help book, *my* self-help book, and I'm certainly not here to insult you, but we need to chat about this one. I've seen way too many women become near or full-on obsessed with self-help, think about changing their life, but not actually *do* anything about it. If you think this might be you, if you read a lot of self-help or listen to motivational podcasts but don't truly address any of the big areas in your life that need to change, you might be in a spot where you feel more comfortable in your pain, uncomfortableness, or stuckness. This isn't that uncommon, so please don't be hard on yourself about it. Sometimes it's better to know that's where you are, know that when you're ready to take action and change, you will, and be at peace with it. But please believe me when I tell you that may very well be your inner critic keeping you stuck and not taking any action.

Once you tell someone, it becomes too real. I once had a friend who private-messaged me on Facebook asking about my son, and the process we went through to test him for special needs years prior. I gave her some information and my phone number, and she said she would call me. She also shared that one of her close family members did not agree about having their son tested, which was proving to be a source of contention. I told her I could help her with that, too.

She never called, and several days later I ran into her at a community event. She awkwardly told me she was sorry she didn't call and would love to talk that day. "Sure," I said, "I'm sitting over there and we can sneak off somewhere quiet." She never came over to talk to me and never called. I know I'll run into her again, and when I do, I'll gently remind her I'm here to talk when she's ready and leave it alone.

My hunch is that she wanted to talk to me but is afraid. She knew that once she does, once I tell her what her options are and what I recommend, once I confirm her fears, she can no longer stay in whatever denial she might be in, and will likely have to face her possible worst fear as a parent.

Sometimes we do this; maybe we know that reaching out and telling someone our pain or asking for help is the best thing for us to do but can't seem to make the leap, because once we do, we can't turn back. It becomes real, like it suddenly takes shape after being more abstract and only swirling around in our minds. Once we tell it, we might be faced with action, and we understand the true pain of *not* taking action.

WHAT HAPPENS WHEN WE STAY THE LONELY ONLY

I had a friend once tell me that although she did see spirituality and her faith as important to her, her relationship with her higher power was spotty. She explained that she called on her higher power for help only in situations such as jumping out of an airplane and her parachute won't open. This hadn't literally happened to her, but her point was that she reached out for spiritual help only when she was in a full-blown emergency, sometimes of epic proportions.

Problems can go from problem to crisis awfully quick, and I assure you it's much easier to ask for help solving it when you have a problem, versus when it's a full-blown crisis.

Even when you don't have an issue that needs solving—if you're just needing an ear or a shoulder to cry on—when you don't release it and instead keep it inside, you can stay stuck. Stuck in feeling despair about it, stuck in your negative self-talk, or stuck in feeling incredibly alone.

Finally, when you keep things bottled up, you're missing out on an opportunity to learn and grow, as well as connection with your friend.

TOOLS

It's a very real pain to tell someone something deep and personal and be met with anything but time, compassion, and love. For some, it happens once and only once, because they vow to never tell a living (or dead) soul anything deep and personal.

While I'm going to get into friendships and communication here in a moment, there is something else I'd like you to dig into first if you're one who tends to hold things inside.

To begin with, as usual, look back at your family of origin and think about what was modeled for you in terms of asking for help. Take Meredith, age forty-four:

"As a child, I was praised for being 'proactive' and taking care of things around me in my studies, with chores and home life, etc.

Being the child of immigrants, an independent woman who didn't need any help was the gold standard to shoot for. But it's become a harmful pattern as I've struggled with postpartum depression, bankruptcy, bouts of depression and anxiety, and my insecurities. I've learned to hide my true emotions from everyone, even my husband and kids, and soldier on with a 'brave face.' It's actually put strain on my friendships, because my friends don't feel I trust them enough with my feelings. It's truly been a struggle to grow on from this pattern."

Meredith illustrates self-awareness around why she struggles in her adult life with reaching out for help. For you, were there any messages you received from your family of origin—whether they were explicit or not—in terms of what was okay and what was not okay to share? Did you grow up with a single mom who did pretty much everything? Or even if you did grow up with two parents, did your mother do the lion's share of the work and never or rarely ask for help? Did your parents encourage your independence, which of course can be a good virtue to have, only you may have run with it a little too far? Like Meredith's story, sometimes the culture of our family's identity can be wrapped up in autonomy.

To put it another way in regard to your family, what was given more value, strong, do-it-yourself independence or asking for support? In some cases, this is tricky to answer because nothing was ever said directly about asking for help in terms of personal problems. But if you have grown up hearing your parents call therapists and psychiatrists "head shrinks" in a negative tone, your parents or other caregivers making fun of people who go to therapy or counseling, or hearing things like "just move on," "forgive and forget," and "suck it up, Buttercup" when it comes to your problems, that is clear messaging that is bound to be picked up on and internalized.

It's important to spend some time here so you can understand where some of your influence has come from, and this one can be a sizable part of your programming.

WITNESSING YOUR DARKNESS

I'll be straight with you, in all of my own personal work I've done on myself, in all of the public transparency and storytelling I've done over the last fourteen years to strangers on my blog, on my podcast, on stages, and in books, nothing has been harder than sharing the darkest moments with my best friends and close family. No matter how much I know how important it is to our relationships and spirits, no matter how much I know those few people care about me and will not leave me no matter what I tell them, I still procrastinate on it and it's still painful to crack my heart open and speak my darkness out loud to others.

Social conditioning runs deep, and rare is the person who grew up in a family where their most vulnerable and difficult emotions and truths were welcomed and encouraged. Rare is the person who felt safe and had a soft place to land when it came to their darkest moments. When we had these dark moments, we learned to keep them quiet, pack them up deep inside, and carry on, hence building up our "baggage."

If you truly want to break free in your life, if you absolutely want more confidence, to walk through life bravely and courageously, you must learn to allow the right people to witness your darkness.

This will not be just any person. You may have someone in mind, or you may draw a blank when it comes to someone you can reach out to. If you're like Meredith, if possible, start with a therapist or counselor. There are online options now for support where you don't have to meet with someone face-to-face. And don't feel like you have to tumble out all of your sorrows at once—a relationship with your therapist can still take time to ease into, and it's normal to feel like you need to develop trust first before you dive into sharing your struggles.

HOW TO MAKE FRIENDS

Finding friendships in adulthood, and more specifically, close friendships where you can create a trusting relationship, is not typically something we make time for. But like anything, as I've said before, if you want to change your life, you have to change your life. One of the questions I get often is "Where are these women? How do I find friends now as an adult?" Creating new, close friendships is much like dating. You have to go out and meet people. Obviously, this becomes a challenge when things like global pandemics are happening, but during normal circumstances, here are some ways and places to meet like-minded and like-spirited women:

Gyms (yoga, CrossFit, spinning)
Book clubs
Moms' groups
PTA or other school extracurricular activities, like
volunteering for your children's sports teams
If you work from home, join a coworking space
Game nights such as Bunko
Facebook groups

Church

Theater or improv group

Sports clubs (softball, running club, tennis, etc.)

Dancing club (ballroom, swing, etc.)

Volunteering

Friendship apps (Nextdoor, Bumble BFF, Meet My Dog)

When you take action one of these ways to meet new friends, set the intention that you're open to meet someone great. Watch if your self-talk sounds like "This is the worst, I'm not going to meet anyone who gets me." Yes, it might be scary and awkward, but the alternative of not sharing your awesomeness with someone equally as awesome is also scary and awkward.

Another way to form new friendships is to ask people you know to more or less "set you up" with women who might be a good match for you. Ask your partner if they know someone at work that you might like. Or your siblings or neighbors. Yes, it's vulnerable, but it takes only less than a minute of conversation between you and the other person. It might be as simple as, "Do you know any women I could potentially be friends with? I'm in the market for new friends." Not only are you taking a big step of action, but you're putting energy out into the world that you're open for these new relationships and experiences.

EXISTING FRIENDSHIPS

I couldn't talk about friendships without talking about the ones you already have. Chances are you have a friend or two that if you aren't close with them now, the friendship has the potential to be closer.

Like any relationship, the health of the relationship is built over time, and takes attention and conscious intention. Maybe you have a friendship from college where you've lost touch a bit, connecting only once a year or so. Intention might be that you reach out to her, express that you know you don't talk that often anymore, but you'd love to connect more regularly. Bonus points if you add something like "I've been missing closer female friendships in my life and you were the first person who came to mind." Be specific about what you want. If she's local, can you have monthly hikes? If you're not geographically near each other, can you FaceTime on the first Saturday morning of the month to catch up and begin to text more regularly?

If it's a newer friendship, it's okay if you're the one who reaches out to make lunch dates or invite her to your gym. It's awkward to say things in a new friendship like "I'd love to take this friendship to the next level" without confusion as to what you mean, but you might consider something kind and light, like "I'm so glad I met you. I enjoy hanging out with you and our friendship." We don't acknowledge these types of things enough, and while it's vulnerable, you're being clear about your feelings.

TELL PEOPLE HOW THEY CAN SHOW UP FOR YOU

My friend Amy says you have to share important and vulnerable things only to "ears that can hear them." In other words, sometimes we try to tell our struggles to the wrong people, people who continually meet us with criticism or judgment or are dismissive, even if they mean well. They don't have the tools to show up for you the way you need them to. In these situations, you have two choices:

Option #1. Stop telling them your struggles. If you keep telling this person or persons your problems and expect to have a different result, if you keep hoping they'll be empathetic and listen, when over and over again they haven't, you're more than likely going to keep being disappointed and hurt. If you're not willing to communicate what exactly it is that you need, nothing will likely change.

Option #2. Ask them how to show up for you. The other person won't know they aren't showing up for you the way you need them to if you don't tell them. They're going to think they're being a great friend or family member, maybe even pat themselves on the back.

A few years ago, my family and I moved across the country and had a very difficult time. Many hard things were happening all at once and I called my mom to tell her about it. My mom is an eternal optimist, a lover of silver linings. One of her favorite replies is "Tomorrow is a new day." When I finished telling her all my woes, she said, "Honey, you and Jason are smart and resourceful, I know it will all work out for you."

Although it was a loving response and her intention was to lift me up, I was too deep in despair for the bright side. I became angry, started crying, and shouted into the phone, "Sometimes when I tell you I'm having a shit time, I need you to say, 'That sucks, honey, I'm so sorry this is difficult for you.' I know we'll eventually figure it out, but right now it's the worst and I need you to acknowledge that." We got off the phone and I sobbed, also realizing I needed to call her back and apologize for my outburst.

Part of why I was so upset when I got off the phone with her was because it was my mom. Had it been a friend, I likely wouldn't have been this upset. When it's a close family member, especially someone in our immediate family, like a parent, sibling, or partner, the stakes can be high. Our vulnerabilities can feel more tender and delicate. Like I always say, families are complicated.

While my delivery of what I said to my mom was not great, it was good that I was communicating what I needed. How could my mom know what I needed if I didn't tell her? In her eyes, she was complimenting my resiliency and reminding me how capable I and my husband were. It wasn't fair that I raised my voice and directed my anger at my mom; she had no way of knowing what it was that I really needed. When I had calmed down, I called her back and apologized for my outburst and reiterated what I needed.

You may have an understanding friend or family member, or perhaps not. My mom could have felt personally attacked, gotten defensive, and been angry back at me. She could have been unwilling to hear my apology or not wanted to hear what it was I needed. If that had been the case, that would have told me she isn't the person I go to when things are especially difficult, unless I want to hear only platitudes and how the sun will come out tomorrow.

Maybe talking to your mom isn't an option for you, and you don't have friendships you'd consider close enough to share your struggles with. Again, use the tools mentioned here to try and cultivate new friendships or nurture ones that already exist. If not, start practicing with a therapist or counselor. At the end of the day, you can still be an independent woman, and at the same time get your needs met by slowly but surely sharing your struggles with those who are deserving of hearing them and who can show up for you as you deserve to be shown up for.

THE
UNLEARNING

NOTICE: Think about the last time you were really struggling with something. Was it the onset of the pandemic? Did you or someone you love lose their job? The 2020 election? Did you reach out for help, and if not, why not?

If you do open up to people, do you tell them "just the facts"? In other words, if you lost your job, do you say, "I lost my job today," or do you say, "I lost my job today and I'm scared I won't be able to find a new one." One is just telling the story and the other is telling the story, how you feel about it, and your fears around it. When you tell someone how you're feeling and what you're going through, it opens up the conversation for connection and intimacy.

CURIOUS: Which cultural and societal myths do you buy into when it comes to reaching out and asking for help? Are you worried about looking foolish or weak or something else to others? Where do you think this came from? Whether you know the answer to that or not, what has it cost you to not reach out and instead keep your struggles quiet? For instance, like Meredith's example, has it put a strain on your romantic relationships or made you feel lonely and isolated?

What do you feel you're missing in your relationships by not accepting or seeking out emotional help from others? What are you worried might happen if you opened up to someone? Have you had a negative experience with this in the past, and if so, what happened?

SELF-COMPASSION: If I were to put a major emphasis on self-compassion in any of these chapters, this would be one of them. In my years as a coach and facilitator, I've seen so many women beat themselves up over their friendships. Wondering if they are a good enough friend, feeling guilty about past mistakes they made, feeling hurt about a friendship and wondering if there was something they did or said to deserve it.

Friendships can be hard. They require effort, they require you to go out on a limb with your heart, and for many of us, we've been brought up to be competitive with other women and not trust them, which makes things more complicated. Whether you're unpacking your internalized misogyny or just focusing on your friendships, give yourself an extra-large dose of grace. As I've said before, beating yourself up doesn't get you closer to what you want. But being kind to yourself does.

KEEP THE MOMENTUM: First things first, take inventory of your friendships and see if you have any gaps. Dig into the curiosity about whether you share, how you share, and whether you could put more effort into it so that your friendships will improve. Notice how vulnerable this feels and practice self-compassion.

If you are someone who could use better friendships, the key is to take action. Use the suggestions I've given here and don't give up. I know it's easy to make everything else a priority, such as organizing your sock drawer versus working on your friendships. I also know it's easy to get discouraged if someone doesn't reciprocate or, worse, ghosts you. It very well might happen. But like any relationship, just because one or two didn't work out, that doesn't mean it's time to give up. You are worth the effort to keep trying. The right friendship is out there for you, as well as the trust and closeness you are looking for and deserve.

15

Stop Making Your Pleasure Optional

In 2020, I hired a new therapist. Like most of us, COVID-19 had kicked my ass up and down the street, and I needed to unpack some old stuff. In our first session, she asked me all the intake questions, and one of them was "What do you do for fun?"

I looked away, thinking deeply. "Ummmmm . . ." I replied. A long pause followed. I'm rarely if ever stumped, and with this simple question, I was.

"Nothing lately," I said. By all means, I had a noble excuse of being amid a global pandemic, but even before that, the only thing I was doing was sometimes playing tennis.

Here I was, a life coach, two books under my belt, teaching people how to live a kick-ass life, and I did hardly anything for fun?

When the session ended it got me thinking about pleasure. Because having fun is about pleasure, and when we think about that . . . how much pleasure was I having in my life?

And it wasn't just me. Pleasure is one of those common things that, for women, tend to fall by the wayside. Last on the priority list, an absolute luxury for a lucky few. It's interesting that this is true for most of the women in my community, when they're all here to create more wellness in their life, have more personal growth, and be happier.

So, if pleasure equals happiness, why not more pleasure?

It might be obvious at this point, but like most things, women tend to put themselves last, and we consider engaging in pleasurable activities that aren't "necessary" to be frivolous and indulgent.

Since we're on the very last chapter of this book, I'm going to directly say, *To hell with that noise.* Fuck that shit that says women are selfish for doing what they want, need, and crave.

Seriously, we get *one life.* In the grand scheme of the Universe, we're here for about a nanosecond. Once we reach adulthood, which I'm assuming you're at, we have loads of responsibilities that tend to take center stage.

Part of why I love listening to eighties music isn't so much because I love the music. I do love it, but what I love just as much is remembering who I was then. A very young person with almost no responsibility and the freedom and time to do fun and pleasurable things. This all changes when we become adults, so it's up to us to make it happen.

Yes, it's a very real thing that some people have more time and resources to create more pleasure in their lives. I want to name that and acknowledge the unfairness of it all. And at the same time, small acts of pleasure can be life-altering.

GETTING TO THE BOTTOM OF YOUR PLEASURE

Since this might be something you haven't thought about in a long time, or ever, let's start with a series of questions. Get out a piece of paper or your journal and answer the following inquiries.

1. What do you want more of in your life?

This is more than simply "What do you want?" That question can feel abrupt and too vague, so I'm more curious about what you want more of. Maybe it's sleep, quiet time, or dresses with pockets. Perhaps you're getting only a little of what you really want, so think about small things you love that you would love even more in larger quantities. Don't be shy here. Watch if you think what you want more of is impractical. If it feels impractical, it belongs on your list. You're not necessarily making a to-do list, just digging around. Think of this as a Christmas list where you get to dream big.

2. What do you want less of in your life?

Sometimes this question is easier to answer than the first one. We tend to know what's bugging the crap out of us. Maybe for you it's that you want less stress, fewer arguments with your kids, less clutter, fewer annoying people on Facebook, or fewer hangovers. There might be certain people in your life you want less of, or certain behaviors or thought patterns that keep you stuck. Write them all down.

3. What are you craving?

This is one of those questions that can feel loaded. Many times, our immediate answer is something like "a chocolate croissant" or "to watch *The Real Housewives of New York City*," or both of those things together. But many times, when we want to reach for food when we're not really hungry, or reality TV when we're feeling stressed, the food and TV are what we call secondary cravings. What we're actually craving and need might be one of the following:

Safety/structure

Certainty

To be seen and heard

Rest

Exercise

Sunshine

Spiritual connection

Human connection

Physical touch/affection

Validation

Comfort

Love

Meaning

Sit with that list, especially any of those words that jump out to you and you feel a reaction to. Or, when you think about these kinds of deeper cravings, what would you add to this list? These are rooted, human experiences that are not frivolous; they are necessary for your vitality. You, as a human being, deserve basic human cravings like the list above.

Typically, when you're reaching for the remote to turn on reality TV, there might be a couple of different things you're seeking when you turn to that kind of entertainment. Perhaps you want to remove yourself from something else going on—work is stressful and taking up too much space in your head and you need to turn on something a bit mindless that you don't have to think too hard about to follow. Or maybe you're lonely and seeking to live vicariously through a group of female friends on TV.

I'm not asking you to investigate every single action you take all day long. But if you're seeking more happiness and fulfillment, you may want to ask yourself these questions to get to the bottom of what it is that your heart and soul are really seeking.

4. What do you need?

I like to ask this question after asking the similar "What are you craving" so that you can consider what it is that you need. My hope is that you begin to conflate what you crave and what you need. To learn to listen to your body and your heart about what you're craving and wanting, so it becomes easier for you to admit and know that it's what you need.

"What do you need?" is a good question to meditate on, or doodle on a piece of paper. You may find it helpful to think of yourself as a child, needing something. Maybe you needed a nap after the school day, a bath after playing outside for hours, or comfort from being frightened by a scary movie. You would never neglect that child.

I invite you to ask yourself this question not just when you're stressed and you find yourself sobbing in to your pillow. Practice now, when small things come up. When you find yourself scrolling through social media going on two hours, or complaining about your coworkers being idiots, ask yourself if there's something else you need. Then, when big things do happen and you're sobbing into your pillow, you have the practice and can more easily access what it is that you need.

Getting closer to and practicing granting yourself what you crave, want, and need will get you closer to recognizing what brings you pleasure and help you create more of that in your life.

LET'S TALK ABOUT SEX

When I was a senior in high school, our house got toilet-papered one night. More than that, the kids who wrapped our house and trees in toilet paper also threw trash all over our driveway. The kicker was that they keyed the word *slut* in large letters on the trunk of my car.

Running my fingers over the letters, wet from the morning dew, I hoped I could rub them off as I could the moisture. Wondering who would do that, who hated me so much to make the word permanent on my car and label me as such. I remember the shame and humiliation when my parents looked at it and said nothing; rather, they walked back into the house, and as my father walked away, he angrily turned around and said, "Clean it up."

I felt absolutely mortified that my parents might think I was a slut, not to mention people at school. It was one of the worst insults we slung at one another as girls, and someone had felt the urge to permanently label me on my car.

I came of age in the nineties, and as we spent our youth in bodysuits and Doc Martens, embracing our sexual pleasure was not something for which we had role models that we aspired to be like. To be a sexually expressive young woman was not okay, although we understood on some level the double binary of feeling like we had to be sexual to attract a relationship, but not so much so that we'd be labeled a slut. We were screwed either way, no pun intended.

While there has been more awareness around this as the decades have passed, not much has changed.

Although my wish is to snap my fingers and shift the culture to accept that women are, indeed, sexual and should not be villainized for wanting, needing, and loving sex, my point is this: Because sex and our sexuality are used as a weapon against us, we tend to not ask for what we want when it comes to sex, especially sex with men. This in some ways is generational; younger women now are more commonly talking to their partners about things like what they want in bed, consent, and previous trauma. But, generally speaking, we have a long way to go in terms of our pleasure.

Laurie Mintz, sexual psychologist, has coined the term *orgasm gap,* which refers to the disparity between cisgender men and women when it comes to the achievement of orgasm during heterosexual sex. Basically, to put it in layman's terms, men are getting off while women aren't. Data indicated that the majority of women—up to 70 percent—do not achieve orgasm during sex with a man, while 90 percent of men do achieve orgasm with a woman. Yes, there are some men who care and make their partner's pleasure a priority. But this isn't the norm.

Scientists, researchers, and sex educators cite many reasons for this: things like lack of sex education in schools, pornography, sexism and misogyny, and poor communication.

It's that last one, poor communication, that I want to point to. Generally speaking, we don't ask for what we want. We don't ask because we tend to think our pleasure is optional, and our male partners many times think the same thing. We don't ask because we have hang-ups about sex, and this is incredibly common. People have a hard time communicating in general—about money, everyday annoyances, when they've been hurt—so sex is one of the bigger, more vulnerable topics that we steer away from and let the showerhead do the work later on.

And not to ignore bisexual and lesbian women. Yes, women tend to be more sexually satisfied when having sex with other women, but it still comes down to communication. If they feel uncomfortable in any way, or still hold on to beliefs that it's best to stay quiet and "go with the flow," they're more likely to be unsatisfied.

Marissa Wilkes, twenty-one, made a video on TikTok and asked her followers a question she was curious about. She asked, "So, as a woman-loving-woman who's never been with a guy, ladies, what's it like to sleep with a guy?" Here are some of the responses from women, all of them getting thousands of likes:

> *Ever been disappointed? It's like that.*
> *You know when you have to sneeze and you're building it up and then it just goes away . . . yeah, like that.*
> *Ever had a cat bring you a dead bird like they did something for you, and you're supposed to like it even though it's vile? Like that.*
> *Like Ubering French fries that you know are going to arrive cold and soggy, but you eat them anyways and will probably order them again next week.*
> *It's like going down a water slide and halfway through they cut the water off and you have to scoot the rest of the way.*
> *It's like getting a birthday card with no money in it.*

Ladies. We have a problem on our hands. Yes, men need to be more educated when it comes to sex and clitorises. Yes, sexism and misogyny need to die a quick death so many things can change for the better, including the assumption that women's pleasure in the bedroom isn't a priority. And, yes, we women need to learn to communicate our needs.

Clearly, sexual pleasure is not solely about orgasm. It's about your connection to yourself, your connection to your body, intimacy with others, and freedom, and maybe sexual pleasure means something else to you.

FIRST THINGS FIRST

Just like it's a thing these days to see YouTube videos of people un-boxing their packages that come in the mail, I want it to be just as normal for people to unbox their hang-ups about sex. Maybe not go through the whole process on YouTube (I mean, you can if you want to), but it's going to be that much more difficult to speak up with your partner and have conversations about what you both want if you're feeling ashamed and resistant and have high anxiety.

If you have some blocks around sex, I invite you to do some inventory on where they stem from, if you're ready to do so. If this feels especially difficult, I encourage you to do it with the safety of a trained and trusted professional, a therapist, counselor, experienced and certified sex coach.

Ask yourself and journal on the following questions:

When did you first learn about sex? How was it presented to you, if at all?

How was sex presented as it pertained to girls versus boys? (In other words, if you had male siblings, did your parents focus on your not getting pregnant or raped, but not discuss the same thing with your brothers?)

Did you grow up in a religion that had strict rules about sex before marriage and purity? If so, how did they affect your beliefs and subsequent behavior?

What did you think of masturbation when you were younger, and how do you feel about it now? Do you or did you have any ill feelings about it, like shame or embarrassment?

Do you have any sexual patterns, like being afraid to ask for what you want in bed?

How do you feel about your body in terms of being sexual with another person? In other words, are you worried about how your body looks, and if so, how much does it get in the way of your sexual pleasure?

How do you feel about women who are sexually free and embrace their sexual selves? Do you find yourself having judgments about them or envy?

Have you been in a relationship for a long time and sex has changed or you feel no desire at all? If so, why do you think that is?

If you are older and feel that you have come a long way in terms of sex and your sexuality, do you still have past behaviors or feelings that might need to be worked on? (For example, maybe you feel much freer now that you're over forty, but still harbor resentment about your upbringing around sex.)

Many, or all, of these can feel like heavy questions. There might be much to untangle. My hope is that the questions can help you tease out what work needs to be done. Remember, especially if you're just starting out here, you've had these patterns, beliefs, and behaviors for a long time, so it will take some time to create new ways of thinking so you can create new ways of being in terms of your relationship with sex, as well as with pleasure. The good news is that it doesn't have to take a lifetime to create something new.

YOU ARE WHAT YOU EAT

When I say "eat" here, I mean "consume." If you're wanting to change how you feel about sex and your sexuality, and feel freer, start following sex educators and people who are sex-positive online. If this has not been on the menu for you before, be prepared to see people talk about vibrators, dildos, and other sex toys, bodies, and sex in general like it's no big deal, because their goal is to educate and make you also feel like it's no big deal. The more educated you are on the topic, the more empowered you are in your own relationship to sex and the more easily you can have conversations with your partners. No matter where you are on the scale of discomfort here, this is about building up a tolerance to seeing it, learning about it, and talking about it.

You can follow these people on social media, purchase books (check the Recommended Reading section of this book), and listen to podcasts. When you find someone you resonate with, you may also look into taking some in-person or online workshops.

COMMUNICATE

Nora Roberts said, "If you don't ask, the answer is always no." So, say your partner or roommate makes coffee for you every day and hands it over with cream and sugar, but you prefer it black. If you keep accepting it, the answer will always be no if you don't ask them to stop putting cream and sugar in it.

I wish the topic of sex were as light as the topic of how you like your coffee. That's why if the topic of sex is burdensome for you, it's important to start to unburden yourself around it before you delve into it with your partner, if you have one. It's not our partner's job to heal our wounds, whether those wounds have to do with sex or not. We all have wounds to heal, and partners can witness it and support us (and my hope is that they do), but the facing and healing are up to us. Revisit chapter 3 on how to have hard conversations and how to ask for what you want.

SIDE NOTE

While we're at it, as we're talking about not making your pleasure optional, let's talk about not making your growth in a relationship optional, either. I can't tell you how many women have come to me for coaching, or stopped me after a speaking event, and told me a problem that has been going on in their relationship, and it's clear it's an issue that needs to be resolved in therapy. In couples counseling, and moreover, it's obvious her partner needs to go to individual therapy. And as we're having this conversation, I'm hoping not to hear: "Oh, he refuses to go to therapy." (I'm using the pronoun *he,* because 100 percent of the time I've heard this story, it's in heterosexual relationships. When clients are in a same-sex relationship, it's been my experience that the partner is open to therapy. I know this is still a generalization, and I am for this example putting the focus on men.)

So he refuses to go to therapy. First, I want to acknowledge that patriarchy tells men that going to therapy is too vulnerable and makes them look weak, and they know it's a place where they will be asked to talk about their feelings and possibly emotions, which is also something they are taught to steer clear of. It's tragic that men have for the most part been taught this. Because many times if and when they do agree to go to therapy and are faced with massive vulnerability and their own trauma, they have very little or no skills to work through them. They have to seriously commit with a therapist they trust, and it takes a lot of work.

Yes, it's hard for them, and at the same time, it's their responsibility to accept the conditioning they've been handed and move past it for the sake of their relationship and themselves. **It is not up to you to save him or the relationship all on your own.** You never did nor should you ever have to fill out a job application to be his rehab for his brokenness. You can be understanding and compassionate, but your limits matter, too. Your mental health matters as much as his, and it's not your responsibility to carry him through his personal journey if it entails your doing all of the heavy lifting.

If you're not married or in a serious relationship, take note: Do not get into a relationship with anyone who refuses to go to therapy. It's a *major* red flag if this person makes fun of you or anyone else who gets professional help for their mental well-being.

Sex and your relationships are just one aspect of pleasure, but when we're talking about your pleasure we're really talking about your enjoyment, fulfillment, and gratification in all aspects of your life. You are entitled to pleasure, simply by living. To embrace your pleasure is to make some noise in your life. Making it a priority can create a positive impact on your life altogether.

THE
UNLEARNING

NOTICE: Note how much pleasure you get in your life. How much enjoyment, joy, and satisfaction? Or are you spending most of your day pleasing others? And if you are, pay attention to your assumptions about "how it's supposed to be." In other words, what expectations do you buy into in terms of your wants and needs? Where does it fall in the lineup of your life?

CURIOUS: I asked what might feel like a million questions in this chapter. To sum it up, after you take inventory of how much pleasure you're getting in your life, the assumptions you have about your own pleasure, and if you're able to communicate about it, get curious about *why* you aren't getting more of it in your life and *why* you feel the way you do about your pleasure, if in fact you have some baggage about it. Women's pleasure matters, and if you want more happiness, you need to make your pleasure a priority.

In addition, get curious about small shifts you can make in your life to put more emphasis on pleasure.

SELF-COMPASSION: If you have beliefs that circle around not deserving pleasure, or that it's frivolous and a waste of time, or that other people's pleasure matters more than yours, this is where I want you to focus your self-compassion. For some of you the concept of self-compassion might feel revolutionary. Something you've never practiced before. If this is you, I invite you to mother yourself, to speak to yourself as someone you love and care about, to treat yourself as you would someone who has top priority in your life. What might that look like? Start small here. Your happiness matters, and your pleasure will be one of the gateways there.

KEEP THE MOMENTUM: Like anything, making your pleasure a priority and not optional might be a lifelong journey. It will ebb and flow if you have children or not, and it will depend on your career, as well as your romantic partners. Two things will matter the most: how you feel about creating and receiving pleasure in your life, and how you communicate it with the people you spend the most time with. The first will require you to unpack, get clear about, and work on healing any wounds or hang-ups you have around pleasure, and the second will require you to learn healthy communication with your partners. Neither of these things are easy, but they're necessary and the payoff is extraordinary.

You, phenomenal women, deserve pleasure. You deserve happiness, joy, bliss, and satisfaction. It's your birthright and up to you to learn what you want more of, what you need, and what you crave.

Closing

This, or any self-help book, isn't about making massive change in your life, moving mountains, and becoming a different person altogether. My apologies if I'm bursting your bubble here now that you've finished this book, but life is a trek of self-discovery. With every relationship, heartbreak, job we didn't get, hard parenting days, and argument—when we decide to look at our part and what we can learn from it, we move closer to the person we were meant to be.

We have to look at our past, our bad habits, our addictions, and relationships, which is mildly dangerous, due only to the fact that you'll learn new things about yourself, some good and, yes, some bad. There is shame, fear, regret, sadness, and disappointment all wrapped up together like a pizza you ordered with toppings that don't combine well. You're not going to want to eat it, but once you do, you realize it's not so bad after all.

Once in an interview I was asked how I got to be comfortable with change. I laughed and replied, "I'm not comfortable with change. But I know it's necessary, and the discomfort is proof that I'm doing it."

I want that for you. I want you to set a place for discomfort at your dining room table, allow the uncomfortable guest to feel welcome enough to do what it came there to do: aid in your change for the better.

I invite you to take the handful of chapters that spoke to you the most and focus on those. Download the workbook at andreaowen .com/msn and do the work. If you're going to make some noise in your life, you must put in the effort, and that is typically unpleasant.

That aside, if there's anything I want you to walk away with, it's the knowledge that . . .

You are not broken.

You are perfectly imperfect in every way.

Love surrounds you.

You are a phenomenal woman.

You are exactly where you're supposed to be.

Recommended Reading

Along with the various titles I've mentioned throughout the book, here are some additional resources:

Ask For It: How Women Can Use the Power of Negotiation to Get What They Really Want by Linda Babcock and Sara Laschever

Boundary Boss: The Essential Guide to Talk True, Be Seen, and (Finally) Live Free by Terri Cole

Burnout: The Secret to Unlocking the Stress Cycle by Emily Nagoski, PhD, and Amelia Nagoski, DMA

Come as You Are: The Surprising New Science That Will Transform Your Sex Life by Emily Nagoski

Health at Every Size: The Surprising Truth About Your Weight by Linda Bacon

Hood Feminism: Notes from the Women that a Movement Forgot by Mikki Kendall

Patriarchy Stress Disorder: The Invisible Inner Barrier to Women's Happiness and Fulfillment by Valerie Rein, PhD

Self-Compassion: The Proven Power of Being Kind to Yourself by Kristin Neff, PhD

The Body Is Not an Apology: The Power of Radical Self-Love by Sonya Renee Taylor

The Seven Necessary Sins for Women and Girls by Mona Eltahawy

Thick: And Other Essays by Tressie McMillan Cottom

White Feminism: From the Suffragettes to Influencers and Who They Leave Behind by Koa Beck

Women & Money by Suze Orman

Continue Your Journey

Personal development is a lifelong exploration, with ebbs and flows, and periods of great self-awareness and sometimes simple reflection. If you're interested in continuing on, join me every week on the *Make Some Noise with Andrea Owen* podcast, where I interview experts, coach listeners, and have solo episodes. You'll walk away with strategies, tools, and insight to have more confidence, resilience, and ways to empower yourself. You can find it on your favorite podcast platform.

We also offer private coaching and programs; visit andreaowen .com to learn more.

Acknowledgments

The seed for this book was planted in 2016. I heard the song "Raise Hell" by Dorothy and thought to myself that women's empowerment is an act of raising hell, and immediately knew my next book had to be on this topic. So *Make Some Noise* was born. I thank my intuition and the Universe, and my guides and angels, for sending me the song and the message when I was ready to receive it.

Success does not happen in a vacuum. Books take a village plus an extra town to be successful, and the following people have been integral to this project, from helping all the way to fielding tearful phone calls from me.

The community and podcast listeners of my show, *Make Some Noise* (formerly *Your Kick-Ass Life Podcast*). Thank you for your time, your ears, and your all-around support. You are the reason I write books, and I think about you as I do my best to call you forth and guide you to empower yourself.

To my team: Emily Kristofferson, you've been with me since 2012, and now through three books. I would be lost without your help. Thank you for keeping me from constantly flying by the seat of my pants. Darlene Gonzales, Christina James, Liz Applegate,

Rebecca Metauro, and Liz Theresa, thank you for your part in making everything work so smoothly. Jessica Sharp, I'm so grateful for your support, both with this book and beyond.

To both Michele Martin and Steve Harris, the best literary agent team a woman could ask for. Michele, thank you for holding my feet to the fire with this book, having high expectations that you knew I could meet. It took me a minute to find my groove (but you kept hearing my fears and encouraging me), and once I did, it felt easy to write. This book had been wanting to be born.

Sara Carder at TarcherPerigee. Thank you for being the last face-to-face lunch I had before COVID-19 hit NYC like it did; it was a dream come true to visit the Penguin Random House offices. Thank you for right from the start believing so much in this book, my message, and my voice as an author. Having an editor who believes in me and the book like you did makes the process fun and fulfilling. And to the whole marketing and publicity team at Penguin Random House. We've been blown away by your support; thank you so much.

The women in my life who support me: I am beyond blessed to have you as friends and colleagues. Amy Smith, I love you to the moon (made of cheese) and back. Amy Ahlers, Samantha Bennett (#conceitedcunt), Kate Anthony, Kate Swaboda, Jenny Fenig, Rebecca Ching, Nicole Whiting, Courtney Webster, and Annamaria Loven, all of you to varying degrees have talked me off the ledge when I become overdramatic and declare writing is too hard. You hear me out and remind me who I am (Andrea MotherFuckin' Owen). My wish is that all women have friends like all of you. And to my therapist, Helen Campbell. Trauma therapy is no joke; thank you for guiding me with compassion and a sense of humor. I needed to surrender to that process in order to move forward and to write this book.

To Jason . . . your patience and dedication to me and our marriage astounds me. Thank you. And to Colton and Sydney, thank you for being great kids and for being proud of me.

To my parents (and Dad, I see you visit me as a cardinal at least weekly). Thank you for never saying no to books (the bookmobile!) and for giving me the DNA that makes me *have to* talk about hard and important things and always notice *and* say it out loud when the emperor has no clothes. Thank goodness being outspoken and direct has served me well.

Last, to you, dear reader. Whether this is the first book of mine you've read or you've been following my work for some time, thank you for your dedication to making yourself a better woman (by the way, you are already great). When you lift yourself up, you lift up others. And if you're the type of person who reads acknowledgments because you imagine writing your own one day in a book you wrote, consider this your sign to do it; write that book and go out and make some noise.

About the Author

Andrea Owen is a mom of two, global speaker, author, podcast host, and retired Roller Derby player. Her books have been translated into eighteen languages and are available in twenty-two countries. She and her team mentor women online and in person. Andrea lives in North Carolina with her family.

Also by Andrea Owen

How to Stop Feeling Like Sh*t: 14 habits
that are holding you back from happiness

Paperback 9781473695795

Ebook 9781473695771

Audiobook 9781473695788